The Geography of
Tropical African Development

A Study of Spatial Patterns of Economic Change Since Independence

by

A. M. O'CONNOR

Lecturer in Geography, University College, London

SECOND EDITION

PERGAMON PRESS

OXFORD · NEW YORK · TORONTO · SYDNEY · PARIS · FRANKFURT

U.K.	Pergamon Press Ltd, Headington Hill Hall, Oxford OX3 OBW, England
U.S.A.	Pergamon Press Inc., Maxwell House, Fairview Park, Elmsford, New York 10523, U.S.A.
CANADA	Pergamon of Canada Ltd., 75 The East Mall, Toronto, Ontario, Canada
AUSTRALIA	Pergamon Press (Aust.) Pty. Ltd., 19a Boundary Street, Rushcutters Bay, N.S.W. 2011, Australia
FRANCE	Pergamon Press SARL, 24 rue des Ecoles, 75240 Paris, Cedex 05, France
FEDERAL REPUBLIC OF GERMANY	Pergamon Press GmbH, 6242 Kronberg-Taunus, Pferdstrasse 1, Federal Republic of Germany

British Library Cataloguing in Publication Data

O'Connor, Anthony Michael
The geography of tropical African development.
– 2nd ed. – (Pergamon Oxford geographies).
1. Africa – Economic conditions – 1945 –
I. Title
330.9'67   HC502   77–30470

ISBN 0 08 021847 4 (hardcover)
      0 08 021848 2 (flexicover)

*Printed in Great Britain by William Clowes & Sons Limited
London, Beccles and Colchester*

CONTENTS

List of Maps   vii

List of Tables   ix

List of Plates   xi

Preface to the First Edition   xiii

Preface to the Second Edition   xv

Acknowledgements   xvi

Chapter

 1. Introduction   1

 2. Agricultural Change   22

 3. Fishing and Forestry   67

 4. Mining   76

 5. Industrial Development   99

 6. The Supply of Power   120

 7. The Role of Transport   138

 8. Urbanization   171

 9. External Economic Relations   189

10. Conclusions   208

Index   221

LIST OF MAPS

	General reference map	*facing page* 1
1.1	Ecological zones	2
1.2	Distribution of population	5
1.3–1.6	Political units: 1956, 1959, 1961, 1965	10–11
1.7–1.10	Political units within Nigeria: 1960, 1963, 1967, 1976	15
1.11	Income levels, 1975	19
1.12	Energy consumption, 1974	20
2.1	Resettlement in the Kenya Highlands	31
2.2	Irrigation schemes in Sudan	35
2.3	Coffee production: 1955-7, 1973-5	41
2.4	Coffee and cocoa in Ghana and Ivory Coast: 1954, 1971	42
2.5	Coffee and cotton in East Africa: 1956, 1966	43
2.6	Cotton production: 1955–7, 1973–5	47
2.7	Sugar production: 1955–7, 1973–5	60
2.8	Change in total agricultural production: 1957–9 to 1973–5	63
4.1	Mineral development: 1956–7, 1974–5	77
4.2	Oil in Nigeria	80
4.3	Development on the Copperbelt	82
4.4	Iron mines, roads, and railways in Liberia	85
5.1	Textile mills	105
5.2	Cement factories	106
5.3	Employment in manufacturing, 1972	109
5.4	Industrial development in Nigeria, 1966	110
5.5	Industrial development in East Africa, 1972	114
6.1	Electricity generation: 1956, 1974	122
6.2	Major power stations,	123
6.3	Zambezi and Kafue power projects	124

6.4	Volta power project	127
6.5	Niger power project	129
7.1	Port of Mombasa	141
7.2	Port of Tema	142
7.3	Port of Abidjan	143
7.4	Five West African ports	143
7.5	Railways	149
7.6	Railways in north-central Africa	151
7.7	Railways in south-central Africa	152
7.8	Motor vehicles in use, 1972	156
7.9	Road construction in Ethiopia	157
7.10	Road construction in Nigeria	158
7.11	Road construction in Angola	159
7.12	Tarred roads	160
7.13	Internal air routes in Gabón	165
7.14	Air routes from Zambia to other African countries	166
8.1	Population of major towns	172
8.2	Administrative boundaries of Kampala	176
8.3	Physical growth of Dar es Salaam	179
8.4	Physical structure of Nairobi	185
9.1	Regional associations, 1961	201
9.2	Regional associations, 1976	202
10.1	National income, 1958	210
10.2	Increase in national income, 1958–75	211
10.3	Growth in real *per capita* income, 1958–75	212
10.4	Areas of intense economic development	215

LIST OF TABLES

1.1	Population	4
1.2	Educational provision	8
1.3	Tropical Africa in the world economy	16
1.4	Exports in the economy	17
1.5	Levels and sources of income	18
2.1	Index of food production	22
2.2	Value of agricultural exports	39
2.3	Coffee production	40
2.4	Cocoa production	44
2.5	Cotton production	46
2.6	Groundnut production	48
2.7	Palm oil and kernel production	50
2.8	Tea production	56
2.9	Rubber production	57
2.10	Sisal production	58
2.11	Sugar production	59
3.1	Fishing	68
3.2	Timber felling and export	72
4.1	Value of mineral production	78
4.2	Oil production	78
4.3	Copper production	81
4.4	Iron-ore production	84
4.5	Diamond production	88
4.6	Role of mining in the economy	89
5.1	Evolution of an export processing industry	102
5.2	Growth of two industries using local materials	104
5.3	Growth of two industries using imported materials	107

List of Tables

5.4   Oil refineries

5.5   Employment in manufacturing

6.1   Electricity capacity and production

6.2   Major hydroelectricity schemes

7.1   Port traffic

7.2   Rail traffic

7.3   Rail construction

7.4   Motor vehicles

7.5   Airline traffic

7.6   Air routes to Europe

7.7   Intra-African air routes

7.8   Airport traffic

8.1   Urban population

8.2   Population growth of major cities

8.3   Town population growth in Ghana

8.4   Town population growth in Tanzania

8.5   Town growth in Zambia

8.6   Town growth in Rhodesia

9.1   External trade of tropical Africa

9.2   Trade pattern of selected African countries

9.3   OECD and multilateral aid

9.4   Share of France in external trade

9.5   West German trade

9.6   United States trade

9.7   Japanese trade

9.8   Soviet trade

9.9   Eastern bloc aid

9.10 Trade within tropical Africa

9.11 Dependence on external trade

9.12 Dependence on official aid

10.1 Increase in *per capita* GNP

10.2 Increase in energy consumption

10.3 Increase in exports from selected African countries

10.4 Regional imbalance in two African states

LIST OF PLATES

Plates 1–8 between pages 40–41

1. Traditional Africa: unproductive country in Tanzania
2. Traditional Africa: densely settled country in Rwanda
3. Commercialization in agriculture: a market in Ghana
4. Commercialization in agriculture: coffee in Uganda
5. New techniques in agriculture: ploughing in Uganda
6. New techniques in agriculture: mechanization in Kenya
7. New structures in agriculture: land consolidation in Kenya
8. Plantation agriculture: sugar in Uganda

Plates 9–16 between pages 96–97

9. Oil drilling in eastern Nigeria
10. Oil pipeline in Nigeria
11. Development on the Copperbelt: Nkana Mine
12. Resource-based manufacturing: cement in Uganda
13. Kariba Dam and power station
14. Volta Dam and power station
15. Kainji Dam resettlement: old Bussa
16. Kainji Dam resettlement: new Bussa

Plates 17–24 between pages 160–161

17. Port development at Mombasa
18. The new port of Tema
19. Railway construction in Uganda
20. Road construction in Zambia
21. The indigenous city: Ibadan
22. The colonial city: Nairobi
23. The University of Ghana
24. Adult education in rural Ghana

PREFACE TO THE FIRST EDITION

OVER much of tropical Africa, life continues today much as it has done for centuries, but in various parts of the region exciting changes are taking place. Indeed, in the minds of many people elsewhere in the world, Africa has been linked throughout the 1960's with "the winds of change". The most outstanding transformation has been in the political map. In 1956 Sudan became only the third independent state in tropical Africa, yet by 1966 there were thirty-three sovereign nations within the region. This process of political emancipation has been accompanied by important social changes, although these have inevitably been taking place more slowly.

Another form of change sought by the people of tropical Africa, and one which is the chief concern of most governments now that political independence has been achieved, is economic development. Most of the people of the region are extremely poor, and an improvement in standards of living is an urgent need. In this respect, too, change cannot be brought about as rapidly as in the political sphere, but many forms of development are taking place, and it is with this economic advance that this book is primarily concerned. At the same time, attention must be directed to the facts that the rate of economic growth in recent years has been in many respects disappointing, and that it has been far from uniform over the region. All tropical African countries fall clearly within the group to which the term "underdeveloped" was generally applied in the 1950's. This was replaced by "developing" in the early 1960's, but recently this has in turn given way in many circles to the term "less developed", and unfortunately this is, in many cases, more realistic.

Much has already been written on current change in Africa, including several studies of problems of economic development. In addition, a number of books have recently appeared on the geography of the continent, examining the spatial patterns of both natural and human phenomena, and the relationships between these patterns. This book is intended to stand between the texts on African geography and the studies of economic development by focusing on the changes in geographical patterns that have taken place in recent years, or, in other words, on the geographical pattern of recent and current economic change.

The area covered is not precisely that lying between the Tropic of Cancer and the Tropic of Capricorn, but is that of the countries which lie mainly within these limits. The countries which lie to the north are very different in character, and while their relationships with tropical Africa are increasing, these are as yet no stronger than their ties with southern Europe and South-west Asia. In the south, the distinction is in some ways less clear, since there is no physical divide comparable with the Sahara; but both political and economic conditions in South Africa are quite different from those in most other parts of the continent. South-west Africa/Namibia, Botswana, Lesotho, and Swaziland are so closely tied to South Africa that they, too, have been omitted from this book. The island of Madagascar, and smaller islands in the Indian Ocean such as Mauritius and Reunion, have also been excluded.

The period of time with which this book is primarily concerned extends from 1956 to 1970. This time span is to some extent arbitrary, but it has been chosen because 1956 was the year in which the process of the transfer of power began. In this way attention has been focused on the pattern of economic development which has accompanied the attainment of independence. An attempt is made to discover the general trends which are being maintained in current change, and it is hoped that this may be of some relevance to the planning of the accelerated development which is so greatly needed in the 1970's.

The development discussed here is essentially that which is following the path already trodden by the prosperous industrial nations of the world, and it is sometimes suggested that this is not appropriate for Africa, which still has time to seek some better way to improve the quality of life. However, this book is concerned with what is happening rather than with what should happen, and rightly or wrongly most African governments have been striving towards a more industrial–urban economy comparable to those which have produced much higher levels of income in North America, Europe, and the Soviet Union. Perhaps priorities will change in the future, as they already have to some extent in, say, Tanzania, but that is for the people of Africa to decide for themselves.

I am greatly indebted to many people who have helped me to produce this book, from my students in Africa who taught me much about their homelands, to my colleagues in London who have kindly commented on parts of the manuscript. I am also grateful to Mrs. E. Jamieson and Mrs. F. Barton for their assistance with typing, and to Mr. A. Newman and Miss C. Hill for their help in producing the maps. Most of the writing was done at home, and my greatest debt of all is to my wife for her help and encouragement at every stage.

London   Anthony M. O'Connor

PREFACE TO THE SECOND EDITION

SUBSTANTIAL changes have occurred in most sectors of the tropical African economy during the early 1970's, partly in response to fundamental alterations in the wider world economy. For instance in Nigeria, the region's most populous country and also its main oil producer, development prospects have been greatly improved by the massive increase in export earnings. Unfortunately this period has also brought setbacks for many countries, such as those afflicted by the disastrous Sahel drought; and there has been all too little evidence of improvement in material well-being for most people in tropical Africa. One very welcome change is the increased attention being given in many African countries to the ways in which economic advance is often widening existing social and spatial disparities in income and welfare, and to the need to formulate development goals that incorporate not merely growth but also a wider distribution of the benefits of growth.

In this second edition, considerable changes have been made in every chapter in an attempt to keep up to date in respect of both the geographical pattern of development and prevailing attitudes to it. However, the discussion remains largely confined to the twenty-year period from 1956 to 1976, and to the economic component of development: an attempt to incorporate a longer historical perspective, and to review social and political development also, would require a much longer book.

I am grateful to Trevor Allen, Alick Newman, and Ken Wass for their help in producing revised maps, and to all at University College who have encouraged me to continue working on the geography of tropical Africa.

London, 1977   ANTHONY M. O'CONNOR

ACKNOWLEDGEMENTS

THE author wishes to thank the following for permission to reproduce photographs: Uganda Ministry of Information (Plates 4, 5, 19); Kenya High Commission, London (Plates 6, 7, 17, 22); Zambia High Commission, London (Plates 11, 13, 20); Ghana High Commission, London (Plates 3, 18, 24); Shell Petroleum Co. (Plates 9, 10).

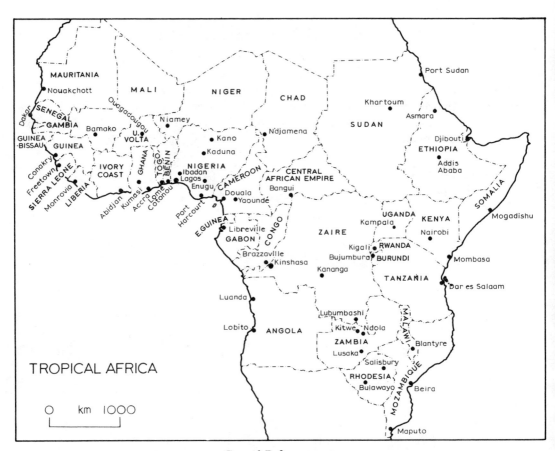

TROPICAL AFRICA

MAURITANIA
Nouakchott
MALI
NIGER
CHAD
Port Sudan
Khartoum
SUDAN
Asmara
Ouagadougou
Niamey
Bamako
U.
VOLTA
SENEGAL
GAMBIA
Dakar
GUINEA-
BISSAU
GUINEA
Conakry
Freetown
SIERRA LEONE
Monrovia
LIBERIA
IVORY
COAST
GHANA
TOGO
BENIN
Abidjan
Kumasi
Accra
Lome
Cotonou
Kano
Kaduna
N'djamena
NIGERIA
Ibadan
Lagos
Enugu
CAMEROON
Port
Harcourt
Douala
Yaoundé
CENTRAL
AFRICAN EMPIRE
Bangui
Djibouti
ETHIOPIA
Addis
Ababa
SOMALIA
Mogadishu
E.GUINEA
GABON
Libreville
CONGO
Brazzaville
Kinshasa
ZAIRE
UGANDA
Kampala
Kigali
RWANDA
Bujumbura
BURUNDI
Kananga
KENYA
Nairobi
Mombasa
TANZANIA
Dar es Salaam
Luanda
ANGOLA
Lobito
Lubumbashi
Kitwe
Ndola
ZAMBIA
Lusaka
Salisbury
RHODESIA
Bulawayo
MALAWI
Blantyre
MOZAMBIQUE
Beira
Maputo

O   km   1000

General Reference map

1

INTRODUCTION

THE LAND

The process of economic development is everywhere influenced to some extent by the nature of the physical environment within which it is taking place, and this influence is perhaps stronger in tropical Africa where most people depend directly upon the land for their livelihood than in many other parts of the world. The environmental conditions of the region range from the desert wastes of Mauritania and Somalia to the humid forestlands of Liberia and Gabon. Even larger areas consist of savanna land with marked wet and dry seasons, and with mixed woodland and grass vegetation. The greater part of the land surface takes the form of plateaux, but certain West African countries are entirely low-lying, while some in eastern Africa, such as Rwanda and Burundi, lie within rugged mountain systems. There are many other states which span several of these environmental zones, the distribution of which is shown in a highly generalized form on Map 1.1. Until the early 1960's there were few sources from which a knowledge of this diversity of physical conditions could be obtained, but recently many books have appeared on the geography of Africa, and most of these provide at least an introduction to the subject. No purpose would be served, therefore, by attempting to cover it again here.

Although little change normally takes place in such features as landforms and climate over a period of a few years, one important change that has occurred is in prevailing attitudes towards the tropical environment. At one time the abundant vegetation of parts of the tropics was interpreted by many people in temperate lands as an indication of boundless fertility, and it is often said that this is still a popular misconception. Yet much has now been written to counter this, and it could be argued that a pessimistic view of the natural resources of the tropics, such as Gourou presented in *The Tropical World*, is now well established. The latest trend is a reaction to this, and is exemplified by Hodder's statement that "the problem of natural resources is not that they are especially poor or inadequate in tropical countries but rather that the facts about these resources are little known" (*Economic Development in the Tropics*, p. 14). Even the appalling Sahel drought of the early 1970's has been seen by some observers less as a natural disaster than as a reflection of "development" ill-adapted to the environment.

1

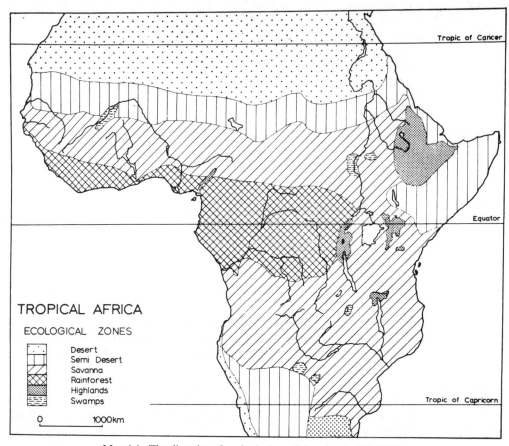

MAP 1.1. The diversity of ecological conditions in tropical Africa.

In certain respects most parts of tropical Africa do suffer from greater problems than most temperate countries. This applies to various aspects of soil fertility, for example, and also to the prevalence of conditions conducive to disease. On the other hand, there are aspects of the physical environment which offer outstanding economic opportunities, notably temperature conditions favourable for plant growth throughout the year. As the facts about the environment become better known, there are signs of a growing appreciation of both the problems and the opportunities.

Increasing attention is also being given to the variations from place to place within African countries in such characteristics as rainfall reliability and soil type, especially from the point of view of "resource assessment". As yet only a little has been done in this field, and this is one form of technical assistance which the developed countries may be able to provide on a much-increased scale in the future. At the same time it presents a great challenge to the growing number of African geographers who, along with people trained in other disciplines, may in this way make a vital contribution to the economic development of their own lands. Perhaps the most distinctive role of study undertaken from within tropical Africa rather than from outside will be to emphasize further the differences between one part of the region and another, thereby countering the over-generalization which has often resulted in the past from a distant viewpoint.

2

THE PEOPLE

The total population of tropical Africa in 1975 was probably about 300 million (although this figure is liable to an error of at least 10% since there are some countries, such as Ethiopia, in which no census has ever been taken, and others, such as Nigeria, where census figures are much disputed). This represents about 6% of the population of the whole world, occupying 15% of the world's land area, and as yet pressure of population upon the land is not characteristic of the region as a whole. However, the average density of 14 people per square kilometre masks great variations from place to place, as indicated by the country figures in Table 1.1 and also by Map 1.2.

There are large tracts with extremely sparse population, not only in the arid wastes of the Sahara but also in many savanna lands such as most of the Central African Empire, Zambia and eastern Angola, and in rainforest areas such as parts of the Congo/Zaire basin and Gabon. It is possible that in some of these areas economic development is actually hindered by the sparsity of settlement. Yet there are places such as south-eastern Nigeria and the small states of Rwanda and Burundi in which people are very densely settled upon the land, and which are suffering from severe over-population at least in relation to their present economies. Elsewhere, as in parts of Upper Volta for example, the density is lower but agricultural resources are so poor that population pressure is equally serious.

Population Growth

The population estimate of 300 million for 1975 may be compared with one of 180 million for 1956, giving an annual growth rate of almost $2\frac{1}{2}$%. This rate is much higher than that prevailing in Europe, and is similar to that in southern Asia, though not as high as that in Latin America. While very few precise data are available on the subject, it seems certain that the rate of growth is currently accelerating, since death rates are falling as a result of improved medical facilities while birth rates probably remain little changed. Because of the lower initial density of population, the implications of this rapid increase are not as serious in most parts of tropical Africa as in much of Asia, but wherever some pressure is already being felt it has very important repercussions for economic prospects. In some of these places an improvement in living standards is impossible without drastic change in the nature as well as the scale of economic activity unless, of course, the population growth can be arrested.

There are probably substantial differences between one country and another in the present rate of growth, although some of the apparent differences suggested by Table 1.1 may result largely from the limitations of the available data. The highest rates are recorded in countries of eastern Africa, such as Kenya, Zambia, and Rhodesia, while rates of increase are certainly lower over much of equatorial Africa. There are also contrasts in official policies towards population growth. Kenya and Ghana are among the countries where it is seen as a major obstacle to development, and where family planning programmes have government support, whereas few of the Francophone countries acknowledge it as a serious problem, and in such a thinly populated country as Gabon rapid growth is regarded as highly desirable. Nigeria, with much the largest population in the region, has so far remained somewhat ambivalent on the matter.

Population growth in tropical Africa as a whole results almost entirely from an excess of births over deaths, since migration to and from other parts of the world is very slight. The

TABLE 1.1. THE POPULATION OF TROPICAL AFRICA, 1956–75

	1956 (million)	1975 (million)	Annual growth, 1970–5 (%)	Density per km² 1975
AFRICA	250	400	2.6	14
TROPICAL AFRICA	180	290	2.6	14
Western Africa	76	124		
Benin	1.8	3.1	2.7	27
Gambia	0.3	0.5	1.9	46
Ghana	6.1	9.9	2.7	41
Guinea	3.5	5.5	2.4	22
Guinea-Bissau	0.4	0.5	1.5	15
Ivory Coast	4.0	6.7	2.5	19
Liberia	1.0	1.7	2.9	16
Mali	3.7	5.7	2.4	4
Mauritania	0.9	1.3	2.0	1
Niger	2.7	4.6	2.7	3
Nigeria	41.0	69.0	2.6	75
Senegal	3.2	5.0	2.4	25
Sierra Leone	2.1	2.9	2.4	41
Togo	1.4	2.2	2.8	40
Upper Volta	3.9	6.0	2.3	22
Eastern Africa	54	87		
Djibouti	0.1	0.1	2.0	5
Ethiopia	19.4	27.9	2.3	22
Kenya	7.4	13.3	3.3	22
Somalia	1.9	3.2	2.5	5
Sudan	9.1	15.6	2.9	6
Tanzania	8.9	15.2	2.5	16
Uganda	6.7	11.5	2.9	48
Central Africa	50	79		
Angola	4.5	5.8		5
Burundi	2.6	3.8	2.2	135
Cameroon	5.0	7.3	1.8	15
CAE	1.2	1.8	2.1	2
Chad	2.9	4.0	2.0	3
Congo	0.9	1.3	2.4	3
Eq. Guinea	0.2	0.3	1.7	11
Gabon	0.4	0.5	1.0	3
Malawi	3.2	5.0	2.4	41
Mozambique	6.2	9.2	2.3	12
Rhodesia	3.6	6.3	3.4	16
Rwanda	2.4	4.2	2.6	157
Zaire	14.0	24.9	2.5	10
Zambia	2.9	4.9	3.1	6

Sources: United Nations, *Demographic Yearbook*; national sources.

Notes: Some sources suggest figures of 75 m. for Nigeria, 2.7 m. for the Central African Empire, and 11 m. for Gabon in 1975. The growth rate for Angola was affected by a large exodus of Europeans in 1975.

estimated average death rate of 23 per thousand is far above the 11 per thousand in western Europe and North America, but the difference in birth rates is even greater, the respective figures being about 49 per thousand and 16 per thousand. These rates differ considerably from one part of Africa to another, and this must explain most of the spatial variation in the rate of population growth. For example, the birth rate in Zambia or Ghana appears to be considerably higher than in Cameroon, Congo, or Gabon, while the death rate is now lower in Kenya and Rhodesia than in most countries.

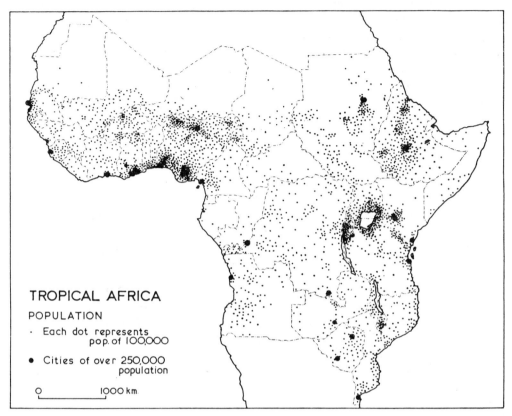

MAP 1.2. The distribution of population in tropical Africa based on data available for the late 1960's.

Differences in growth rates between countries are certainly small in comparison with those between one district and another within individual countries. In a few districts there has been an absolute decline in population, whereas in others, especially those which include the main cities, it has doubled over the past ten or twelve years. Even on a local scale, variations in birth and death rates may be important. Thus the slow growth of population in Rufiji district of Tanzania and in Bunyoro district of Uganda seems to result mainly from unusually low birth rates. Even so, the chief cause of most local contrasts in the rate of population increase, unlike national contrasts, is probably migration.

Migration

The massive movements of people which were a common feature of tropical Africa in the past were largely halted by the drawing of political boundaries in the late nineteenth century. However, examples of advancing frontiers of rural settlement may still be found, as in parts of Ivory Coast and Tanzania, although these rarely extend across national boundaries. A distinctive and distressing feature of recent years has been a series of refugee movements, notably from Rwanda and southern Sudan. These have rarely been of suffi-

5

cient scale to affect national population figures, but they pose problems for the local areas to which the refugees have moved as well as involving great suffering for the people concerned. The main direction of migration today is from the rural areas to the towns, and this urbanization forms the subject of Chapter 8. This is rarely taking place on a sufficiently large scale to bring about rural depopulation, but in many countries it is having a clear impact on the total distribution of population.

There are many other types of migration which are widespread in tropical Africa but which are short-term in nature. These include much movement both to the towns and to areas of highly commercialized agriculture for periods of employment lasting only a few months. The distribution of employment opportunities does not match that of population at all closely, the Copperbelt of Zambia and Zaire, for instance, lying within a very sparsely inhabited zone; and the willingness of large numbers of people to move long distances for work has greatly assisted the course of economic development as well as greatly influencing its distribution. Yet in many instances, such as the migration of Mossi from Upper Volta to Ivory Coast, the pattern of movement has remained remarkably stable in recent years, and it has therefore contributed little to spatial variations in population growth.

There have been certain exceptions to this stability in the pattern of short-term migration resulting in part from the political developments of the past two decades. The most outstanding exception is provided by Rhodesia, where internal migration has increased as people have found it ever more difficult to gain a livelihood in the "Tribal Trust Lands". This has offset a decrease from 100,000 a year in 1955–7 to 15,000 a year in 1965–7 in the numbers coming in from Mozambique, Malawi and Zambia. The numbers travelling further south to work in the Witwatersrand have also decreased, the flow having virtually ceased from such countries as Tanzania. In a number of other countries, including Zaire and Nigeria, internal movements have been disrupted by political strife. In addition, it should be noted that while the extent of short-term labour migration has not changed greatly over the region as a whole, its relative importance has declined as long-term migration, and even permanent settlement in areas of employment opportunity has increased.

Alien Groups

One type of migration that has greatly affected economic development in tropical Africa throughout this century has been the influx of people from Europe, and to a lesser extent, from Asia. These people have had an influence out of all proportion to their numbers and, since they are very unevenly distributed, the effects on the spatial pattern of economic activity have been great.

During the mid-1950's the rate of European immigration into several countries was greater than ever before, but as these approached and attained independence it slackened, and in some instances it was reversed. The most notable examples are Kenya, where the European population reached a peak of 61,000 in 1960 but had dropped to 41,000 by 1969, and Zambia, where a peak of 77,000 was reached in 1962, and the subsequent fall was to 43,000 in 1969. The situation is rather different in Rhodesia, where the European population is still rising, though more slowly than in the 1950's. It is different again in Angola and Mozambique, where much Portuguese colonization was still taking place in the 1960's, but where a great exodus began in 1974.

Elsewhere in tropical Africa, Europeans were always fewer in number and were mostly expatriates involved in administration or Europe-based business rather than permanent settlers. In most of these countries the numbers engaged in administration have fallen as local people have taken over their tasks, but in many this exodus has been counterbalanced by an increasing number of short-term expatriates who are employed in such activities as teaching. Often these people are coming not only from the former metropole but also from a variety of other European countries and from North America, although Ivory Coast provides one case where the numbers of Frenchmen have increased eightfold since independence.

The Asians live mainly in East Africa, where they have always outnumbered Europeans and where they have dominated commerce, at least in the towns. Despite the efforts of the independent governments to help Africans to participate more fully in trading activities, the numbers and role of the Asians have decreased only slightly in Kenya and Tanzania, although in Uganda the majority were expelled in the early 1970's.

Social Change

The great changes now taking place in most African societies both influence, and are influenced by, the pattern of recent economic development. If any generalization can be made about the diverse peoples of tropical Africa in this context, it is that most appear remarkably willing to change, and especially to adopt European ideas, attitudes, and standards. Nevertheless, there are marked differences between one area and another. It is possible that more rapid change is currently taking place in East and Central Africa than in most of West Africa where there is a longer tradition of trade and urban life and where there are stronger indigenous traditions of art, music, dress, and so on.

Within East Africa many of the pastoral groups in particular exhibit much more conservatism than the majority of the population. It is likely that social characteristics, along with many other factors, have contributed to the relatively slow rate of economic development in Ethiopia and Somalia. They certainly contribute to differences in the pace of economic advance between one part of Kenya and another. Similarly, the influence of some forms of Islam may have retarded economic change in the interior of West Africa, contributing to the contrasts between northern and southern Nigeria, for example. Yet here, too, change is now occurring, as Islam increasingly accommodates Western ideas of development.

By no means all the social changes that are taking place are to be welcomed. Countries striving for economic development may be sacrificing a great deal that is of value in traditional ways of life. A breakdown of close family ties and an increase in crime are two phenomena which unfortunately seem to be closely associated with economic change and especially with urbanization in many places. If these are particularly characteristic of East and Central Africa today, another problem which is perhaps more serious in West Africa is corruption, which by its nature is closely bound up with the growth of the money economy.

Some other developments of recent years are obviously changes for the better. One has been a rapid expansion of educational and medical facilities, leading to improvements in literacy rates, availability of skilled manpower, and standards of health. Even these advances are welcomed with reservations, for education may lead to frustration if economic development does not proceed rapidly enough to provide adequate employment opportunities, while efforts are needed to ensure that the falling death rate is accompanied by some fall in the birth rate if excessive population growth is not to act as a brake on improvements in living standards. In these respects, too, there have been substantial differences between one country and another. There were sharp contrasts in educational levels in the 1950's, and there have been equally great contrasts in the rate of expansion of educational facilities. There is no close correlation between the two sets of differences, but there is some evidence that the changes have reduced the widest disparities. Thus Ghana and Rwanda were relatively well provided with schools at that time, and therefore less priority has been given to further investment in education in these countries than in many others.

The most rapid increase in the number of children attending school has taken place in

TABLE 1.2. EDUCATION IN SELECTED AFRICAN COUNTRIES

	Population (millions)	Primary pupils (thousands)		Secondary pupils (thousands)		All pupils per 100 population
	1973	1955	1973	1955	1973	1973
Nigeria	60.0	1703	4662	63	517	9
Ethiopia	26.5	145	860	4	191	4
Zaire	23.6	1164	3292	33	320	15
Sudan	14.8	161	1082	14	231	9
Tanzania	14.4	327	1126	12	52	8
Kenya	12.5	433	1816	11	186	16
Ghana	9.4	508	1455		95	16
Cameroon	7.0	291	1014	7	108	16
Ivory Coast	6.4	69	606	4	90	11
Malawi	4.8	245	537	2	16	12
Zambia	4.6	195	810	4	61	19
Niger	4.3	10	110	0.4	11	3
Rwanda	4.0	231	398	4	11	10
Chad	3.8	21	198	0.5	13	5

Source: UNESCO, *Statistical Yearbook.*

certain of the poorer French-speaking countries such as Mali, Niger, and Chad (Table 1.2). In these, educational facilities were still pitifully slight in the mid-1950's, but the last years of French rule brought much improvement which has continued since independence. Thus the proportion of all primary-age children actually in primary schools rose between 1955 and 1970 from 3% to 22% in Chad, and from 3% to 15% in Niger. In these countries, secondary school enrolments increased at a comparable rate, although the numbers involved are far smaller. In other countries such as Malawi primary education has expanded less, since it was already relatively well developed in the 1950's, but secondary school enrolments have risen very rapidly. In Zambia, where secondary education was provided initially mainly for Europeans, the number of African children in such schools increased from 900 in 1955 to 12,800 in 1965 and 54,000 in 1970. An exceptionally great expansion of secondary schools has also occurred in Ethiopia. In yet other countries the most obvious deficiency was in higher education, and the greatest development has taken place in this field. A notable example is Zaire, where university enrolment rose from 200 in 1956 to 4600 in 1965 and 12,300 in 1971. In numerous other countries a university was established for the first time in the 1960's.

The geography of education in Africa involves the spatial variations not only in the extent of education at each level, but also in its nature. There have been sharp differences between one country and another in the emphasis given to practical rather than academic training, and to activities outside the school system such as adult literacy campaigns. Within the school system the merits of preserving the features inherited from the colonial period have been questioned to a far greater extent in countries such as Tanzania and Guinea than in others such as Ivory Coast and Ghana. In some cases the syllabus has been made much more appropriate to local needs, and the use of the local language for instruction has increased at least at the primary level. In these respects, and also in simple terms of school enrolments, the extent of change has often differed substantially between various regions within African countries. In Nigeria, for instance, both primary and secondary school enrolments have increased far more rapidly in the northern states than in the south, thereby reducing, though by no means eliminating, the wide regional disparity in educational provision.

There has been a rapid increase in the numbers of hospitals and dispensaries in most tropical African countries, although change has not been as rapid or as widespread as in education. Up to the 1950's medical facilities in many countries depended on missionary activity to an even greater extent than the provision of schools, and while the role of government has increased everywhere, more has been achieved where mission hospitals have been supplemented than where effort has been devoted to taking these over. Similarly, the number of qualified doctors has often increased greatly, for instance from 420 to 2680 in Nigeria and from 150 to 1170 in Sudan between 1955 and 1970. However, the equivalent increase was only from 460 to 640 in Tanzania and from 220 to 320 in Zambia, while in Zaire and in Rhodesia there are no more doctors today than in the mid-1950's.

As in the case of schools there is some evidence that the differences in the rate of expansion of medical facilities and personnel have brought about some reduction in spatial disparities at both international and inter-regional scales: but there has not always been an inverse correlation between existing levels of provision and the extent of new additions. Thus the ratio of doctors to population still ranged in 1972 from 1 to 6000 or 8000 in Rhodesia and Gabon to 1 to 50,000 or more in Upper Volta, Chad, Burundi, Rwanda, and Ethiopia. Within Nigeria the number of hospital beds per 10,000 people in 1970 ranged from under 15 in Kano State to 75 in East-central State, even excluding the figure of 200 for the highly urbanized Lagos State; and even the present Tanzanian administration has been criticized for concentrating too much of its medical expenditure on specialized facilities in Dar es Salaam, although there, as in Uganda, special efforts were being made in the late 1960's to provide better health services for the rural population.

The importance attached to improved educational and medical facilities has been reflected in the high proportion of total government expenditure which has been devoted to them, reaching 15% for education alone in several countries. Yet there is an urgent need for still more to be done in both fields, and therefore current development plans often allocate equally large, or even larger, sums for these purposes in the years ahead. The degree of priority given to them will vary greatly from one country to another, however, sometimes reflecting differences in needs, but sometimes merely reflecting different government policies. Perhaps this is inevitable, since there is no means of assessing the relative merits of investment in social services and in more directly productive activities.

CHANGING POLITICAL PATTERNS

The political map of Africa has been constantly changing for centuries, but there have been two brief periods during which change has been especially rapid. The first was between 1885 and 1895 when almost the whole of tropical Africa was partitioned and occupied by the competing European colonial powers. The second was between 1955 and 1965 when the majority of the colonies gained their independence. Economic development in this region in

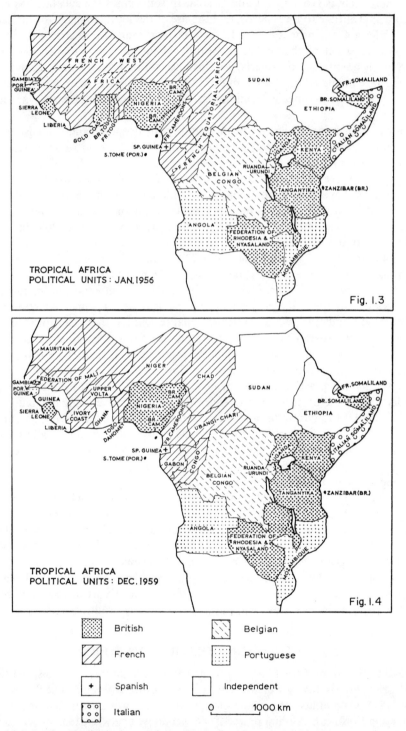

MAPS 1.3–1.6. The transformation of the political map of tropical Africa between 1956 and 1965

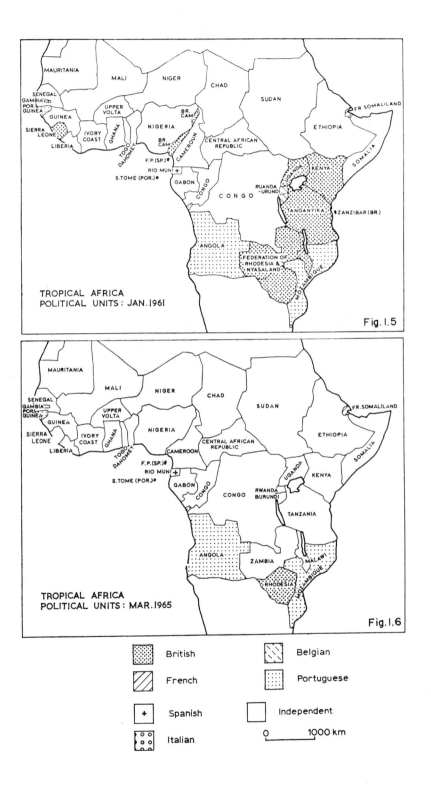

TROPICAL AFRICA
POLITICAL UNITS: JAN.1961

Fig.1.5

TROPICAL AFRICA
POLITICAL UNITS: MAR.1965

Fig.1.6

British	Belgian
French	Portuguese
Spanish	Independent
Italian	0 1000 km

recent years has therefore taken place in a situation of dramatic change in political patterns, and has been affected in many ways by these changes. After 1965, however, the political map altered very little until 1975, when change eventually came in Angola and Mozambique.

The transformation from colonial status to independence is illustrated in Maps 1.3 to 1.6. In 1955 the only sovereign states in tropical Africa were Ethiopia and Liberia. Ethiopia has a history extending back over many centuries, and was occupied by the Italians only between 1936 and 1941. Liberia as a political entity was set up by the United States in 1847 as a home for freed slaves (but it is often suggested that the relationship between the Americo-Liberians and the indigenous population is still essentially a colonial one). In 1956 these two states were joined by Sudan, which had been an Anglo-Egyptian condominium since 1899, although administered primarily by Britain. In the following year, Gold Coast became the independent state of Ghana, a nationalist movement having developed there in the 1940's and early 1950's more rapidly than in most other colonial territories.

When in 1958 a referendum was held throughout the French colonies, Guinea chose immediate independence, but the other territories passed through a two-year transitional period before becoming republics within the French Community in 1960. That year witnessed the greatest transformation of the political map, for in addition to thirteen former French states, independence was also granted to the former Belgian Congo (now Zaire), to Nigeria, and to Somalia. During the next five years the process continued more slowly, but it eventually extended to the countries of eastern and south-central Africa where European influence was stronger, and to countries such as Gambia, which a little earlier had been considered too small to be viable entities. Between 1965 and 1973 the only tropical African country to become independent was Equatorial Guinea, where Spanish administration ended in 1968. The other new states to appear on the African scene during this period were Botswana, Lesotho, and Swaziland, which all lie to the south, and the island of Mauritius, which lies far out in the Indian Ocean. In 1974, however, the first stage of Portuguese decolonization took place in Guinea-Bissau followed in 1975 by withdrawal from Mozambique and Angola after a decade of armed conflict. Then in 1977 the French Territory of the Afars and Issas (formerly French Somaliland) gained independence as the Republic of Djibouti.

In some cases the change has not only been from a colony to a sovereign state, but has also affected the extent of the political units. There has been a general agreement not to attempt to move boundaries, even though these were drawn by alien powers, but there have been several instances of subdivision or amalgamation of states. Thus independence brought the break-up of the large confederations of French West Africa and French Equatorial Africa, although some of the successor states have re-established various forms of co-operation. Even the small unit of Ruanda–Urundi split into the two quite separate countries of Rwanda and Burundi. Among the most important changes was the disintegration of the Federation of Rhodesia and Nyasaland. While two of its components have become the independent states of Zambia and Malawi, in 1977 Rhodesia remained legally under the authority of Britain, despite the unilateral declaration of independence in 1965 by a white minority government.

Examples of amalgamation are provided by the republic of Somalia, which was created out of the formerly separate entities of Italian and British Somaliland; and the republic of Cameroon, which includes part of the former British Cameroons as well as the former French trust territory. Both of these unions have proved successful, but elsewhere there have been attempts which have failed, as between Senegal and Mali. In 1964 a union took place between Tanganyika and Zanzibar to form the republic of Tanzania, and although implementation was slow at first it is now becoming effective. A much more widespread development has been a move towards economic integration among African countries, discussed in Chapter 9, and it is hoped greater political integration may follow from this.

The pattern of economic development in each country since independence has sometimes been greatly affected by the character and policies of the regime in power. Military coups have become a distinctive feature of tropical Africa since 1960, but it is not possible to generalize about the effects of these. In some of the French-speaking countries, and perhaps in Ghana, they have been a stabilizing influence and have assisted the development process: but those which took place in the Central African Republic (now Empire) in 1965 and in Uganda in 1971 brought to power leaders whose impetuous actions have caused much misery and disruption in many aspects of national life.

Certain other trends, such as that towards one-party parliaments, have been almost universal, but the political outlook of these parties ranges from extreme conservatism to radical socialism. Within West Africa there is a sharp contrast between Ivory Coast, where private enterprise is vigorously encouraged and ties with France are still extremely strong, and Guinea, which favours state control of as large a part of the economy as possible and has developed close relations with the communist world. In East Africa suprisingly good relations have been maintained between Kenya and Tanzania in view of the fact that Kenya favours a predominantly private-enterprise economy, while Tanzania has pressed ahead with a policy of "African Socialism", or "Ujamaa" in Swahili, in which there are severe constraints on the accumulation of individual wealth. The latter has perhaps to some extent been pursued at the expense of maximum economic growth, although it can be argued that it is assisting development in terms of bringing improved living conditions to a wider range of people. It is quite impossible to explain why this policy has emerged in Tanzania rather than elsewhere, although in addition to the obvious factor of Nyerere's leadership another is the lack of powerful vested interests in inequality, social or spatial. Thus, while a similar philosophy has been propounded by Kaunda in Zambia, the inherited structures there have prevented a comparable degree of implementation; and in West Africa the markedly dualistic economies that had developed up to the 1950's in Guinea and Ivory Coast provided a basis for advance more suited to the latter's capitalism than the former's socialism.

While some forms of socialism may tend to limit growth in present African circumstances, conservatism of the type epitomized by Liberia may so confine the effects of growth to limited groups and limited areas as to hinder real economic development for the majority of the population. There are signs, therefore, of a general move away from extreme positions, as exemplified by the recent establishment of state enterprises in Ivory Coast, and attraction of American private capital to develop vast bauxite deposits in Guinea.

Spatial Political Patterns within the New States

In many of the new states the transition from colonial status to independence has brought little change in internal political patterns, but unfortunately there are some in which the period has been marked by serious upheavals and conflicts. Indeed, disorder first in Zaire, then in Nigeria, and finally in Angola, focused world attention on tropical Africa more sharply than did the process of attaining independence. While many of the military coups have had virtually no impact on geographical patterns, certain of the most

13

serious internal conflicts are to a large extent problems of political geography, for these have been between the inhabitants of different parts of each country rather than between different social groups spread throughout each.

The crisis in Zaire perhaps resulted largely from the lack of preparation for independence, but it was aggravated by the sheer size of the country and the problems of administering a population that is widely scattered with clusters all around its borders. The difficulties were especially great in the case of Katanga (now Shaba), which lay 1500 km from the capital, had close links with neighbouring countries, and had the economic strength to put up an extended fight for secession. However, although the conflicts have had serious repercussions in retarding economic development (even perhaps discouraging foreign investment in other parts of Africa), no major change has taken place in the political map of the country. After several reversals of policy, the 1969 pattern of a strong central government and eight provinces with limited powers differed little from that left by the Belgians in 1960.

Nigeria inherited a federal constitution which in the early 1960's showed outward signs of stability, but serious regional rivalries soon became felt. These culminated in terrible massacres of Ibos from the east who were living in the northern region, and, in the opinion of many northerners, occupying a disproportionate number of the more responsible jobs there. The return of most of the surviving Ibos to the east was followed by the attempted secession of that region as the republic of Biafra, an attempt naturally resisted by the Nigerian Federal Government, especially since the former eastern region was the home of many other groups in addition to the Ibo. The resulting civil war lasted from 1967 to 1970, and seriously disrupted many sectors of the Nigerian economy including, perhaps most seriously, the growing of basic foodstuffs throughout the areas of conflict. But it seems that the course of economic development was only temporarily retarded, especially since the oil industry, which had been growing mainly in the east and which gave that region the initial strength to resist, was already reviving rapidly even by 1969. Among the steps taken to achieve greater national integration have been the replacement of large partly-autonomous regions inherited from the British by more numerous states with more limited powers (Maps 1.7 to 1.10).

Within East Africa the greatest changes have occurred in Uganda, where the political structure inherited in 1962 was extremely complicated. In the heart of the country lay the kingdom of Buganda which had a federal relationship with the central government, and in the west there were three other kingdoms with more limited powers. Perhaps inevitably, relationships between the central and Buganda governments became very strained; and in 1966 all the kingdoms were overthrown, the whole country coming under central authority. Since the military coup of 1971 further changes in the administrative areas have been made. In Kenya a substantial decentralization of authority took place soon after independence, but after the next election the new regions which had been created lost most of their powers and were relegated to a much lower status as provinces.

Sudan suffers from problems of political geography as serious as those anywhere else in tropical Africa, although they have not been allowed to come to the surface as clearly as elsewhere. Yet a resistance movement was active in the south of the country for some time, as the Negro peoples there, most of whom are either Christian or pagan, bitterly resented dominance by the Arab Islamic north. In some respects the conflict may have forced Khartoum to pay more attention to the south, e.g. by extending the railway there: but in others it greatly hindered development until better relations were restored around 1972. More recently internal conflict has been gathering momentum in neighbouring Ethiopia.

14

NIGERIA: Political Units

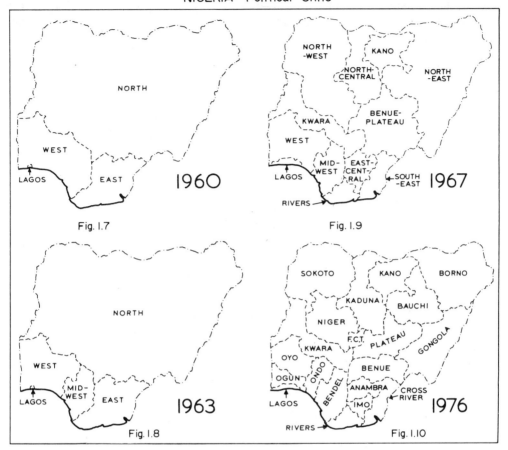

Maps 1.7–1.10. Changing internal political units within Nigeria: 1960, 1963, 1967, 1976.
F.C.T.=the new Federal Capital Territory.

THE LEVEL OF ECONOMIC DEVELOPMENT

Tropical Africa is in every sense an economically underdeveloped region. The vast majority of the population is extremely poor, and it is the effort being made to alleviate this poverty which is the chief concern of this book. Now that most tropical African countries have attained political independence, and except where the problems of national integration loom even larger, their governments acknowledge that their most urgent task is to improve the standard of living of the people. The limited provision of medical and educational facilities noted previously is a clear reflection of the present stage of economic development in most parts of the region. Precise measurement of levels of development is not possible, but a valuable indication is provided by the estimates now made in every country of the national income, gross national product, or gross domestic product. In areas where much economic activity is undertaken for subsistence rather than exchange, these estimates cannot be very accurate; and the increasingly difficult process of converting the data to a common currency further reduces the precision. Yet the general picture which emerges

15

from the figures published by the United Nations and the World Bank closely matches the impression formed by anyone moving between tropical Africa and other parts of the world.

The average income per head in tropical Africa as a whole is probably only one-sixth of the world average (Table 1.3), and although higher than in India, it is substantially

TABLE 1.3. TROPICAL AFRICA IN THE WORLD ECONOMY, 1974

	Gross National Product	
	Total ($ m.)	*Per capita* ($)
TROPICAL AFRICA	60,000	220
India	80,000	140
China	250,000	300
Latin America	300,000	1,000
USSR	600,000	2,400
EEC	1,200,000	4,700
USA	1,400,000	6,700
WORLD	5,500,000	1,400

Source: World Bank Atlas.

lower than in most countries of South-east Asia or Latin America. After rising slowly from about $80 in 1956 to about $130 in 1971, the crude figure for tropical Africa rose sharply to about $230 in 1974, but much of this increase reflects merely inflation. Fortunately, national incomes have generally been rising faster than population even in real terms, but the rate of increase is no higher than that in most parts of the world, and therefore the relative position of this region has changed little; while as elsewhere a rising average may mask complete stagnation for large sections of the population.

While real incomes have risen year by year, the rate of increase has been far from constant. During the mid-1950's it was very rapid in many parts of tropical Africa, and in some years more rapid than in any other large region of the world, but since then it has generally been much slower. By 1957 African primary production for export was beginning to exceed the demand from the main importing countries, and the terms of trade were swinging against the producers of agricultural and mineral commodities in favour of the producers of manufactured goods. Throughout the 1960's the prices obtainable for most African exports were substantially lower than in the mid-1950's, and this has profoundly affected the whole course of economic development. The early 1970's brought a marked improvement in the prices obtained for some of these exports, but the greatly increased oil prices harmed far more countries than they helped, while the costs of most imported manufactures have also risen substantially.

The Nature of the Economy

The importance of changing world market conditions reflects the nature of the economy of most African countries. Before the beginning of this century most of the economic activity taking place in tropical Africa was for subsistence only, though local trade was important in certain areas. Even today there is still a high degree of self-sufficiency on the part of each family in many countries. Indeed, the greater part of the labour of the total population of the region is probably devoted to the production of goods or the performance of services for themselves and their families. Nevertheless, over the past eighty years the cash economy has greatly expanded, and there are now few people who have no direct contact with it. This process continues today, and whereas a few years ago subsistence production was even more dominant in tropical Africa than in other underdeveloped areas, it is now probably no more important than in much of southern Asia. More and more people are producing some goods for sale or entering some form of paid employment. Perhaps one should say seeking employment, for one of the most serious problems now arising throughout the region is that the demand for unskilled labour is not rising fast enough to absorb all those who are seeking work.

The cash economy which has spread through tropical Africa depends very heavily upon the export of primary products to Europe and other developed regions, and upon the import of manufactured goods from them. Exports represent over a quarter of the total national income of many African countries (Table 1.4), compared with about 15% in most

TABLE 1.4. EXPORTS IN THE ECONOMY OF CERTAIN AFRICAN
COUNTRIES, 1974

	Exports as % of GNP	Leading export as % of total export value	
Gabon	110	Oil	69
Liberia	80	Iron ore	66
Mauritania	80	Iron ore	73
Nigeria	50	Oil	93
Zambia	50	Copper	93
Ivory Coast	40	Coffee	23
Zaire	40	Copper	69
Ghana	20	Cocoa	72
Kenya	20	Coffee	24
Sudan	20	Cotton	38
Ethiopia	10	Coffee	28

Sources: United Nations, *Yearbook of International Trade Statistics;* and national sources.

of western Europe, 5% in the United States, and 5% in India. Furthermore, many countries are heavily dependent upon just one or two commodities, and would face economic disaster if the demand for these products fell sharply. Strenuous efforts have been made during the past decade to diversify exports, but the dominance of cocoa in Ghana or copper in Zambia is still almost as great as ever.

Even if exports can be diversified, heavy dependence on the traditional type of overseas trade is not a satisfactory situation in the light of recent world economic trends, and most African countries are now giving particular attention to the expansion of the internal exchange economy. To some extent this can be achieved by changes in the pattern of agriculture, which is much the most important sector of the economy in nearly all parts of the region (Table 1.5): but it also involves the development of manufacturing industry, and there are those who see industrialization as the panacea for the problems of all poor countries—in Africa as elsewhere. Until the internal exchange economy is enlarged, tropical Africa will continue to be marked by a high degree of economic dualism with a sector oriented primarily to subsistence and a sector oriented primarily to distant export markets juxtaposed. It is sometimes suggested that dualism implies the absence of any interaction

TABLE 1.5. THE LEVEL AND SOURCES OF INCOME IN CERTAIN AFRICAN
COUNTRIES, 1974

	GNP ($ m.)	GNP per capita ($)	% contribution to GDP of Agriculture	Mining	Manufacture
Nigeria	17,800	280	23	45	6
Zaire	3,700	150	14	22	10
Angola	3,400	580			
Ghana	3,300	350	45	2	9
Mozambique	3,000	340	42	0	12
Rhodesia	2,900	480	16	7	24
Ivory Coast	2,600	420	28	0	16
Kenya	2,600	200	31	0	14
Sudan	2,600	170	38	0	9
Ethiopia	2,500	90	55	0	10
Zambia	2,300	480	9	34	13
Tanzania	2,300	140	40	1	11
Uganda	1,800	160	53	1	8
Cameroon	1,700	240	33	0	13
Senegal	1,300	270	26	3	16

Sources: World Bank Atlas; United Nations, *Yearbook of National Accounts Statistics;* and national sources.

Notes: All the figures given above are estimates liable to a large margin of error. For most African countries the GDP is slightly higher than the GNP. The sectoral shares in the GDP are affected by variations in definition, especially of manufacturing.

between the two sectors, but that is hardly possible when many individuals are involved in both: it does, however, imply a serious lack of interaction in many national economies, with serious problems resulting from this.

The heavy reliance of most African countries on overseas trade is only one facet of the situation in which the attainment of political independence has not brought a comparable degree of economic independence. In many ways African economies function as part of the periphery of an economic system centred on Europe and North America, in a relationship which is often termed "neocolonial". The currency of most West African countries, for example, is tied to the French franc, while long-independent Liberia uses the American dollar. Any understanding of the African space economy must recognize the extent of these links, which often mean that the decisions which govern the local economies are made in Paris, London, Brussels, New York, or Washington. In one sense the degree of external economic control may even be increasing as a result of a change that has been occurring at least in some countries since independence. As indicated above, ever more people are being drawn into the cash economy, and this is perhaps contributing to some breakdown of the economic dualism which to different degrees African countries inherited from the colonial period: but where the interpenetration of the indigenous and alien sectors is increasing, the external control exercised through the alien sector may be widening its sphere of influence.

Changes in the structure of the economies of African countries are partly the direct result of government policies, and one feature of these economies that should be noted is the extent to which they are under government control. Even sixty or seventy years ago the colonial governments were active in such fields as railway building, but after World War II it came to be assumed that the administration was responsible for promoting economic activity to a much greater degree than previously. This view has carried over into the present independent nations, and it is exemplified by the importance which almost every country has attached to the drawing up of development plans. It is further encouraged by the increasing importance of overseas government aid rather than foreign private investment as a source of funds for development.

The Spatial Pattern of Development

While every country in tropical Africa is poor in comparison with those in North America and Europe, there are great variations in the present level of economic development between one part of the region and another as reflected in Map 1.11. The estimated income

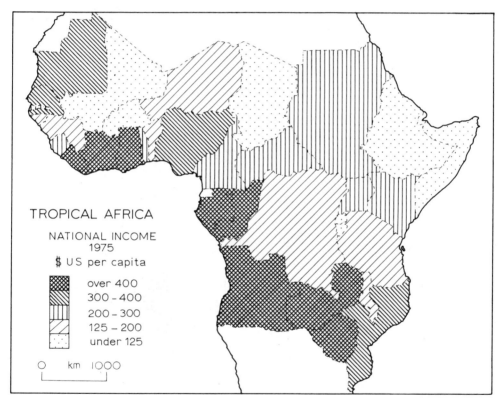

MAP 1.11. The level of national income *per capita* (1975) in the countries of tropical Africa. Despite its many deficiencies, this is the best single indicator of relative prosperity or poverty.

per head in a number of individual countries is given in Table 1.5. There are several in which it now exceeds $300 a year, but there are others where it is still less than $100. Even greater contrasts exist within countries, the level of income in the district which includes the capital city often being ten times higher than that in certain outlying districts. Regional differences in prosperity are a matter of public concern in such countries as the United States and Britain, but in view of the much greater disparities, they are surely of even more significance in most African countries.

There are also marked differences between one place and another in the extent of

19

continued dependence on subsistence rather than commercial activity, and on farming rather than mining or industry. In such countries as Niger or Rwanda, most people are still occupied very largely in producing their own food. Elsewhere, as in Ghana and Ivory Coast, much more production for cash takes place, though there, too, agriculture still dominates the economy. A third situation is found in Zambia, Liberia and Gabon, where most farming is concerned with staple food crops for the farmers' own use, but where there is also a thriving commercial sector based on mining. While no tropical African country yet has an economy dominated by manufacturing, there are great differences in the extent of industrialization that has taken place as reflected in the map of commercial energy consumption (Map 1.12), and within each country industrial development is highly localized.

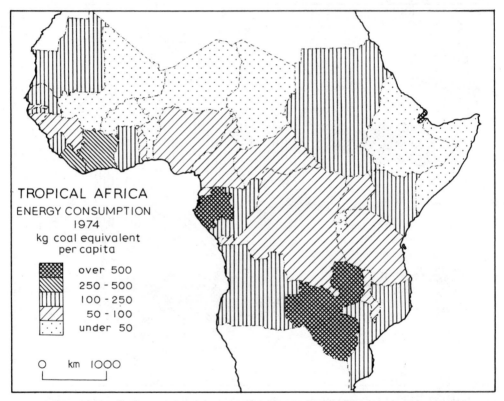

MAP 1.12. Energy consumption in tropical Africa (1974). It should be noted that the data represent only inanimate energy such as that obtained from coal, oil and hydroelectricity.

It is these spatial variations in each aspect of economic development, at both the international and the national scale, which are the main concern of the chapters that follow. A constant theme must be the concentration of intensive economic activity in scattered "islands" separated by vast areas where little change of any type has occurred for centuries. A constant question must be whether current development is contributing to a breakdown of this pattern and a dispersion of economic activity, or is rather consolidating it and bringing about ever greater disparities between areas of prosperity and areas of poverty.

20

SELECTED READING

One of the most valuable geographical studies of tropical Africa is:
  G. H. T. KIMBLE, *Tropical Africa* (New York, 1960), which forms a starting point for this book since it provides a comprehensive survey of the region as it was in the 1950's

Other books complementary to the present volume are:
  W. A. HANCE, *African Economic Development* (New York, 1967), which provides a set of case studies;
  B. W. HODDER and D. R. HARRIS (ed.), *Africa in Transition* (London, 1967), which considers change over a longer period region by region;
  C. G. KNIGHT and J. L. NEWMAN (ed.), *Contemporary Africa* (Englewood Cliffs; 1976), which includes interesting essays on a wide range of topics.

The best study of the economic geography of Africa is:
  W. A. HANCE, *The Geography of Modern Africa* (New York, 1975).

Recent texts which cover the physical, as well as human, geography of the continent are:
  J. I. CLARKE *et al.*, *An Advanced Geography of Africa* (London, 1975);
  A. T. GROVE, *Africa* (London, 1978).

A discussion of tropical development which is cautiously optimistic about the physical environment is:
  B. W. HODDER, *Economic Development in the Tropics* (London, 1973).

A more pessimistic view is expressed in:
  P. GOUROU, *The Tropical World* (London, 1966).

New insights on the physical environment and development are provided in:
  P. RICHARDS (ed.), *African Environment: Problems and Perspectives* (London, 1975).

Of the volumes on population in Africa, the most relevant are:
  S. H. OMINDE and C. EJIOGU (ed.), *Population Growth and Economic Development in Africa* (London, 1972);
  J. C. CALDWELL *et al.*, *Population Growth and Socio-economic Change in West Africa* (New York, 1975).

Many aspects of social and political change are reviewed in:
  J. N. PADEN and E. W. SOJA (ed.), *The African Experience* (Evanston, 1970).

Very useful data on these aspects are provided in:
  D. G. MORRISON *et al.*, *Black Africa: A Handbook for Comparative Analysis* (New York, 1970).

A geographical study of changing political patterns is:
  R. D. HODGSON and E. A. STONEMAN, *The Changing Map of Africa* (Princeton, 1968).

There are several valuable essays on problems of national integration in:
  D. R. SMOCK and K. BENTSI-ENCHILL (ed.), *The Search for National Integration in Africa* (New York, 1975).

For an exposition of Tanzania's distinctive development policies, see:
  J. K. NYERERE, *Freedom and Socialism* (Dar es Salaam, 1968);
  J. K. NYERERE, *Freedom and Development* (Dar es Salaam, 1973).

A helpful introductory study of African economic development is:
  A. M. KAMARCK, *The Economics of African Development* (New York, 1971).

Useful economic surveys are provided in:
  IMF, *Surveys of African Economies* (6 volumes, Washington, 1968–75);
  UN ECA, *Survey of Economic Conditions in Africa* (New York, annual).

An outstanding study of economic change over a long period is:
  A. G. HOPKINS, *An Economic History of West Africa* (London, 1973).

For analyses from a radical viewpoint, see:
  S. AMIN, Underdevelopment and dependence in Black Africa, *Journal of Modern African Studies* **10**, 503–24 (1972);
  G. ARRIGHI and J. SAUL, *Essays on the Political Economy of Africa* (New York, 1973);
  P. C. W. GUTKIND and I. WALLERSTEIN (ed.), *The Political Economy of Contemporary Africa* (London, 1977).

A notable case study from this viewpoint is:
  C. LEYS, *Underdevelopment in Kenya* (London, 1974).

An invaluable reference source on all current political, social and economic developments in Africa is:
  C. LEGUM (ed.), *Africa Contemporary Record* (London, annual).

2

AGRICULTURAL CHANGE

MOST people in tropical Africa depend primarily upon the land for their livelihood. Indeed, farming is the main activity of between 75% and 85% of the working population, although the level of productivity is such that in most countries it accounts for little over half the national income. The relative importance of agriculture is now generally falling, and this must surely continue for the economy of tropical Africa as a whole is still very unbalanced. It cannot forge ahead rapidly without a substantial swing to industrial activity, especially in view of the trend for the purchasing power of agricultural exports to fall in relation to the cost of imported manufactures. Yet in most countries farming must remain the dominant activity for the forseeable future, and most of the national development plans recognize the need for an increase in agricultural productivity as a prerequisite for industrial development. In particular, the growth of industry is at present limited by the size of domestic markets, and these can expand rapidly only if the income of the farming population rises. At the same time there is an even more urgent need for agricultural improvement to ease the fundamental problems of seasonal hunger in some parts of Africa and permanent malnutrition resulting from unbalanced diets over much larger areas. There is all too little evidence of improved food supplies in most countries (Table 2.1), and the effects of the droughts of the early 1970's demonstrated how precarious life is for many people.

TABLE 2.1. INDEX OF FOOD PRODUCTION IN SELECTED AFRICAN COUNTRIES

Per capita food production 1975 (1961–5 average = 100)					
Sudan	127	Tanzania	97	Ethiopia	79
Cameroon	124	Kenya	95	Niger	73
Ivory Coast	121	Rhodesia	91	Mali	64
Malawi	114	Nigeria	83	Chad	62

Source: FAO, Production Yearbook.

Economic historians such as Hopkins have shown that the patterns of agriculture in pre-colonial Africa were by no means static as is sometimes suggested, but change was certainly greatly accelerated during the early part of this century as a result of the contact between the farming population and the colonial powers. In such countries as Kenya, Zambia, and especially Rhodesia, European settlers occupied large tracts of land and established their own brand of agriculture on these. Elsewhere plantations were developed for the intensive production of export crops. Much more widespread, however, was the introduction of cash crops into the existing system of peasant farming. The rural economy in much of tropical Africa was thus very different in 1930 from what it had been in 1900.

The rate of agriculture development slowed considerably during the depression and World War II, and did not greatly accelerate even in the late 1940's. Then there was a period of rapid expansion of most forms of export crop production in the early 1950's, when world prices for many commodities were exceptionally high and when the colonial governments directed more of their effort than formerly to promoting economic development. Unfortunately, by about 1956 this period of rapid growth had ended in most countries, and since then the pattern of agriculture has remained remarkably stable, or even disturbingly stagnant, in much of the region. Nevertheless, there have been some changes almost everywhere, including an expansion of crop and livestock production at least matching the growth in population, while in certain countries some very significant developments have taken place.

In Kenya, for example, changes have occurred not only in the level of production of each crop, but also in the whole structure of agriculture. Consequently the present agricultural geography of Kenya is very different from that existing around 1960, both in terms of the contrasts between that country and others and in terms of spatial patterns within the country. One result of change there and elsewhere has been some blurring of the formerly very sharp distinction between small-scale African farming and large-scale alien, largely European, agriculture. Yet the distinction is still clear enough over tropical Africa as a whole for each to be considered separately. Many of the problems which are characteristic of small-scale African farming do not apply to large-scale farming, and it can even be argued that the large plantations have as much in common with mining and manufacturing enterprises as with peasant agriculture.

SMALL-SCALE AGRICULTURE

Just as agriculture dominates the whole economy of tropical Africa, and has changed less than other sectors, so small-scale peasant farming dominates the total agricultural pattern, and has changed less than other types of farming. The great majority of the people of the region still farm their small plots in much the same way as their fathers did thirty years ago: some in the same way as their forefathers did a hundred years ago. Unfortunately, this often means that they expend great effort for pitifully small returns. Nevertheless, various important changes have taken place, some common to most parts of the region, some highly localized. Many affect mainly cash cropping, but others affect traditional patterns of subsistence production also.

Stabilization

One of the most fundamental and widespread changes is one that has been taking place for many decades and will continue for many more. This is the increasing stabilization of farming as pressure on the land rises and it has to be used more intensively. There are parts of tropical Africa, such as Lake Victoria zone of Uganda, which have a long tradition of fixed agriculture, but the normal pattern of land use in the past throughout most of the region was shifting cultivation. This term has been used by different writers to mean different things, but it is generally considered to involve the clearing of successive patches of ground around a homestead, each of which is cropped for only two or three years, and then the removal of the homestead to another site. Some observers are prepared to defend shifting cultivation as an appropriate farming system for areas with very sparse settlement; but others argue that it is a system in which no substantial economic development is feasible, and which should be abandoned wherever possible. All agree that where there is pressure of population on the land, every effort must be made to assist the transition from shifting to fixed agriculture.

Throughout the more heavily settled parts of tropical Africa shifting cultivation has already given way to a system of "bush fallowing", in which the settlement remains fixed and land which has been tilled and then left to revert to bush is brought back into use again after a few years. In some areas of very dense population such as the country around Kano and also the south-east of Nigeria, the fallow period has become progressively shorter, field boundaries being clearly maintained from one period of cultivation to another; and in a few places it has disappeared altogether in recent years. No precise data are available on this change in any area, but it is widely reported, even in countries which have not been notable for their agricultural progress, such as Sierra Leone and Benin.

However, there are still some thinly populated areas, such as the interior of Liberia and much of Gabon, where little stabilization has occurred and shifting cultivation is still widespread. Although the great majority of people in tropical Africa are primarily cultivators, there are areas, such as large parts of Mauritania and Somalia, where nomadic pastoralism is still the dominant form of land use. Even in these areas, however, there is a trend towards stabilization. Sometimes it is associated with the provision of water supplies at fixed points, sometimes with the adoption of cultivation as a subsidiary activity, at least by the women. In Somalia in particular this trend was intensified by the effects of the droughts of the early 1970's.

New Techniques

A prerequisite for improved productivity in tropical African agriculture is the adoption of a wide range of new techniques such as the use of more efficient implements and the application of fertilizers. The majority of farmers employ no labourers and have no machinery, and are therefore able to cultivate only as much land as they can clear, till, weed, and harvest with their own energy and simple hand tools. They can combat the infertility of the soils of most areas only by constantly clearing new land, and have no means of overcoming most pests and diseases. In some cases effective methods of tackling the problems posed by the tropical African environment have been evolved by the local farmers, but in others no satisfactory solutions have been found either by them or by advisers from outside. In yet others lines of possible advance are known, and the chief difficulties lie in putting them into general practice. Vast numbers of farmers have to be made aware of the possibilities and often have to be given assistance where new techniques involve a capital outlay. However, various forms of progress are taking place in at least some parts of the region.

Many of the new developments are related to the increasing stabilization mentioned above. Some, such as the application of manure or fertilizer, permit greater intensification of land use in areas of population pressure. In the case of others, such as mechanization, agriculture may be just as extensive as before but can take place from a fixed base. These contribute to greater productivity per man rather than per unit of area, and there is most scope for such developments in areas where land is not in short supply, and sometimes therefore where there is no spontaneous trend towards stabilization.

OX PLOUGHING

Several important lines of advance involve greater integration between the cultivation of crops and the rearing of livestock. Most farmers in tropical Africa engage in both activities, but regard each as quite separate from the other. Animals have been traditionally used as beasts of burden in very few parts of tropical Africa, but there are a number of countries in which ploughs drawn by oxen were already widely used in the mid-1950s (Plate 5).

One of these is Ethiopia, and the widespread use of ploughs there probably contributes to the relatively high level of food production achieved. Elsewhere ox ploughing was practised by very few farmers until recently, but is now of increasing importance, as in the cotton-growing areas of Mali and Chad, in northern Nigeria, and in the Sukumaland area of Tanzania. In all these areas much of the land is level, the natural vegetation is not too difficult to clear, and the people are already familiar with cattle.

This is a development which is greatly favoured by some writers on African agriculture, such as Dumont, and which could be extended over far larger areas in the future. A farmer can often cultivate three or four times as much land with an ox-plough as with a hoe, without having to change his whole farming system or to incur any large capital outlay. The chief obstacle in many areas seems to be the tradition that cattle are the concern of the men, while cultivation is the women's responsibility. Where this is the case the spread of ox ploughing clearly involves a major social change. There are also other problems, such as the difficulty of weeding the larger area that can be cultivated and because of these, ploughing has not brought a marked increase in productivity everywhere that it has been adopted.

MECHANIZATION

A tractor-drawn plough increases the area that can be cultivated much more than one drawn by oxen, and in many African countries there is a wish to bypass the latter and to move straight into mechanized farming. Unfortunately, few of the attempts that have so far been made within the context of small-scale farming have proved successful. The problems that have arisen include difficult terrain, the small size of plots, the limited resources of each farmer, and the seasonal nature of the tasks to be performed. The tractors generally have to be provided by the Government for use by a number of farmers, and problems of organizing their use, and especially their maintenance, have been very great. In addition, the difficulties presented by the possibility of mechanizing some operations but not others are even greater than in the case of ox ploughing. As a result, where tractors have been introduced they have rarely brought a return adequate to justify the large amounts of foreign exchange required for their import.

Nevertheless, there are places where mechanization has taken place with some success, such as on the Grimari scheme in the Central African Empire, and especially in the central rainlands of Sudan. Conditions in this part of Sudan are particularly favourable. The land is very flat and almost treeless, and although the cultivation is undertaken by peasant farmers, much of the land is owned by wealthy businessmen who have the capital to pay for the tractors and holdings large enough to keep them occupied. Mechanization has also played an important role in the highly successful Gezira irrigation scheme, a little to the north, and in other irrigation schemes such as at Richard-Toll in Senegal.

There are other countries, such as Tanzania, where programmes of mechanization have begun very recently. It is as yet too soon to pass judgement on these developments, but even when the extent of their impact does become clear it will not be possible to give a simple answer to the question of the merit of mechanization in African agriculture. The only point on which there will be no doubt is that conditions are more suitable for it in some areas than in others. Where the land is rugged, the vegetation is dense, farms are very small or labour is abundant, as in most of south-east Nigeria, the highlands of Rwanda and Burundi, and the Kikuyu country of Kenya, the scope for mechanization is much more limited than on the flat and sparsely populated plains found in parts of Sudan, the Central African Empire, and Tanzania.

FERTILIZERS AND INSECTICIDES

Although the amount of fertilizer used in small-scale agriculture in tropical Africa is still extremely small even in comparison with countries such as Algeria and Egypt, it is now rising year by year in certain areas. Nitrogenous fertilizers are now applied to many irrigated cotton fields in Sudan, total consumption in that country having risen from around 10,000 tons in the mid-1950's to 40,000 tons in 1966 and 70,000 tons in 1973. In parts of Senegal, where years of groundnut cultivation have exhausted the soils, phosphates are now being applied with very beneficial effects on yields, and the practice is likely to increase greatly now that these are being produced locally. Potash is also being used increasingly in both these countries, and also in Ivory Coast, where it is playing a part in the rapid increase of cash-crop production. In East Africa, fertilizer consumption is rising on small farms in Tanzania, where trials on Ukerewe Island in 1962–3 were so successful that a big campaign was launched for their use throughout Sukumaland: but large farms in Kenya still account for most fertilizer use in East Africa, in the same way that Rhodesia has by far the largest consumption among all the countries of tropical Africa by virtue of its flourishing large-farm sector.

Sufficient is now known about the benefits of fertilizer application to justify its encouragement over far larger areas of tropical Africa. Yet there is still a need for more study in this field, with an emphasis on establishing which types are most appropriate in each part of the region. There is often a temptation to apply the results of an experiment in one place to wide areas, but since the soils differ greatly from one district to another in the nature of their mineral deficiencies, this is often unwise. It must also be established in each case that the undoubted benefits will outweigh the costs incurred, and this may depend on many other considerations such as marketing facilities.

A more widespread development has been the application of insecticides, especially to the main cash crops. Thus many farmers in Ghana, Ivory Coast, and south-western Nigeria are now using gamalin (BHC) to protect cocoa-trees from capsid bug. In Nigeria this was first tried only in 1957, yet by 1964 almost 180,000 hectares were being sprayed, with excellent results. In Tanzania a great expansion of cotton production has been assisted by spraying against bollworm, and in Kenya the use of insecticides has contributed to the success of the extension of coffee growing to the Kikuyu farmers. Even so, the consumption of insecticides in tropical Africa as a whole is still very small, and there is great scope for the further expansion of agricultural production by this means.

Where fertilizers and insecticides are now being widely used, this is to a large extent due to government assistance, for most farmers have difficulty both in realizing the benefits that they can bring and in finding the cash to pay for them. In all the countries mentioned above, publicity campaigns have been undertaken, and either subsidies or loans provided for the farmers. However, these forms of development involve much less change in existing farming patterns than the introduction of mechanization, or even ox ploughing; and once the benefits are seen and the farmers have built up some capital, the use of fertilizers and insecticides becomes more spontaneous, at least in the case of cash crops. Effort may then have to be focused on their application to food crops, which presents greater problems especially in areas where these are the women's concern and yield no cash income.

Indeed, the use of fertilizers and insecticides illustrates clearly the importance of considering the agricultural system of any area as a whole, as well as in terms of individual components. If income obtained from cash crops can be used in part to buy fertilizers for food crops grown for subsistence, the resulting higher yields will mean that there is more land and labour to spare for an expansion of cash crop production. At the same time the benefits of a given investment in fertilizer or insecticide may be much increased if it forms part of a "package" of improvements which may also include, for example, new varieties of seed.

IMPROVED VARIETIES AND QUALITY OF CROPS

The past twenty-five years have witnessed considerable progress in the development of new varieties of crops and in the spreading of those known earlier among larger numbers of farmers. A striking example is provided by Amazon types of cocoa, which yield quickly and heavily and seem to be resistant to swollen-shoot disease. Seedlings of this type were distributed to many farmers in Ghana in the late 1950s, and this has contributed to the great expansion of production since then. The new varieties have also been introduced in the other cocoa-producing countries of West Africa with equal success.

New varieties are more easily introduced in the case of annual crops as long as there is some mechanism for producing and distributing the new types of seed. They have been particularly important in the case of cotton, new types which either give higher yields or are more resistant to disease having been introduced in most of the main producing countries at some stage during the past two decades. Again the task is much harder in the case of food crops, although recent experiences with wheat and rice in Asian countries, sometimes termed "the Green Revolution", indicate the potential benefits. One problem limiting the spread of new maize varieties in Africa is that some of these are higher yielding only in the sense of being more responsive to fertilizer. Even where the maize can be sold to provide cash for the fertilizer, further problems arise if the increased supply merely lowers the local price that the farmer can obtain for his maize, again indicating the need for improvements in marketing facilities.

Perhaps the form of agriculture advance in which the greatest degree of success has been achieved in tropical Africa in recent years has been the improvement in quality of most of the export crops. This has done something to offset the general trend towards falling prices for these crops on world markets. In Ivory Coast, for example, there has been a great improvement in the quality as well as the quantity of coffee produced, the proportion classified as first-grade rising from 18% in 1959 to 93% in 1964. In Nigeria around 1955 less than 10% of groundnut purchases in that country were classed as "special grade", but by the late 1960's only nuts of that grade were bought for export. A special effort is now being made in many countries to raise the quality of the coffee crop in the face of quotas on the quantity of exports to traditional markets. In some cases the improvement has taken place in the harvesting or sorting of the crop by the farmer, while in others it has occurred in the primary processing operations. In either case it has usually resulted from governmental efforts to bring about this change, often by the setting of artificially high price differentials until the improved practices have become generally accepted.

THE PRODUCTIVITY OF LIVESTOCK

There are probably about 120 million cattle in tropical Africa, and an even larger number of sheep and goats, and in general these numbers are steadily rising, although the disastrous droughts of the early 1970's brought a setback over vast areas of the Sahel zone from Mauritania, across Mali, Upper Volta, and Niger, to Chad, and also in Somalia and parts of Ethiopia. The majority are owned by people whose chief concern is cultivation, but some are owned by people who grow no crops and depend entirely upon their flocks and herds for their livelihood. These pastoral groups are usually very conservative in outlook, and change their ways only slowly. Attempts are being made to improve the quality of their animals by controlled breeding and an assault on disease, but with limited success. Efforts to persuade these people to tackle problems of overgrazing by reducing the size of their herds have, of course, met with even less success.

Many of the people who depend largely on cultivation have an almost equally conservative approach to their cattle, partly because they are often kept more for social than for economic reasons. As noted above, they are not usually employed for ploughing, and their manure is rarely applied to the land. Furthermore, their milk yield is extremely low, and they provide much less meat than they could with different management. Partly because of this low productivity and the consequent obvious scope for improvement, livestock are sometimes considered to offer the greatest opportunities for development in the rural sector. This is suggested, for example, in several national development plans.

The present picture is not an entirely static one, however. One long-term change in progress is the blurring of the distinction between pastoralists and cultivators as more of the former take up some cultivation and more of the latter regard their livestock as an economic asset. Not only has there been some integration in the form of ploughing and manuring the land, but also meat and milk production is slowly rising and new methods of disease control are being applied. But whereas livestock numbers are increasing almost everywhere, most of these improvements are highly localized. One of the most striking developments has taken place in Kenya, where dairying has extended from European farms to many areas of small African farms, especially in the vicinity of Nairobi. Many farmers there have fenced their land, bought a few cows of European breeds, and now regard milk as one of their chief sources of income. Yet elsewhere in the country, among the sedentary Luo as well as the nomadic Masai or Turkana, animal husbandry is changing very little.

In neighbouring Somalia, stock rearing dominates the economy, and there improved marketing arrangements have allowed livestock to contribute substantially to increased exports. The value of sales of live animals, especially to Saudi Arabia, has increased from $4 million in 1960 to $35 million in 1974, and now far exceeds the value of the previous major export commodity—bananas, while exports of canned meat have now begun.

Many development plans lay particular stress on the scope for raising productivity, and

28

especially for improving diets, by expanding pig and poultry raising. The case for this seems strong, especially where feeding stuffs are readily available in the form of such cash-crop residues as groundnut cake, yet little has yet been achieved. Pigs are, in fact, of very small importance in tropical Africa, though it is notable that they have formed one of the very few growth points in the farming pattern of Benin. Chickens are much more widespread and the chief source of meat in many areas, though data on this subject are even more scarce than for most other agricultural activities. There are some countries such as Uganda in which numbers are thought to have risen greatly in recent years, but there are many more in which they are assumed to have remained almost static. Perhaps it is indeed in such modest ways as keeping more and better poultry that most can be done to ensure that the people of tropical Africa are better fed, and especially that improvement shall be spread over large areas rather than confined to a few favoured areas.

Structural Change

LAND TENURE

There is little doubt that land-holding arrangements present a serious hindrance to agricultural development in much of tropical Africa. These differ from place to place, but the usual system is one in which all land is owned by the community as a whole but each farmer has some security of tenure on the land which he (or she) is cultivating. Among the direct consequences of this system, the most serious is the impossibility of using the land as a security for obtaining credit: but it is also widely considered that there is less incentive for the farmer to improve his land, with fertilizers for example, than if he owned it. Grazing normally remains a communal right, so that the individual progressive farmer may not fence his land to improve the pasture and protect his livestock from contamination by others. A further widespread problem is the fragmentation of the land, to which each family has a right, into many scattered parcels.

There are several areas where this pattern has been undergoing change for many years as a tradition of individual ownership has developed. Often this has been associated with the establishment of permanent tree crops, as in the cocoa districts of Ghana. This process is continuing to spread there, as also in neighbouring Ivory Coast. It is also taking place in various parts of East Africa, as on the densely settled slopes of Mount Kilimanjaro and Mount Elgon. In Kenya it has been greatly accelerated by government policy, as noted below.

In certain other countries, notably Ethiopia and Sudan, much of the agriculturally productive land has been privately owned for decades, but a few rich landlords rather than by the cultivators themselves. In Sudan this situation appears to have assisted certain types of change, such as mechanization, and if land reform is needed it is for social rather than economic reasons: but in Ethiopia, where the tenure system is sometimes described as "feudal", the landlords have rarely instigated change, and, as in so much of Latin America, land reform is considered by most outside observers as essential for any substantial agricultural development.

REORGANIZATION OF SMALL-SCALE FARMING

In several parts of tropical Africa the agricultural scene has changed over the past two decades through the direct intervention of governments, which have decided that rapid improvement can be effected only by the planned reorganization of small-scale farming. In some cases this has involved major modifications in the techniques of farming, while in others the main emphasis has been upon changing the land tenure arrangements.

One of the most successful developments of the 1950's was the creation of *paysannats* by the Belgians in many parts of Zaire. These did not aim to change the traditional system of land tenure, or even to abandon all aspects of shifting cultivation: instead they retained communal tenure, and modified the farming system into a more regular land rotation, often by clearing and cultivating for a few years successive "corridors" through the forest. These *paysannats* appear to have brought increased productivity in many areas, and to have assisted the spread of cash crops, especially cotton: but as a result of the political disturbances since 1960, most of the ground thus gained has now been lost. Similar *paysannats* established by the French also proved successful in many areas, including cotton-growing districts in northern Cameroon, and these continue to operate today. In other former French territories, however, notably the Central African Empire, they seem largely to have failed to have any impact on agricultural production.

Efforts by the British to transform peasant agriculture in Malawi and Rhodesia during the 1950's also largely failed, partly because they aimed to bring about fundamental changes, especially in land tenure, without any immediately obvious benefit to the farmers, and partly because they were seen as an attempt by the increasingly unpopular colonial authorities to gain more control over African land. The programme of agricultural reform arising out of the 1951 Land Husbandry Act in Rhodesia was pushed ahead with great vigour in the late 1950's, but within a few years it was largely abandoned. It is generally agreed that the programme was sound in principle, but often pointed out that it could not be applied in practice in many areas unless the African farmers were given access to a larger area of land.

The most successful programme of reorganization in English-speaking Africa has undoubtedly been that implemented in Kenya as a result of the 1954 Swynnerton report (Plate 7). This has involved the registration under individual title of a vast area of central Kenya together with smaller areas in the west of the country and, in many cases, the consolidation of formerly fragmented holdings. At the same time a comprehensive farm-planning service has operated, and the success of the scheme has depended to a large extent on the fact that it has coincided with the first major government effort to encourage cash-crop cultivation on small farms in these parts of Kenya. It is generally accepted that this programme has brought about a great increase in agricultural productivity and that it has contributed to the emergence of a new class of farmers, especially in the Kikuyu areas, who are now determined to improve their farms in every way possible. The new land-tenure pattern has been especially significant for the growth of the small-scale dairy industry mentioned above.

RESETTLEMENT

Kenya is one of a number of countries where agricultural change has included a substantial programme of resettlement of the rural population. There the problems of transforming the farming system of large areas of dense African settlement have been eased by the possibility of offering land elsewhere to some of those who do not have a holding large enough to provide a reasonable livelihood however it were organized. During the late 1960's more than 400,000 hectares of land in the former "White Highlands" were transferred from about 1000 European farmers to 30,000 African farmers (Map 2.1). Most of the areas chosen for this resettlement have been on the margins of areas of dense African settlement, and therefore movement over only a short distance has been involved.

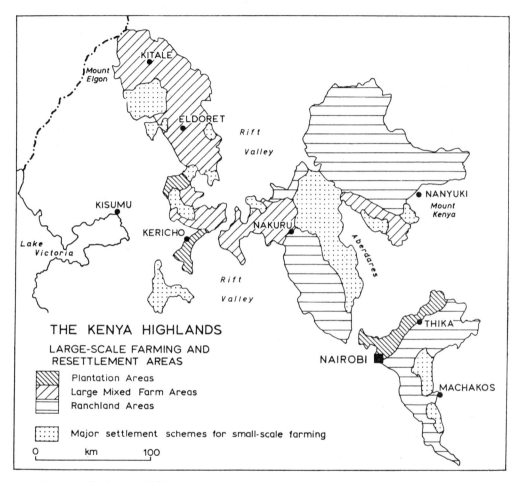

MAP 2.1. The former "White Highlands" of Kenya, indicating the extent of resettlement areas and the pattern of large-scale farming which remains.

Various problems have arisen in connection with the allocation of schemes between different tribal groups, the selection of settlers, and the type of farming to be established. In most cases these have been resolved sufficiently well for the resettlement to be considered successful. There is no doubt that the farmers concerned are more productive than before they moved, although it is not yet clear whether the land they are now working is yielding more or less than when it was under European ownership. It is likely, of course, that productivity has increased in some places but fallen in others.

Major resettlement programmes were also implemented by the Portuguese in both Angola and Mozambique, though in these cases on newly opened land rather than to replace large-scale European farmers. Some of the schemes, indeed, involved European as well as African settlers. Others, such as several in Uige district of northern Angola, were attempts

31

to improve the productivity of peasant agriculture through a new start on new land rather than by reorganization *in situ* as on the French and Belgian *paysannats*. There were some disappointments, but many of the schemes certainly brought about a considerable increase in production, although at the cost of strict control by authorities which the African settlers regarded as alien.

In both south-west and south-east Nigeria, resettlement schemes have been established with the aims of providing employment for school-leavers and creating growth points in the countryside from which new techniques might be spread by example. Opinions about the success of these schemes differ considerably. They have rarely provided the settlers with an income high enough to justify the heavy expenditure involved, perhaps in part because control there has not been as strict as it might have been: but it may be too early to judge the extent of their demonstration effect. As far as south-east Nigeria is concerned, however, these small schemes were overwhelmed by the civil war, and the chaos that this caused has demanded completely new and far larger programmes of resettlement.

Special cases of resettlement have had to take place where land has been flooded behind dams on the great rivers of Africa. Both the Kariba and Kainji schemes, for example, involved the movement of about 50,000 people, and the Volta scheme rather more. These resettlement projects are not outstanding for their agricultural achievements, and are considered by some to represent missed opportunities. They have sometimes been regarded as an unfortunate necessity, and although the new settlers have managed to feed themselves within one or two years, their cash income is generally little higher than before they were moved. Greater productivity has been achieved in Sudan, where the people whose lands have been flooded by the Aswan High Dam have formed the settlers on an important new irrigation project on the Atbara River.

The most ambitious of all the resettlement programmes in tropical Africa is that being undertaken by the Tanzanian government under the name of *ujamaa vijijini*. It is intended that almost the entire rural population should move from their previously highly dispersed homesteads into new nucleated villages, and that in many areas the whole organization of farming should be changed. In particular, the previous trend towards individual ownership of land is being reversed, although plans for the cultivation of most of the village land on a collective basis have had to be modified in most districts. It is important to note that increased agricultural productivity is only one of the aims of the programme: others include the greater prospects of providing social services in nucleated villages, and in the words of the 1969–74 Development Plan (p. 26) to create "communities with no divisive class distinctions, and a healthy and stable social system where corruption, exploitation and inequality of wealth unrelated to work done can be eliminated".

In view of the diversity of aims it will be many years before the success of the programme can be judged. Two observations that may be made, however, are that the resettlement itself has made remarkably rapid progress, with an estimated 2 million people moving between 1969 and 1973, and that despite President Nyerere's insistence that such movement should be voluntary there was disturbing evidence of compulsion, at least at the local level, around 1974–5. A further feature of particular geographical interest is that whereas all parts of the country are due to be involved simultaneously, the enthusiasm for the programme has been far greater in poor regions such as Dodoma and Mtwara, where immediate benefits such as piped water supplies in the villages provide a great incentive, than in the relatively prosperous areas such as Kilimanjaro and West Lake where farmers with individual holdings, a steady income from cash crops, and reasonable access to water supplies, schools, and medical facilities do not see it as being in their interests. *Ujamaa vijijini* has already brought undoubted benefits to people in some parts of Tanzania, but it is not yet clear that it has had much impact on the broad pattern of agricultural production within the country.

It should be noted that not all the resettlement taking place in tropical Africa results from government initiative. The process of moving in search of new land is a well-established tradition for many peoples, and it continues in many areas today. In East Africa, for example, a spontaneous movement of people has taken place from the crowded parts of Sukumaland in Tanzania into Biharamulo, Geita and Maswa districts, and from many directions into the Bugerere area in Uganda. An outstanding example of such movement in West Africa is that occurring in Ivory Coast as farmers move into empty areas especially in the west of the country, thereby extending the zones of coffee and cocoa cultivation.

CO-OPERATIVES

An important development of recent years in many parts of tropical Africa is the growth of a strong co-operative movement. By grouping together in this way, peasant farmers can overcome some of the problems resulting from the small scale of their activities. It is in the field of marketing, especially at the primary level, that the co-operatives have a particularly great role to play. In some cases perhaps they have merely taken over the functions of other organizations such as private Asian firms in East Africa, but even there the identification of the farmers with the marketing and processing of the crop may have provided an incentive for greater production. In other cases the co-operatives have undoubtedly brought an improvement in marketing facilities and ensured for the farmers a better price for their crops.

The most remarkable growth of co-operatives since the mid-1950's has taken place in the Sukumaland area of Tanzania, where they are particularly concerned with the cotton crop. There has also been a considerable expansion in Kenya, where they have played a vital role in assisting the spread of tea cultivation on small farms. In several of the French-speaking countries, efforts to promote co-operatives have brought much less success, perhaps partly because they have been imposed from above rather than arising largely spontaneously.

CREDIT

One field in which the co-operative movement can be of great value is in the provision of credit facilities for small farmers, for there is a need for some link between the banks or government institutions which can provide this, and the vast number of potential small borrowers. Undoubtedly the problems of administering loans have formed the chief obstacle to a greater provision of credit in recent years.

There is conflicting evidence on the importance of credit for African agricultural development. Much striking advance has taken place without it where farmers have managed to acquire some capital either by periods of employment or by savings out of crop sales: and while several new organizations for providing loans have been established in recent years, not all the funds made available have been taken up. Yet in the right circumstances, especially where farmers have made some progress on their own but could make more with assistance, it can be very important in accelerating the types of development discussed

33

above. It may, for example, be used to buy equipment, fertilizers, or insecticides; or, in areas such as central Kenya, to buy dairy cattle; or, occasionally, even to buy more land.

AGRICULTURAL EXTENSION AND EDUCATION

All the changes discussed above have required a great deal of effort from workers in agricultural extension services who have the task of encouraging the individual farmers to put into practice the policies formulated by governments and the new techniques evolved in research institutions. While the nature of these services perhaps lies outside the field of geography, it should be noted that they themselves differ from place to place. Thus in most of the countries formerly under British administration, a structure has been inherited in which extension forms an integral part of the work of government agriculture and veterinary departments; whereas in many former French territories it has been delegated to French public corporations such as the Compagnie Française pour le Développement des Fibres Textiles, which has assisted the expansion of cotton cultivation in Mali and Cameroon, or the Compagnie Internationale de Développement Rural, which has encouraged *animation rurale* in the Bouaké region of Ivory Coast. Those responsible for extension work always have to decide to what extent they should concentrate attention on the more promising areas within each country, or alternatively help the poorest areas to catch up with the more prosperous; and there are differences between one country and another in the policy that has been adopted.

A further essential element in agricultural development is the improvement of agricultural education. Much criticism has been levelled at the type of education brought to tropical Africa by the colonial powers, which has tended to produce dissatisfaction with work on the land. Again there are differences between one country and another in the extent to which new educational programmes designed specifically for people whose work will be in farming have been established, whether at school or university level.

Irrigation

An important element in the improvement of tropical African agriculture, which involves both new techniques and new forms of organization and sometimes also resettlement, is the adoption of irrigation. One of the greatest problems faced by many parts of the region is the inadequacy and unreliability of the rainfall, and the most obvious way of tackling this problem is by harnessing the water of the rivers. Unfortunately, this is generally a costly operation, and where it has been attempted it has not always proved worth while in terms of returns on investment. Irrigation has, of course, been vital to Egypt for centuries; and the extension of the practice up the Nile into Sudan, notably in the Gezira area in the 1920's, proved extremely successful. But the scheme for irrigating the inland delta of the Niger in what is now Mali, initiated in 1932 and developed further in the early post-war years, produced extremely disappointing results.

The most important developments in irrigation in tropical Africa over the past two decades have been the extension of the Gezira scheme and various smaller schemes also in Sudan (Map 2.2). Between 1958 and 1962 irrigation using the waters of the Blue Nile was extended from the 400,000 hectares in the Gezira to a further 300,000 hectares to the southwest. Farming in this Manaqil extension is organized in a similar way to that in the older Gezira area, although the land, which is worked by tenant farmers who pay rent to a government board, is rather more intensively used. One-third of the land is under cotton, one-third

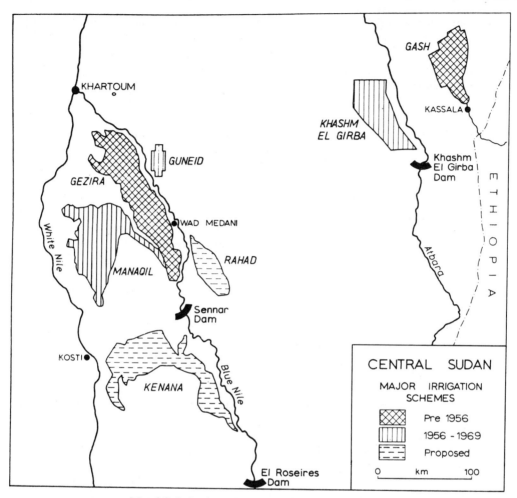

MAP 2.2. Irrigation schemes in the Republic of Sudan.

under other crops, and one-third under fallow each year, compared with one-quarter, one-quarter, and one-half respectively in the older areas. Furthermore, in order that the benefits of the scheme might be spread more widely, the average size of holding has been reduced from 16 to 6 hectares.

On the eastern side of the Blue Nile a new scheme was begun at Guneid in 1955, and this too has proved very successful. More pumping is needed than in the Gezira, and costs are higher, but the project has assisted a very poor area, and it has also helped to diversify the Sudanese economy since the chief crop grown is sugar rather than cotton. The supply of water for Guneid and for proposed southward extensions to Rahad and Hawata, as well as for the Manaqil development and for many smaller private pump schemes, has been greatly increased by the completion in 1967 of the $89 million Roseires Dam. This dam, the building of which was made possible by the 1959 Nile Waters Agreement, holds back a far larger part of the annual Blue Nile flood than did the older Sennar Dam. The Rahad scheme is due to cover over 300,000 hectares, and finance for development of the first 100,000 hectares for the cultivation of cotton, groundnuts, and wheat was secured in 1973.

35

Among other schemes in Sudan one of particular interest is that at Khashm el Girba, where a dam built across the Atbara River between 1961 and 1965, and costing about $20 million, has permitted an irrigation project which could extend to 200,000 hectares. This scheme has provided a new home for about 40,000 people from around Wadi Halfa, whose land has been flooded by the new Aswan Dam in Egypt, and appears to be progressing very successfully. Here, too, sugar is being grown as well as cotton, while sugar cultivation on a far larger scale is to be a major activity on the ambitious Kenana scheme which, unlike the Gezira and its extensions, is to draw water from the White Nile.

A second country in which irrigation has made an important contribution to recent expansion of agricultural production is Rhodesia. About 30,000 hectares have been brought under cultivation in the formerly little-used Chiredzi–Hippo Valley Triangle area of the lowveld, with the aid of the regular supply of water provided by the opening in 1960 of the Kyle Dam. However, this development is taking place on European-owned land and is in every sense large-scale farming. Some effort has been directed to the irrigation of African-held land also, notably in the Sabi valley, but the extent of this is very limited. A larger area of land has now been brought under irrigation for the benefit of African farmers in neighbouring Mozambique, where several of the most important of the settlement schemes mentioned above depend upon the waters of the Limpopo, Zambezi and other rivers. In the other countries of central and eastern Africa, irrigation has been largely confined to schemes for the production of sugar on a plantation basis, although one notable exception is the Mwea–Tebere project in Kenya, where rice production on plots of $1\frac{1}{2}$ hectares each by 1250 families has been successfully established. While minute in area in comparison with the schemes in Sudan, this scheme is to be followed up by others of much greater extent. In western Africa, too, developments in the field of irrigation have been very limited in recent years, although some efforts have been made to revive and expand both the Niger Inland Delta scheme in Mali and the Richard–Toll scheme in Senegal on which the French had also previously spent large sums with little return.

The expansion of irrigation as a means of increasing the productivity of African farmers during the past decade has therefore been localized. The greatest development in this, as in so many other ways, has taken place where most had already occurred. However, this may not necessarily continue to happen in the future, for plans have been made for the irrigation of vast areas in countries where it is now of limited importance. These include 200,000 hectares on the Volta Plains in Ghana, 200,000 hectares on the Kafue Flats in Zambia, and 100,000 hectares near the Cuanza River in Angola. At the same time it is widely recognized that a large number of small schemes may be of equal benefit to a vast scheme costing a similar amount, and there are plans for some development of this nature in most countries of tropical Africa.

Crop Production

The spread of new farming techniques and new agrarian structures are not ends in themselves but rather means to achieve greater agricultural productivity. To some extent this is achieved if the same quantities of crops are produced by fewer people, but in tropical Africa the number of people working the land is not falling. The increasing opportunities for employment in other activities are fully taken up by the general growth of population. Improved productivity therefore implies an increase in crop production, and this has been achieved to a greater or lesser extent in most countries.

In many places changes in techniques and organization have been accompanied by a change in the crop pattern. Over tropical Africa as a whole the pattern is very diverse, and the trend is towards ever greater diversity as new crops spread to particular parts of the region. Many of the changes are associated with a breakaway from a subsistence economy, and the crops discussed individually below are the main cash crops. It is, of course, often these which provide the funds required for changes in techniques which should in turn contribute to greater productivity. At the same time, modifications have been taking place in the patterns of subsistence-crop cultivation and, despite a decline in its relative importance, the total production of food crops for the farmers' own use has probably increased slightly.

INCREASING COMMERCIALIZATION

The increasing commercialization of agriculture, which has been taking place throughout this century, has continued during the past two decades. Probably the majority of farmers still spend the greater part of their time growing crops for their own use, but the time is now approaching when effort will be roughly equally divided between production for subsistence and for sale. Even in the early 1950's there were a few areas such as southern Ghana and western Senegal where the growing of cash crops was the chief activity; and in these areas the swing from subsistence to cash crops, and the consequent purchase of food, has continued. Meanwhile cash crops have come to play an important part in the farming pattern of other areas for the first time, as in central Kenya and the Lake Victoria area of Tanzania.

In addition there have been increasing opportunities for selling any surplus of the crops grown primarily for the farmers' own use, especially as a result of the expansion of the urban population. The fact that rapid urbanization was not in most countries accompanied by a great increase in the prices of basic foodstuffs until the 1970's indicates that with the incentive of a growing market farmers had little difficulty in producing a surplus of these food crops. Thus in Zaire there was a rapid expansion in sales of cassava to supply both the capital and the urban areas of Shaba during the 1950s, while in southern Uganda a sizeable urban market is at last developing for the surplus of bananas which can easily be produced there. In West Africa the requirements of the urban dwellers and the cash-crop farmers, especially for rice, have not so easily been met locally, and food imports have risen rapidly. An attempt to reverse this trend by increasing food crop production for sale has dominated the economic scene in Ghana in the early 1970's, while in Nigeria food supplies for the towns became a critical problem and prices rose steeply in 1975–6.

In many countries the change from subsistence to commercial production was deliberately checked by governments in the past, largely because of the fear of famine if adequate local food supplies were not guaranteed. The new independent governments have inherited this preference for self-sufficiency, especially at the national level, but there is increasing recognition that, at least at the local level, improved communications and marketing facilities make self-sufficiency in foodstuffs less necessary. This does not mean that subsistence agriculture should be abandoned everywhere, but there are areas where priority could now be given to increasing local trade in place of subsistence production. The opportunities for this are particularly clear in West Africa, where the prospects for export-crop expansion are still much better in the coastal zone than in the interior, and where the best prospects for the interior are probably for supplying increasing quantities of food

37

to the coastal zone. However, on a more local scale similar opportunities exist in many parts of Equatorial and East Africa.

The trend towards increased commercialization, and perhaps especially the prospects for its acceleration, concern the raising of livestock as well as the cultivation of crops. In general the pastoral peoples have demonstrated their conservatism in this respect as well as in relation to new techniques of husbandry; and even many of the cultivators who keep stock have shown less interest in obtaining a cash income from these than from crops. Nevertheless, the number of cattle from the pastoral areas sold to provide meat for people elsewhere has increased substantially, while among various cultivating peoples a start has been made in organizing sales of milk by those with large herds of cattle.

Kenya provides examples of both these developments, as sales of cattle from the Masai and other pastoral peoples have been organized by the Kenya Meat Corporation, and a remarkable development of small-scale dairying has taken place in Kikuyu country. In West Africa, on the other hand, the supply of cattle from Mali and Niger to the coastal states has increased very little, and the expansion of such trade offers one of the most obvious lines for future advance.

FOOD CROP CHANGES

While the most striking alterations in crop patterns in tropical Africa over the past twenty years, as over the whole century, concern the spread of various export crops, there have been some significant changes in the distribution of the crops grown primarily to provide local food supplies. The most widespread change has probably been the expansion of maize growing at the expense of the traditional African grains, finger millet, bulrush millet, and sorghum. This process of substitution has been taking place ever since maize was first brought from the Americas centuries ago, but it has gathered momentum in recent years. Maize is easier to grow than millet or sorghum, gives higher yields per hectare, is less liable to attack by birds, and in many areas is preferred as a food. Unfortunately, it is more demanding on the soil and is probably of lower nutritional value, and therefore in some countries, such as Uganda, the government has to some extent discouraged this change. It is also a more demanding crop climatically, and in many semi-arid areas a change from millet or sorghum to maize would spell disaster in years of drought. Among the areas where the change to maize has been most marked are parts of Kenya and Malawi where rainfall is quite adequate, though seasonal, and there is severe pressure of population upon the land.

Another change often associated with population pressure is the expansion of cassava cultivation, for this crop gives very high yields per hectare even in areas of low rainfall and poor soils. Its expansion is also closely associated with the development of cash crops and of seasonal or part-time wage earning, since it can provide a basic food supply with a minimum of both land and labour, and since the availability of cash allows the purchase of other foods which make up for its low nutritional value. Its cultivation has expanded particularly rapidly in the cash-crop areas of Ghana, Ivory Coast, and Senegal, and in the immediate vicinity of the rapidly growing towns in other countries such as Uganda. By contrast, there are other areas in East Africa, in Malawi, in the Central African Empire, and elsewhere, in which cassava cultivation expanded early in this century by government order as a precaution against famine; and in these areas relaxation of this compulsion, resulting from the greater availability of food supplies from other areas in times of shortage, has been followed by a reduction in the amount of cassava planted.

The food crop which has increased in importance at the most rapid rate in recent years is rice, which is the main staple in some West African countries and which is growing in popularity elsewhere also. Total production in tropical Africa is thought to have risen from just over 1½ million tons in the mid-1950's to 3 million tons today, although the consumption of this food has risen even faster, necessitating growing imports from Asia. Both because of these imports, and because of the high yields and nutritional qualities of the crop, governments in many countries have taken active steps to encourage increased local production. In Sierra Leone, Ivory Coast and parts of Nigeria these efforts have been rewarded with a rise in both area and yields. According to the FAO figures there has also been a modest increase in area planted in Guinea and Zaire. In most cases the increase in yields results in part from an increase in the proportion of the crop grown on floodlands rather than as upland rice.

Efforts have also been made to encourage more rice growing in Tanzania, in Rwanda and Burundi, in Malawi and elsewhere, but generally with limited success. The crop requires different techniques of cultivation from those to which farmers are accustomed, and involves hard and rather unpleasant work. Only when the benefits have been very clearly demonstrated, perhaps now—with the aid of new high-yielding types—will large numbers of farmers choose to take up rice growing.

Cash Crops

The most important of the crops grown on small farms primarily for sale are coffee, cocoa, cotton and groundnuts (Table 2.2). The production of each of these has increased

TABLE 2.2. VALUE OF AGRICULTURAL EXPORTS FROM TROPICAL AFRICA

	Exports in $US m. including derived products			
	Average 1955–7	Average 1965–6	Average 1971–2	Average 1974–5
Coffee	350	550	810	1220
Cocoa	340	390	670	1320
Cotton	260	280	440	430
Groundnuts	220	310	230	400
Palm kernels	93	110	80	150
Palm oil	78	60	41	100
Tobacco	76	160	90	200
Rubber	68	75	75	120
Sisal	45	62	35	130
Tea	26	62	92	130

Sources: FAO, *Trade Yearbook;* and national sources.

substantially in recent years, although, because of unstable prices, this has not brought a proportionate rise in income in every case. Annual fluctuations in the size of the harvest hinder exact comparisons, but as indicated in Tables 2.3 and 2.4 coffee and cocoa production have increased particularly rapidly.

COFFEE

Coffee growing has in fact expanded so much that the share of tropical Africa in world production has risen from 16% in 1955–7 to 26% in 1973–5 (Table 2.3). This crop has

TABLE 2.3. COFFEE PRODUCTION IN TROPICAL AFRICA

	Production in 000 tons		
	Average 1955–7	Average 1964–6	Average 1973–5
Ivory Coast	98	202	241
Angola	78	210	168
Uganda	70	190	201
Ethiopia	53	155	166
Zaire	37	57	90
Tanzania	22	42	56
Kenya	21	44	70
Cameroon	18	62	84
TROPICAL AFRICA	450	1030	1130
WORLD TOTAL	2800	4130	4420

Sources for Tables 2.3–2.9: FAO, *Production Yearbook;* and diverse commodity reports.

certainly had more effect than any other in bringing relative prosperity to various parts of the region during the past two decades. Coffee has long been a profitable crop to grow in the well-watered parts of tropical Africa, but the incentive to plant it was particularly great around 1953–5 when world prices were exceptionally high. However, the trees take four or five years to come into bearing, and when the greatest increase of production occurred, around 1960, prices had fallen sharply. The export price of Uganda robusta coffee, for example, dropped from its 1954 peak of $1200 per ton to only $370 per ton in 1961. Fortunately, there was subsequently some improvement, partly as a result of the acceptance of export quotas under the International Coffee Agreement, and while prices in the 1960's never approached their 1954 levels they still brought farmers a better return for their labours than they could obtain from most other crops. Coffee did not even share fully in the commodity price boom of 1974, but African countries have benefited from a trebling of prices during 1975 and 1976 largely as a response to devastating frosts in Brazil.

Although production rose throughout the 1960's as young trees came into full bearing, little new planting has taken place since about 1964. In face of an inelastic world demand, and the consequent need for export quotas, the emphasis in government policy has now generally switched from increasing quantity to improving quality as a means of earning greater income. The arabica variety normally fetches a higher price than robusta, and although their ecological requirements differ there is a marginal zone in which the latter is sometimes being replaced by the former. Where there is no alternative to robusta production, its quality can be improved by replacing the dry-processing technique by wet-processing, and this change is taking place in many areas. Even in these ways the scope for increasing income is limited, and effort is therefore also being directed everywhere to the expansion of other crops instead of coffee.

The expansion of coffee growing has been remarkably evenly distributed over the areas where physical conditions are suitable for the crop (Map 2.3). In Ivory Coast some coffee has been grown throughout this century, but planting increased greatly around 1950, bringing a sharp rise in production from 1954, and it was renewed around 1956, bringing the great expansion of production of 1960–2. The coffee growers were assisted by having free access to the large protected French market and by the payment of a guaranteed price there when prices on the open world market were falling. With the full implementation of

PLATE 1. Traditional Africa: among the areas where little change is taking place, and where prospects for development are poor, are the semi-arid zones such as this part of northern Tanzania.

PLATE 2. Traditional Africa: a very different type of problem area is exemplified by these highlands in Rwanda, where the main change occurring today is ever-increasing pressure of population on the land.

PLATE 3. Commercialization in agriculture: in much of West Africa there is a well-established tradition of internal trade as exemplified by this market in northern Ghana.

PLATE 4. Commercialization in agriculture: in most of East Africa internal trade is less well developed, but in certain areas export crops are now of great importance, as in this part of southern Uganda. The coffee being dried in the foreground is grown alongside the staple food crop, the banana.

PLATE 5. New techniques in agriculture: ox ploughing in eastern Uganda. Few parts of tropical Africa have a long tradition of using animal labour, and there is often scope for much closer integration of cultivation and stock rearing.

PLATE 6. New techniques in agriculture: mechanization on a large farm in the Kenya Highlands. In many countries there is a wish to avoid the stage of animal traction in peasant agriculture and to move directly from hand cultivation to mechanization.

PLATE 7. New structures in agriculture: land consolidation is contributing to a transformation of small-scale farming in parts of central Kenya such as that shown here.

PLATE 8. Distinctive structures in agriculture: the role of plantations in tropical Africa is gradually increasing, and one crop which many countries are beginning to produce on this basis is sugar, following the lead taken by estates such as this one in Uganda.

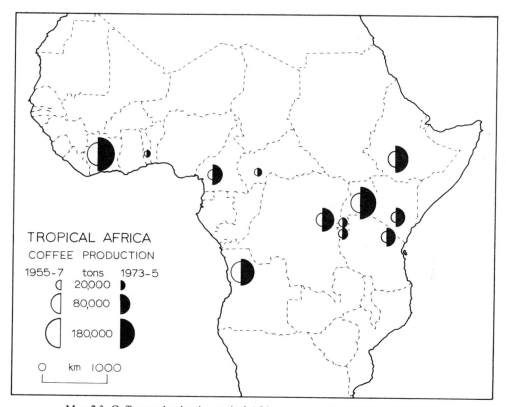

MAP 2.3. Coffee production in tropical Africa: averages for 1955–7 and 1973–5.

the EEC treaty this situation ended in 1968, and Ivory Coast is having to accept lower prices for its coffee; but at least the coffee boom has lasted long enough to give a considerable impetus to the growth of the whole national economy. It has also assisted a slight dispersion of prosperity away from Abidjan, since the crop is now widely distributed over the well-watered southern half of the country (Map 2.4), on about 300,000 farms.

In Uganda the expansion of coffee cultivation has followed a similar pattern, with great spurts in production taking place there in 1955 and 1960. Cotton had already provided the Ganda with experience of cash cropping, while coffee could be fitted into their agricultural system based on the perennial banana with no loss of food production. The government has been anxious to avoid overdependence upon one export crop, and no guaranteed market ever existed comparable to that which France provided for Ivory Coast, and so while coffee largely displaced cotton throughout Mengo and Masaka districts, it was not greatly encouraged in adjacent Busoga, where ecological conditions are almost equally suitable (Map 2.5). The government had intended to assist a spread of production in the early 1960's into western districts which lack other cash crops, but as world market conditions deteriorated this policy had to be largely abandoned just as Britain was handing over power.

In neighbouring Kenya in the 1950's, coffee production was much smaller, was expanding more slowly, and was largely confined to European estates. More recently, however, remarkable development has taken place, especially in the Kikuyu areas where coffee growing was formerly prohibited. Ecological conditions there are so favourable, and the

41

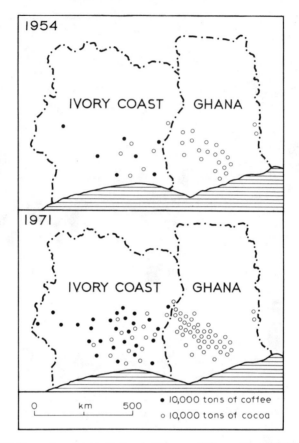

MAP 2.4. Coffee and cocoa production in Ghana and Ivory Coast: 1954 and 1971.

farmers have responded so readily to the reversal of government policy, that this has become the chief producing area of the country. The total area under coffee on African farms in Kenya rose from 1600 hectares in 1953 to 28,000 hectares in 1963. Kenya's adherence to the International Coffee Agreement then forced the curtailment of new planting, but so much of the area was newly planted that production continued to rise rapidly, until coffee-berry disease brought a check in the late 1960's.

The rate of expansion in Tanzania has been comparable to that in Uganda and Kenya. The areas that are climatically suited to coffee are rather limited, and in two of these, on the slopes of Kilimanjaro and west of Lake Victoria, the crop was already well established by the mid-1950's. Yet it is in these areas that most of the increased production has taken place. In the southern highlands there is more suitable land, but that area has suffered greatly from isolation, and there, too, plans for new development have now been shelved because of fixed export quotas.

In Angola up to 1974, coffee production was as large as in Ivory Coast and Uganda and had been expanding equally rapidly. From the old-established areas of cultivation near the Luanda–Malange railway it had been spreading both northwards over the Uige plateau, especially around Carmona, and south in the hinterland of Porto Amboim. The most distinctive feature of this development was that much planting took place on Portuguese

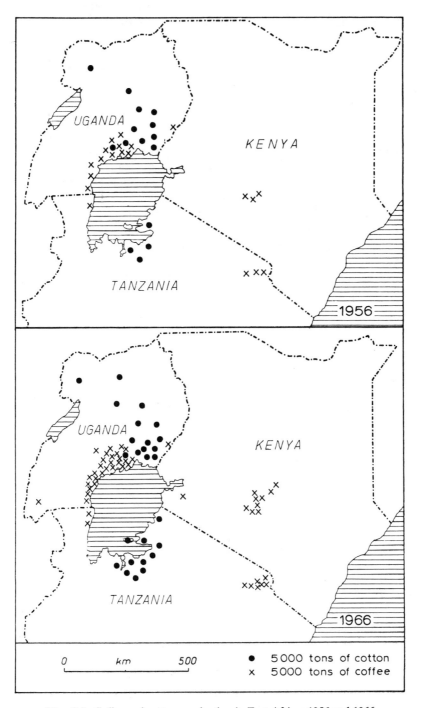

MAP 2.5. Coffee and cotton production in East Africa: 1956 and 1966.

settler farms and company estates: coffee growing on African farms had been spreading only slowly, so that these still accounted for only a quarter of the land under the crop in 1970. It is therefore not surprising that the political changes of 1975 brought a sharp fall in production.

Ethiopia and Cameroon have both shared in the increase of coffee production, and indeed had the most rapid and sustained expansion during the 1960's. In the past much of the Ethiopian harvest came from wild trees, but in the 1950's their share fell as the crop was planted on many farms both large and small. Notable among the new large estates are those around Harar, while much coffee is now being grown on small farms in formerly inaccessible areas south and west of Addis Ababa, such as around Jimma and Gimbi. Yields are lower than the African average, but quality is particularly high. Cameroon, in contrast, produces mainly high-yielding but lower quality robusta coffee from the coastal area around Douala, although increasing quantities of the superior arabica coffee are also being grown in the western highlands. Even in Zaire, coffee growing expanded during the 1960's, mainly in the Kivu region of the east but disturbed political conditions limited the rate of growth there, as also in Burundi and Rwanda, both of which depend on coffee as their chief export yet contribute very little to the total African production.

COCOA

Whereas Africa still produces only the lesser part of the world's coffee, it dominates world cocoa production (Table 2.4), and trends in the total supply largely reflect trends

TABLE 2.4. COCOA PRODUCTION IN TROPICAL AFRICA

	Production in 000 tons		
	Average 1955–7	Average 1964–6	Average 1973–5
Ghana	245	472	374
Nigeria	115	234	216
Ivory Coast	63	120	218
Cameroon	61	86	109
Eq. Guinea	23	33	13
Togo	6	16	15
TROPICAL AFRICA	525	980	1002
WORLD TOTAL	850	1320	1510

within Africa. Also in contrast to coffee, the main development of cocoa growing took place before World War II, and the size of the crop was smaller in 1956 than it had been in 1936. The main reason for this lay in the ravages brought by swollen-shoot disease during this period; and the success of the efforts to control the disease by cutting out all infected trees has played a large part in the rapid expansion of production which has taken place since 1957 and especially between 1958 and 1960. As in the case of coffee, a powerful incentive to plant new trees was provided by the very high prices obtainable in the mid-1950's. The operation of marketing boards in several countries limited the impact on the farmers to some extent, but although part of the proceeds in years of exceptional prices such as 1954 was withheld from them, a satisfactory price was still paid to them in the late 1950's by drawing on the funds which had accumulated earlier.

After 1960 the incentive to extend the area under cocoa was much reduced, world prices falling from $500 to $800 per ton in 1956–60 to around $400 per ton in 1965–6, and growers' prices falling similarly. Since 1967 there has been some improvement and cocoa shared in the 1973–4 boom in world commodity prices, but demand for cocoa is rising only slowly, and any great expansion of production would quickly depress prices again. There is some scope for increasing income from cocoa by improving quality, but less than in the case of coffee. A start has also been made on processing into cocoa butter and powder within tropical Africa, but the well-established processing firms in the consuming countries will not allow this to develop rapidly. In general, the main cocoa producers must look to other crops for their agricultural development in the near future, and those countries which hoped to join the ranks of producers now have to proceed very cautiously.

The area of tropical Africa physically suited for cocoa cultivation is much more restricted than that in which coffee can be grown, and production is largely confined to a zone extending from Ivory Coast to western Nigeria, together with a small zone in Cameroon. The rate of expansion in the 1950's and the early 1960's was fairly similar in each of the producing countries, so that the broad pattern did not change greatly: Ghana accounted for just under half the total, Nigeria for just under a quarter, and Ivory Coast and Cameroon for most of the remainder (Table 2.4). There is some indication, however, that Ghana's dominance is now decreasing, production having fallen there, and also in Nigeria, since the mid-1960's. This situation is generally attributed to poor maintenance, and especially decreased spraying with insecticides during the period of low prices, contrasting with sustained agricultural extension work in Cameroon and especially Ivory Coast, where production has continued to expand.

There has been more change in the geographical pattern of production within than between countries, as cocoa cultivation has extended to new areas. In some cases production in the old-established areas has actually declined as a result of disease, the ageing of the trees, and the impoverishment of the soils. In Ghana the north-westward shift from the country near Accra to Ashanti which had been taking place for some decades has continued; and it has extended onwards across the Western region and especially Brong–Ahafo region (Map 2.4). At the same time there has been some consolidation and some replanting in parts of the south, especially in Central region. The Yoruba areas of the south-west continue to account for nearly all the Nigerian production, but there has been some decline in the area around Ibadan, while expansion has taken place further to the east around Ife, Ondo and Owo. Within Ivory Coast there has been no marked change in the distribution of cocoa growing, partly because there has been more land available for new planting within the existing areas of production than in either Ghana or Nigeria. The great expansion of the crop has therefore reinforced the great disparity in income between the south-east and the rest of the country.

COTTON

The expansion of coffee and cocoa growing in the wetter parts of tropical Africa has been matched by a similar development of cotton and groundnut cultivation in the drier savanna lands. Cotton-lint production has increased from around 350,000 tons a year in 1955–7 to nearly 700,000 tons in 1973–5, and the share of tropical African countries in the world total has risen from $3\frac{1}{2}\%$ to 5% (Table 2.5). An expansion of the area planted each year, and the improvement of yields through the use of new varieties and the application of

45

TABLE 2.5. COTTON PRODUCTION IN TROPICAL AFRICA

	Lint production in 000 tons		
	Average 1955–7	Average 1964–6	Average 1973–5
Sudan	91	137	217
Uganda	68	79	55
Zaire	49	10	20
Nigeria	30	44	42
Mozambique	29	36	35
Tanzania	26	67	60
Chad	24	38	53
CAE	13	11	15
Angola	7	6	23
Cameroon	6	17	15
Ethiopia	5	4	20
Mali	2	9	22
Ivory Coast	2	6	23
Rhodesia	1	6	37
TROPICAL AFRICA	360	500	680
WORLD TOTAL	9,500	11,100	13,300

insecticides, have both contributed to this. World market prices fell in the mid-1950's for cotton as for coffee and cocoa, so that the income obtained from the crop at first rose very little (Table 2.2): but prices rose again even before the general price boom of 1973–4, and while improved synthetic fibres present a constant threat, export prospects are at present fair. In addition there is an expanding local market as the textile industry develops in African countries. Yet the income that can be obtained for a given amount of effort is still much lower than with coffee or cocoa, so that cotton cultivation is expanding only where tree crops cannot be grown. It is still rarely replacing food-crop production in peasant economies, but rather supplementing it, and the amount grown by each farmer is generally extremely small.

Map 2.6 indicates that cotton growing is widespread in tropical Africa, and the distribution has tended to widen further as the crop has developed in countries such as Cameroon, Ivory Coast, Ethiopia and Rhodesia where it was of little significance a few years ago. Nevertheless, there is an outstanding concentration in Sudan, which remains unchallenged as the leading producer. The size of the harvest there varies greatly from year to year according to the weather, but there was a general expansion as more land was planted with cotton until a peak was reached in 1962. The expansion took place on the Gezira extensions discussed earlier, on many private estates beside the Nile, and on a smaller scale in other parts of the country such as near the Nuba mountains in Kordofan province. Since 1962 government policy has emphasized the need for diversification of cash crops, and for some years no clear trend in cotton production was apparent; but cotton has been planted on much of the land in the new Khashm el Girba irrigation scheme, and a new peak was reached in 1971. At that time the Gezira and Manaqil areas accounted for 45% of the total area under cotton and for 60% of the total production.

In East Africa there has been a striking contrast between Uganda, where cotton production has not increased very much since its establishment as the main export crop early in the century (and where it has slumped to very low levels since 1974), and Tanzania, where rapid expansion took place between 1956 and 1966. In Uganda cotton growing became more

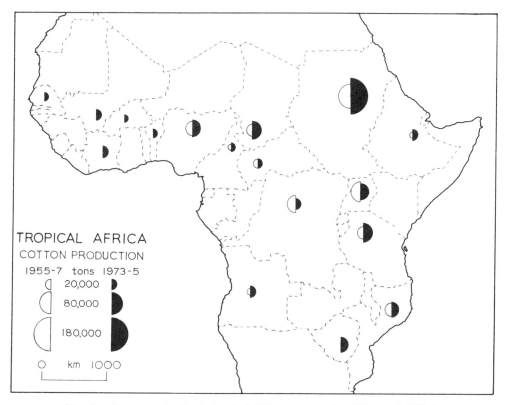

Map 2.6. Cotton production in tropical Africa: averages for 1955–7 and 1973–5.

widespread in northern districts in the 1950's and 1960's, but this has done little more than offset the contraction which took place in the south as farmers switched attention from cotton to coffee (Map 2.5). In no part of Tanzania has there been such a contraction, and in the area to the south of Lake Victoria there has been a remarkable spread of cotton cultivation as many farmers have for the first time devoted a large share of their effort to a cash crop. In the 1950's most of the increase resulted from an expansion of the area planted, both through a reduction in the fallow period and through a spread of settlement to new areas; but in the 1960s there was also an improvement in yields. In Mozambique cotton production has remained remarkably stable for many years, even the ending of Portuguese rule bringing no immediate change. In Rhodesia, by contrast, it expanded rapidly after UDI as European farmers switched from tobacco to a crop for which there was a local demand previously met by imports.

In West Africa cotton cultivation was spreading in several parts of the savanna zone until drought brought a setback in the early 1970's. In northern Nigeria production increased substantially in the 1950's, but little subsequent development has occurred there despite the creation of new markets in the Nigerian textile industry. As this has taken an increasing share of the crop, exports have ended. French efforts to establish a second Gezira on the inland delta of the Niger in Mali brought little success, but during the 1960's there was some increase in production in that country, both on the Niger scheme and in the higher rainfall areas in the south-west. Cotton growing has also spread in Benin, Upper Volta, and the

47

Niger Republic, as those poor countries have sought new sources of income, though as yet on a very modest scale. Indeed, their production has been quickly surpassed by that in Ivory Coast, which is intended to extend development within that country from the well-watered south to the drier north, and which is largely absorbed in the local textile industry.

In Cameroon, too, efforts have been made to spread agricultural development more evenly, and the rapid increase in cotton growing in the north around 1959–63 has contributed to this. In adjacent Chad, cotton cultivation already dominates the commercial economy, but since there are few alternative cash crops, and despite great problems such as the high cost of transport to the coast, the government is engaged on a massive programme to increase production. Up to 1965 the rate of increase was slow, but since then the size of the crop has almost doubled, mainly as a result of increased productivity on existing farms. Similar efforts in the Central African Empire have had little success: there cotton growing seems very unpopular, perhaps because of memories of forced cultivation in the distant past. Further south the situation in Zaire is different again for production slumped when marketing arrangements were completely disrupted after 1960, and although there are signs of revival the annual harvest is still far smaller than in the 1950's.

GROUNDNUTS

Groundnuts differ from cotton in that they are grown for subsistence as well as for cash, but they are cultivated in similar areas, and their production also increased during the 1960's. Groundnut production was, however, hit much harder by the drought in the Sahel zone in the early 1970's (Table 2.6), and in some areas it had still not recovered by 1976.

TABLE 2.6. GROUNDNUT PRODUCTION IN TROPICAL AFRICA

	Production in 000 tons of nuts (in shell)			
	Average 1955–7	Average 1965–7	Average 1970–2	Average 1973–5
Nigeria	1,020	1,570	1,200	350
Senegal	760	1,030	730	1,050
Niger	160	290	250	90
Uganda	160	200	210	200
Zaire	160	110	180	250
Sudan	120	310	360	910
Mali	120	130	140	120
Malawi	100	180	190	170
Gambia	80	120	110	150
Cameroon	80	130	200	170
TROPICAL AFRICA	3,250	4,800	4,700	4,500
WORLD TOTAL	13,300	16,400	17,400	19,200

Groundnuts, like cotton, being a relatively small return for the labour involved in growing them, especially in inland areas where transport costs absorb a substantial part of the export value: but at least world prices remained fairly stable from 1956 to 1966 when those for other crops had fallen, and they rose sharply in the mid-1970's. In some countries it has been possible to increase the value of the crop by crushing an increasing share into oil before export, and in all the internal demand for vegetable oils is gradually rising. Thus while the value of groundnut exports from tropical Africa did not rise greatly during the 1960's, the total value of the crop including that crushed locally increased substantially.

The cultivation of groundnuts is as widespread as that of cotton, and before the severe drought some expansion had taken place almost everywhere. The largest producer is normally Nigeria, and although the crop there has always fluctuated sharply from year to year, it showed a general increase from about 1 million tons in the mid-1950's to 1½ million tons in the mid-1960's. There was little evidence of major changes in the distribution of production within Nigeria, the Kano area remaining the most important zone, but there was a notable increase in Bauchi in the early 1960's. A factor which may prove to have brought some change when total production returns to normal is the recent adoption of a uniform grower's price in all areas irrespective of varying transport costs.

The second major producer is Senegal, and there, too, production rose steadily up to 1967 although the increase was rather slower than in Nigeria, partly because the country was already far more dependent on this crop and the government was reluctant to increase this dependence. Groundnut exports from Senegal were rapidly shrinking even before the drought, but this was largely due to local milling which provided oil for export. The distribution of production within the country has not changed greatly since the 1930's, but there has been some spread from the old-established areas around Thiès and Kaolack to the Diourbel region and even further inland. Within Senegal lies the small state of Gambia, where groundnuts provide well over 90% of total exports. The rate of expansion has been higher there than in Senegal, and the current development plan aims at maintaining this growth. The government has decided that the prospects for groundnut exports are better than for any other crop which the country could produce, though more could be done to increase the share of the crop exported in the form of oil rather than nuts.

The most rapid expansion in West Africa in the early 1960's took place in Niger Republic, where many farmers began to grow a cash crop for the first time during those years, and where groundnuts became much the most important export despite the high cost of transport to the coast. One factor favouring expansion of the crop in this country, as in Senegal, was the provision of a guaranteed market in France at prices above general world levels, and both countries suffered as a result of the abolition of this preferential treatment in 1967. But in Niger drought later brought a much more serious setback. The production of groundnuts has also increased in Upper Volta, Chad, the Central African Empire, and especially the north of Cameroon, but in each case primarily for local use.

The cultivation of groundnuts as a subsistence crop is more important in Uganda than anywhere else, but there is no evidence of much expansion there. Efforts to encourage the production of a surplus for export have frequently been made but without much success. Much more success has been achieved in Sudan, where groundnut exports developed rapidly in the early 1950's, increased further between 1960 and 1964, and surged forward again in the early 1970's. More have been planted both in dry-farming areas such as the Qoz, and also on the Gezira and Guneid irrigation schemes, where much land formerly planted with lubia fodder has been turned over to groundnuts, mainly to reduce the overdependence on cotton for export income. Sudan has thus taken the place formerly occupied by Nigeria in world markets for groundnuts, and this crop has contributed greatly to the increased income of many Sudanese farmers since 1970.

OIL PALM

The oil palm was once the most important source of revenue in West Africa, providing both palm oil and palm kernels for world trade as well as palm oil for local domestic use, but it has now been far surpassed in value by cocoa (Table 2.2). In contrast to all the crops just considered, cultivation of oil palms has not expanded in tropical Africa in recent years, but has stagnated. There was no boom in prices comparable to that for cocoa which might have stimulated expansion, and West African peasant production has suffered from competition from plantation production in Malaysia which has been increasing very rapidly. The tree grows wild throughout the forest belt from Guinea to Nigeria, and often the crop is not really cultivated at all, but rather wild trees are preserved and allowed to spread. In many areas the productivity of these trees is falling, but farmers have shown little interest in planting new trees to replace them. A further factor holding back production of oil and kernels has been a great increase in the practice of tapping the palms for toddy.

Exports of both palm oil and palm kernels have declined quite sharply over the past two decades. In the case of palm oil this is partly due to increasing local consumption, both for domestic purposes and for new oil-using industries, but even total production has probably risen only slightly in most countries. In the case of kernels it is partly due to the development of local crushing industries, which permit the export of kernel oil, and the value of exports of kernels and kernel oil together remained steady through the 1960's. Although prices have risen in the 1970's less than for coffee and cocoa, there is some evidence that market prospects are better for palm products than for most African cash crops, and little doubt that much more could be sold if production could be increased.

The largest producer of oil palms is Nigeria (Table 2.7), and the picture there is as has

TABLE 2.7. PALM OIL AND KERNEL PRODUCTION IN TROPICAL AFRICA

	Production in 000 tons			
	Palm oil		Palm kernels	
	Average 1955–7	Average 1973–5	Average 1955–7	Average 1973–5
Nigeria	440	480	440	280
Zaire	220	180	140	80
Sierra Leone	40	50	60	50
Benin	40	40	50	70
Cameroon	30	60	30	40
Ivory Coast	10	140	10	30
TROPICAL AFRICA	890	1100	820	680
WORLD TOTAL	1140	2720	990	1310

been described for West Africa in general. There was an improvement in both quantity and quality of palm-oil production in the 1950's as pioneer mills for processing the fruit spread through the growing areas, but since this advance was completed there has been little further progress. Indeed, the most recent change has been a serious decline in the whole industry as a result of the civil war, for the former Eastern Region was the main area of production. The reconstruction of the industry has been a vital task in the process of rebuilding the economy of that unfortunate area, although the opportunity has also been taken to bring about some diversification of the area's agriculture. Meanwhile the smaller production west of the Niger has remained little changed.

In Guinea, Sierra Leone, Togo, and Benin, as also in Zaire, virtual stagnation has prevailed throughout the post-independence period. This has been especially serious for

Benin, where the oil palm provides the greater part of exports, and where stagnation of the whole economy has resulted. The government of that country has made efforts to improve the situation, but has failed to arouse enthusiasm from the farmers almost everywhere: the only significant development has been the establishment of mills to crush most of the palm kernels before export.

The one major exception to the general stagnation is provided by Ivory Coast, where the many-faceted agricultural expansion programme has included the establishment of large-scale oil-palm production. Until the last few years the country had to import palm oil, but production rose from 8000 tons in 1956 to 28,000 tons in 1964, and then a massive planting programme raised it to 100,000 tons by 1973 and 165,000 tons by 1975, sufficient to meet local needs and to earn $50 million in exports. In sharp contrast to production by small farmers from semi-wild trees in Nigeria, this development has taken place on state-owned plantations with funds from the EEC and intensive technical assistance. A programme similar in nature, though much smaller in scale, has begun in Cameroon; and it is perhaps only through the revival of plantations in Zaire and their establishment on a large scale in Nigeria that the oil palm could recover its former importance in these countries. For the individual farmer other crops may offer better prospects.

OTHER CASH CROPS

In comparison with the crops discussed so far, all other cash crops grown on small farms are of small importance for tropical Africa as a whole. Some, however, are very significant for individual countries, especially in terms of diversifying the economy, and some have been expanding at a rapid rate. Two examples are cashew nuts and pyrethrum, which have been of increasing value to small farmers in the coastal and highland areas respectively in East Africa. Cashew-nut production has long been dominated by India, but now Tanzania, along with Kenya and Mozambique, has broken in on the market so successfully that production there has risen from 30,000 tons worth $3 million around 1957 to 160,000 tons worth $35 million in 1974. Kenya and Tanzania together dominate world production of pyrethrum, used in insecticide manufacture, and found sufficient markets for it to treble their sales between 1956 and 1961. At that stage the Kenya crop came mostly from large farms, and the resettlement process brought a sharp decline in production; but it has now reached the 1961 level again as the crop has provided the chief source of cash on many of the settlement schemes. Meanwhile expansion on small farms in Tanzania has continued, and production there by 1967 was four times larger than in 1961. Other examples of diversification of agricultural exports are provided by the rapid expansion of sales of oilseeds such as sesame from Sudan and Ethiopia to supplement cotton and coffee respectively.

Several crops which are still grown mainly on large farms have been spreading into areas of small-scale African farming over the past decade. The most striking example is the spread of tea cultivation from plantations to small farms in Kenya, the latter accounting for a third of the total area planted by 1967 and over half the total by 1972. Outgrower schemes around existing plantations have been developing in tea-growing areas elsewhere, and the same process has been taking place in the sugar industry. Tobacco has been grown by peasant farmers in several countries for a much longer period, although nowhere is the crop as important as on the large European farms of Rhodesia, which were earning over $100 million a year from the crop before UDI. It is of greatest significance in Malawi, and although the size of the crop there has fluctuated sharply the general trend has been upwards.

By 1972 tobacco exports were there worth $30 million, or 40% of all export earnings. Within Rhodesia it does not appear that much priority has been given to the spread of tobacco growing to areas of small-scale African farming. The chief West African producer is Nigeria, but production there has risen little in recent years: on the other hand, it has been developing in other West African countries, such as Ghana and Ivory Coast, to supply the local cigarette industries.

LARGE-SCALE AGRICULTURE

Only a very small proportion of the land in tropical Africa is used for any form of large-scale agriculture, but this type of farming should receive some special attention both because it makes a large contribution to the economy of a number of African countries and because it has undergone some substantial changes during the past twenty years. The term is used here to cover several types of farming, but in all of these large tracts of land are under a single management. They include mixed farms owned by European settlers and worked with a large amount of machinery and labour; farms worked in similar ways but established by governments; plantations which specialize in the production of a single crop and often incorporate factories to process it; and ranches which use vast stretches of land for cattle raising. No sharp divisions can be made between these, just as there is no clear-cut distinction between small-scale and large-scale agriculture. Tobacco farming in Rhodesia, for example, lies somewhere between the mixed farms and the plantations, for one crop is clearly dominant yet others often occupy a larger area. Nevertheless, it is easier to examine the changing patterns if this rough division into four types is made.

Large Mixed Farms

On the high plateaux of parts of eastern and central Africa, Europeans found land which appeared to be little used, and which provided opportunities for settlement based on a type of farming which differed little from that practised in much of Europe. The most important area for such settlement was Rhodesia, where Europeans own half the land and completely dominate the agricultural scene. In Kenya, too, European farmers have played a major role in the economy since the early years of this century. Even in Zambia they dominated commercial agriculture before independence, though there they were always overshadowed by the mining economy. Similar settlement also took place in the Portuguese territories.

On the whole the changes of the 1960's tended to accentuate the concentration of large European-owned mixed farms within only a small part of tropical Africa. In Rhodesia, Angola, and Mozambique this type of farming expanded considerably, but in Zambia the expansion was much more modest, while in Kenya growth before 1962 was more than outweighed by subsequent contraction.

In Kenya strong political pressure against the occupation of land by European settlers built up during the 1950's, and since independence land in the former "White Highlands" has no longer been reserved for this group. Indeed, some has been compulsorily purchased for African settlement schemes, and many European farmers have left the country (Map 2.1). The total number of large farms in Kenya (over 8 hectares) has fallen from 3600 to 3100, and their area from 3.1 million to 2.7 million hectares: and since the plantation sector has expanded rather than shrunk, the relative decrease in the extent of large mixed farms is greater than these figures suggest.

However, the extent of the resulting decrease in production from this sector is often exaggerated. After a drop around 1963–4, production of both wheat and maize on large farms has risen to new record levels, and the only crop in which there has been a large fall has been pyrethrum, now produced mainly on small farms. The share of the large farms in the dairy industry has also fallen, the number of dairy cattle on these farms having fallen from 413,000 in 1960 to 245,000 in 1967; but they had recovered to 308,000 by 1972, while the numbers of beef cattle and sheep have fallen much less. One of the main effects of the changes in Kenya has been to bring about a concentration of large mixed farms into a smaller part of the country, for those farmers who have had to sell their farms for resettlement schemes in areas such as the Kinangop plateau, but who wished to remain in Kenya, have often taken over the farms of those who have left voluntarily from the areas which remain untouched.

In Zambia, European agriculture expanded at an even more rapid rate than in Kenya during the 1950's, and it continued to expand, even if much more slowly, during the 1960's. The growth during the first period took the forms of a doubling of tobacco production, mainly through increased yields, and a trebling of the value of livestock and dairy product sales. More recently, these forms of activity have remained nearly static, and the main growth has been in the production of maize to feed the growing urban population. Far more maize is, of course, grown on small farms, but in most years these produce only a small surplus above subsistence requirements.

The pattern of development of European farming in Rhodesia between 1955 and 1965 was similar to that in Zambia, but on a much larger scale. The total value of sales from these farms rose from $98 million in 1955 to $140 million in 1960 and $185 million in 1965. By contrast, sales of produce from African farms were worth only $14 million in 1955, and were no higher in either 1960 or 1965. As in Zambia, the chief crops grown on the large farms are tobacco and maize, and the production of each of these doubled during this period mainly as a result of increased yields. Increased use of fertilizers, improved rotations, and new varieties all contributed to this. The improved rotations incorporated planted leys, and it is these which account for most of the increased extent of cultivated land. The farming system was thus moving from monocultures towards more truly mixed farming, the grass leys being used to feed increased numbers of cattle.

UDI and its aftermath has necessitated various rapid changes in the farming pattern since 1965. Despite the sanctions on exports, the government has continued to buy the tobacco crop, but its size was cut from 110 million kg in 1965–6 to 60 million kg in 1968–9. Some of the tobacco land has been used for a further increase of maize production, but with the encouragement of the authorities who are striving for self-sufficiency in the face of trade sanctions, some has also been used for wheat and cotton—both previously of very little importance. With the help of these adjustments the large-farm economy is surviving the political crisis. But even if this can be resolved the position of this sector in the future economy of the country poses problems. On the one hand, it is so efficient and so important in the economy that it should be preserved, though of course no longer on a racial basis; but, on the other hand, priority for agricultural development in this country must go to the desperate need to improve the lot of most small-scale farmers, including their access to a larger area of land. The experience of Kenya indicates that this might be possible without reducing the value of production from the large-farm sector.

In Angola and Mozambique the distinction between large settler farms and other types of farm was even less clear than elsewhere. Most of the European settlers were Portuguese peasants who were much poorer than their British counterparts in Rhodesia or Kenya, and their farms were generally much smaller. In Angola much coffee has been grown on such medium-sized farms as well as on small African holdings and large company-owned estates. In both Angola and Mozambique there are a number of settlement schemes on which both European and African farmers were originally included side by side. Up to 1974 these countries also differed from neighbouring states in that the process of European settlement was continuing as rapidly as ever, for land is still abundant and until Lisbon released its hold on these territories the prospects still seemed very attractive to many farmers struggling to survive in Portugal. But by 1976 new governments committed to socialist policies in both countries faced the challenge of how to deal with large numbers of abandoned large and medium-sized farms.

State Farms

Soon after independence, some African states embarked upon a policy of experiment with new forms of agricultural organization. One of these forms was the state farm, following the example of the Soviet Union. In both Ghana and Guinea such farms were established primarily to produce food crops by modern methods, with a considerable emphasis on mechanization. On some farms, livestock were incorporated into the system, though others were located in tsetse-infested areas where this was not possible. Yet others were concerned mainly with new cash crops, and thus differed little from government-owned plantations.

In both Ghana and Guinea these farms generally proved very unsuccessful, the value of their production by no means matching their costs of operation. As in the case of colonial schemes undertaken elsewhere in Africa in the early post-war period, the effective use and especially maintenance of mechanical equipment presented great problems; and as in the Soviet Union, it has been very difficult to persuade those employed to put as much effort into the farming operations as they would on their own individual holdings. Thus in Ghana the majority of the state farms have now been sold off or abandoned, and most of those remaining are being turned into plantations designed to diversify the economy by producing rubber or oil palms.

In East Africa a more cautious approach has been adopted in the establishment of large-scale mixed farms under government control. In Uganda this has been attempted, but in the form of "group farms" which involve less radical departures from traditional systems than the state farms of Ghana and Guinea. Mechanization is playing a rather smaller part in the operations, and in some cases the identity of each farmer's land has been preserved, even though all the land is worked together.

Plantation Agriculture

While the extent of large European-owned mixed farms has contracted somewhat in recent years, and while efforts to establish state farms have brought little success, a third type of large-scale agriculture—the plantation—has been increasing in importance in several parts of tropical Africa. Despite the fact that plantation agriculture is traditionally closely associated with colonialism, many of the new African states have accepted that it has an important part to play in their economic development. Frequently, as in Nigeria and Uganda for example, progress has been made in this field without altering the long-established policy of preventing the alienation of land, since most of the estates are owned by government corporations. Furthermore, the sharp distinction between plantations and peasant farms has been reduced in many places by the establishment of out-growers schemes. Under these schemes such crops as tea and sugar are grown on small farms in the neighbourhood of a large estate and are sent to it for processing.

In the 1950's plantation agriculture was much more firmly established in Zaire than anywhere else in tropical Africa, and there it has been somewhat disrupted by political upheavals; but it has been less disturbed than the production of cash crops on small farms, and it continues to play a major role in the national economy. Most of the large plantations such as those owned by Unilever have survived the period of unrest and have maintained their production at about the 1959 level; but conditions have not favoured much new investment. Liberia is another country in which plantations are of great importance to the economy, and there, too, relatively little advance has taken place, most attention having been focused on mineral development. The expansion of plantation agriculture has in fact occurred mainly in countries where its role in the past was very small, and where it is still far from dominant but rather contributes to the diversification of the economy. The result has been a marked dispersal of this type of land use.

It has, of course, not only been on small farms that opportunities have existed for increased efficiency through the changes such as improved equipment and crop varieties mentioned earlier. Some of the increased production from plantations also has resulted from higher yields rather than an enlarged area under cultivation. Much more fertilizer is being used now than twenty years ago, for example, and new techniques of disease control are usually quickly applied in this form of agriculture. Irrigation, too, has played an important part in recent plantation development. Such intensification of production has been especially important where the opportunities for occupying more land are limited, as on most of the privately owned estates in East Africa.

Plantation Crops

Among the crops grown in tropical Africa mainly on plantations, the most important are rubber, sisal, and tea, which are grown mainly for export (Table 2.2), and sugar cane, which is grown mainly for local use. The production of dessert bananas for export is also undertaken mainly in this way, while, as noted earlier, there is some estate production of coffee and oil palms. Some increase of production has taken place during the past twenty years in respect of each of these crops, although for some falling prices prevented much increase in the value of exports until the 1970's. Development has been particularly rapid in the case of tea and sugar, and these will receive most attention as the various crops are considered individually.

TEA

Tea production in tropical Africa doubled between 1948 and 1956, and this rate of growth has continued since, the total rising from 34,000 tons in 1956 to 70,000 tons in 1965 and 150,000 tons in 1974. As a result, Africa's share of world production has risen since the mid-1950's from 4% to 10%. Prices have remained more stable than those of most crops, and the value of tea exports from African countries has increased fivefold over this period (Table 2.2). Production costs are lower than in the major Asian producing countries, and tea was one of the most profitable crops to be grown in tropical Africa during the 1960's. More

TABLE 2.8. TEA PRODUCTION IN TROPICAL AFRICA

	Production in 000 tons				
	Average 1955–7	Average 1960–2	Average 1965–7	Average 1970–2	Average 1973–5
Kenya	10	14	23	44	56
Malawi	9	13	15	20	24
Mozambique	6	10	13	18	19
Uganda	3	5	10	20	21
Tanzania	2	4	7	10	13
Zaire	2	3	4	5	8
TROPICAL AFRICA	32	50	74	121	148
WORLD TOTAL	850	1000	1170	1320	1560

recently market prospects have become less bright, and the price of tea in world markets has risen much more slowly than that of coffee and cocoa.

The expansion of tea cultivation has brought no striking change in its distribution, for development has taken place in all the countries in which the crop was grown in the 1950's, and no major new producers have emerged (Table 2.8). However, growth has been slower in Malawi than elsewhere, so that country has lost the leading place among African producers which it held up to 1955. The amount of land there that is suitable for the crop is very limited, and the large companies operating there have increased the area planted only slowly, although much replanting has taken place on old estates. Outgrower production has as yet hardly begun. In Malawi more than elsewhere emphasis is now being placed on improved quality rather than increased quantity of tea production. If this increases the value of the crop it will contribute greatly to Malawi's development, for tea ranks second to tobacco among the country's exports.

In East Africa there is more land climatically suited to tea, and the governments of Kenya, Tanzania, and Uganda have all actively encouraged the development of this crop, especially as a means of diversifying exports which are heavily dependent on coffee. In addition to offering favourable conditions for new investment by private firms such as Brooke Bond, the governments have themselves established new estates and have assisted the spread of tea growing on small farms. In Uganda, for instance, production has risen eightfold since 1956 as a result of new planting by both the Uganda Development Corporation and private firms, and recently also by outgrowers around both types of plantation. Most of this expansion has taken place in the west of the country, which offers the most suitable environment, but the remoteness of which had discouraged European entrepreneurs in the past.

The most impressive development has occurred in Kenya, where tea production rose from 9700 tons in 1956 to 57,000 tons in 1973. This is partly the result of the expansion of the European estates in the Kericho area in the late 1950's, but the rate of growth has since been maintained mainly through the spread of the crop to small farms in several districts, notably those with dense Kikuyu settlement such as Nyeri. The establishment of 10,000 hectares of tea on 38,000 small farms between 1957 and 1968, and a further 20,000 hectares on these and 42,000 more small farms by 1973, has required close supervision through the Kenya Tea Development Authority: but it has been so successful that it has utterly disproved the widely held assumption that tea could be grown in Africa only on a plantation basis. This has been one of the most promising agricultural achievements of the past decade in the whole of tropical Africa, and it would be extremely unfortunate if further expansion were prevented by problems of world overproduction comparable to those which have beset the coffee industry.

A new area of production of the post-war period was Kivu province of Zaire, and this development is notable for the fact that production was maintained, and even increased, in the 1960's while other sectors of the economy were disrupted. The crop was originally established on European estates, but now small African farms account for half the area planted. Expansion of tea cultivation also provides one of the few bright features in the economy of Rwanda, although its contribution to total African production is very small.

RUBBER

Rubber, like tea, is much less important in Africa than in Asia, but it has long been a mainstay of the commercial economy in Liberia, and of some significance in Nigeria and Zaire (Table 2.9). Total African production has increased substantially over the past two

TABLE 2.9. RUBBER PRODUCTION IN TROPICAL AFRICA

	Production in 000 tons				
	Average 1955–7	Average 1960–2	Average 1965–7	Average 1970–2	Average 1973–5
Liberia	40	46	55	74	84
Nigeria	37	59	65	54	92
Zaire	31	37	27	37	36
Cameroon	4	7	12	14	16
Ivory Coast	0	0	5	13	17
TROPICAL AFRICA	112	150	165	195	247
WORLD TOTAL	1930	2100	2430	2990	3390

decades, although not to the same extent as that of tea, but falling prices resulted in the value of exports remaining almost static until the 1970's (Table 2.2).

In Liberia rapid expansion took place during World War II, when Japan occupied the main Asian rubber-growing areas, but production rose only slowly during the 1950's. Since 1964 it has risen faster again, for on the old Firestone plantations much effort has been devoted to the replacement of ageing trees, while in the late 1950's planting began on three new estates, the largest of which is that established by Goodrich to the north-west of Monrovia. Two further estates in other parts of the country came into production in 1967. Many observers have noted the limited impact of the alien rubber industry within Liberia, and its effects on the peoples of the interior are certainly still slight, but the growing of rubber on smaller Liberian-owned farms has now begun, and accounted for 30% of the production by 1974.

In Nigeria and Zaire, rubber growing has developed mainly after 1945. In Zaire most expansion occurred between 1950 and 1956, but some continued up to 1959 as new plantations in the heart of the Congo basin came into production. No new investment has been undertaken since then, but output was at least maintained through the 1960's. In Nigeria there have been several periods of rapid expansion since 1954, and in some years production has surpassed that in Liberia. Most comes from trees growing on small farms in Bendel State, but new plantations have also been established in several parts of the coastal rainforest zone, largely as a result of co-operation between the former regional governments, the Commonwealth Development Corporation, and private interests. Although the civil war brought a setback in 1967, there are plans for much further expansion, both by improving maintenance and replanting with improved strains on small farms, and by laying out new plantations in such little-developed areas as the Cross River plains.

In Cameroon, as in Nigeria, rubber growing has been encouraged as a means of diversifying exports, while a further factor has been the need to find a substitute crop on banana plantations devasted by disease. It is also being developed on government-owned plantations, rapidly in Ivory Coast, and more slowly in Ghana, as a step towards agricultural diversification, partly to supply local rubber-using industries which initially depended on imports.

SISAL

Sisal is a much less important commodity in world trade than either tea or rubber, but it also differs in that tropical Africa is the main area of production. The crop is of particular value because it can be grown in areas of poor soil and low rainfall which are unsuited to most other commercial crops. Until recently it was much in demand for the manufacture of rope and string, and especially baler twine, and tropical African production rose from 300,000 tons in 1955–7 to 396,000 tons in 1964. Subsequently, however, the figure has fallen (Table 2.10), for competition from synthetic products brought a drastic reduction

TABLE 2.10. SISAL PRODUCTION IN TROPICAL AFRICA

	Production in 000 tons				
	Average 1955–7	Average 1960–2	Average 1965–7	Average 1970–2	Average 1973–5
Tanzania	185	208	222	180	142
Angola	41	62	63	65	66
Kenya	40	63	58	44	63
Mozambique	29	28	31	25	24
TROPICAL AFRICA	300	361	374	317	338
WORLD TOTAL	490	610	650	630	710

in prices, and a number of sisal plantations have consequently gone out of business. Since the synthetics depend on oil sisal prices have now risen again (Table 2.1) but it would take some time to establish new plantations in response to this.

The most important producer in Tanzania, which has vast areas of marginal agricultural land where there are few alternative crops. Many new European-and Asian-owned plantations were established there in the early post-war years, but after about 1953 expansion took place only slowly. Despite a government takeover of a large share of the industry, the trend of production since 1966 has been steadily downwards, with a marked decline in areas where costs are high, notably in the Moshi–Arusha district, and an increasing concentration in the immediate vicinity of the port of Tanga and along the central railway. In the late 1950's there was more rapid development in Kenya than in Tanzania, but first the reduction of the extent of European-owned land and then falling prices brought production there down again. In Angola a similar growth took place with very active government support;

but even in that country production reached a plateau in 1964 and has now fallen with the departure of the Portuguese.

SUGAR

Sugar differs from the crops just discussed in that it is produced in tropical Africa not primarily as an export crop but for local consumption. Partly for this reason, it also differs in that production has expanded rapidly in recent years, and is likely to continue to grow at the same rate. World market prices for sugar are very unstable, and are affected not only by such diverse factors as hurricanes in Mauritius and politics in Cuba, but even by policies on sugar-beet production in temperate countries; but many African countries can establish a sugar industry without becoming dependent on the world market since their own sugar consumption is increasing rapidly. The absence of a sugar industry until recently in such countries as Nigeria and Sudan clearly reflects the "colonial" character of their past economic development, and the replacement of imports by local production was an obvious step after independence wherever it was an economic proposition.

Thus sugar production in tropical Africa has not only increased in volume from 330,000 tons in 1956 to 1,500,000 tons in 1975, but has also widened greatly in its distribution (Table 2.11 and Map 2.7). Much the most important producer in the mid-1950s was Mozam-

TABLE 2.11. SUGAR PRODUCTION IN TROPICAL AFRICA

	Production in 000 tons					
	Average 1955-7	Average 1960-2	Average 1965-7	Average 1970-2	1973	1975
Mozambique	142	172	181	312	298	210
Uganda	77	99	126	140	74	34
Angola	53	69	69	82	80	40
Ethiopia	26	43	79	118	140	140
Kenya	23	32	42	127	149	179
Tanzania	19	32	69	96	115	110
Zaire	19	38	32	45	58	67
Somalia	11	12	34	49	35	37
Rhodesia	5	47	220	175	243	260
Congo	2	17	62	66	38	32
Sudan	—	—	40	89	122	140
Nigeria	—	—	16	28	30	39
Zambia	—	—	—	45	58	85
Malawi	—	—	—	35	53	69
Cameroon	—	—	—	14	21	30
TROPICAL AFRICA	380	580	1010	1420	1560	1520

Sources: FAO, *Production Yearbook;* International Sugar Organization, *Statistical Bulletin.*

bique, but little expansion has taken place there apart from a short period around 1970. The sugar industry in that country, which in some ways can be considered an extension of that in South Africa, was largely dependent on exports to metropolitan Portugal up to 1975, and was able to expand only as far as this export market allowed. Meanwhile, there are some countries which were minor producers fifteen years ago in which the crop has increased four- or fivefold, and several others in which it has been established for the first time during the past decade.

The most striking development has occurred in Rhodesia, where production rose from

59

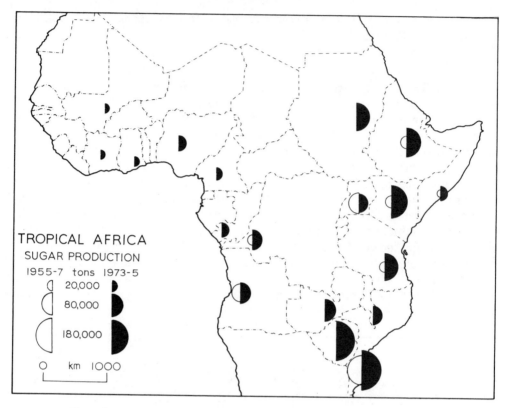

MAP 2.7. Sugar production in tropical Africa: averages for 1955–7 and 1973–5.

a mere 5000 tons in 1956 to 231,000 tons in 1965. Some attempts to grow sugar were made before World War II, but little was achieved until large-scale schemes were begun in the mid-1950's in the Chiredzi–Hippo Valley–Triangle areas of the lowveld. The physical environment is not highly favourable, but Rhodesia has had the financial resources to supplement the 500 mm of rainfall with irrigation and to improve the soils with fertilizers. Private and government sources together contributed over $80 million for the development of the industry, which was providing one of the most important growth points in the Rhodesian economy in the early 1960's. Production rose so rapidly that there was soon a large surplus over local requirements. Even the markets of Zambia and Malawi were soon satisfied, but Britain was willing to add Rhodesia to its suppliers. Since UDI this market has been closed, and Zambia and Malawi are now developing their own sugar industries, and therefore sugar quickly changed from a growth point to a thorny problem, partly as a result of the actions of the Smith regime. The new production in Zambia and Malawi is based in each case upon a single estate just large enough to supply the national market. That in Zambia is at Nakambala on the Kafue flats, only 80 km from Lusaka, and that in Malawi is in Chikwawa district by the Shire river, only 32 km from Blantyre, so that both are well placed in relation to market potential.

Uganda was the second tropical African producer in the 1950's, supplying most of the requirements of all three East African countries, and production there doubled between 1956 and 1966 (Plate 8). This took place mainly through an increase of yields on the two major estates near Jinja rather than an increase in the area planted. New estates further north were due to be established in the early 1970's, but meanwhile production has fallen sharply following the expulsion of Asians, including those who owned and managed the sugar estates. Increased production might in fact have posed marketing problems since, as in the countries to the south, a policy of national self-sufficiency is now being followed in East Africa. Tanzania has steadily expanded its formerly very small sugar industry over the past two decades: and while Kenya still obtained sugar from Uganda up to 1970, it is rapidly expanding its own production as new estates are developed in the vicinity of Lake Victoria in both Nyanza and Western Provinces.

A third area in which a common market assisted the growth of a sugar industry is Equatorial Africa, and there too problems have arisen for the initial producer. A plantation was established at Jacob in Congo in 1957, and production there expanded rapidly in the 1960's, so that sugar was exported both to neighbouring countries and to France. By the early 1970's further investment was needed simply to maintain production, but this was discouraged by the policies first of Cameroon and then of Gabon and Chad to set up their own small sugar industries.

In West Africa sugar cultivation developed surprisingly late, for physical conditions are suitable in many places and imports are substantial. This was recognized in Nigeria at the time of independence, and an estate at Bacita by the Niger River in the centre of the country began production in 1964: but this was satisfying less than a third of national consumption by the early 1970's, and so additional estates are now being established in both the north-west and the north-east. Similar opportunities exist in most other West African states, and although the estates set up by Ghana in 1967 have been beset by both technical and management problems, others were successfully established in 1975 at Ferkessédougou in Ivory Coast and at Banfora in Upper Volta. In Ivory Coast there are ambitious expansion plans, so that sugar may diversify its exports yet further while providing a much-needed source of income for the north of the country. In Senegal and Mali sugar cultivation sufficient to satisfy local needs is intended to assist the economic operation of the costly Richard–Toll and Niger Inland Delta irrigation schemes inherited from the French.

Ethiopia and Somalia each diversified their agriculture and saved some foreign exchange by developing a local sugar industry in the 1950's and expanding it as demand increased in the 1960's. A similar pattern followed in Sudan, where sugar provided an alternative to cotton on the Guneid and Khashm el Girba irrigation schemes: but there sugar is now seen as the spearhead for future agricultural development. On the Kenana irrigation scheme near Kosti work began in 1976 on what may become the world's largest sugar plantation, with a production of 300,000 tons by the early 1980's. Although 51% government-owned, it is being managed by the British firm Lonrho and largely financed by Arab oil revenues, the total cost exceeding $200 million. Four other estates are also being developed, of which the first near Sennar is due to begin production in 1978. Kuwait is the main source of finance in this case also, and it is expected that the oil-rich Middle Eastern countries will provide the main market for the huge surplus of sugar that Sudan should soon be producing.

Ranching

It was mentioned earlier that livestock are often thought to offer the best prospect for development in the rural sector in many African countries, but also that changing this aspect of traditional African farming has generally proved particularly difficult. One possible solution is the expansion of livestock rearing as a distinctive form of large-scale enterprise, especially where this can make use of the vast tracts of country which are unsuited to crop production because of low rainfall and poor soils.

Ranching has already proved very successful on vast stretches of European-owned land in Rhodesia, and on a rather smaller scale in Zambia and Kenya also. In Rhodesia this type of enterprise was already well established early in this century, but such rapid expansion of ranching for beef production has taken place in recent years that the value of meat exports from that country rose from $6 million in 1959 to $18 million in 1965. Since then the industry seems to have continued to expand in spite of sanctions on exports by many buyers.

In Kenya, too, ranching provided the basis for a major expansion of the meat industry in the late 1950's, and there it is now spreading from European-owned lands through the establishment of ranches by African farmers' co-operatives. In Tanzania some of the land cleared for the post-war groundnut scheme was taken over by the government for cattle ranches when this collapsed, and these are now being developed further and supplemented by others in several parts of the country. Uganda is also experimenting with ranching, both in the form of government enterprises in the north and in the form of smaller private ranches on land newly cleared of tsete-fly in Ankole towards the south-west.

Government schemes are also being implemented in several parts of West Africa. Thus in Nigeria ranches in the north are designed to fatten stock before they are moved south, while others have been set up in tsetse-free areas in both the south-west and south-east. In Senegal an 80,000 hectare ranch has recently been opened as the first part of a plan designed to assist the diversification of commercial agriculture and its extension into the drier parts of the country. Other ambitious plans have been announced for the Accra plains in Ghana where there are large tracts of little-used land close to a large market for meat that has at present to be supplied by imports. Clearly this presents a great opportunity for Ghana, although unfortunately it also presents a threat to the export prospects of Upper Volta which is already so much poorer than Ghana and which has far fewer alternative forms of development. Indeed, in Upper Volta as also in Mali, Niger, Chad, and Somalia, ranching prospects are being investigated in relation to rehabilitation after the 1970's droughts.

CONCLUSIONS

There has undoubtedly been a substantial increase in agricultural production in tropical Africa over the period since the mid-1950's. However, the rate of population increase has been such that over the region as a whole there has been very little advance in *per capita* terms. Since the greatest expansion has been in respect of export crops, it is not clear that there has been any improvement in the level of supply of basic foodstuffs. Most African governments have expressed concern about the lagging agricultural sector of the economy and many development plans have indicated that priority must be given to its improvement, but rarely has it in fact been given a share of attention remotely commensurate with its importance as a source of livelihood. (Indeed, it is only because this book is discussing what has been happening rather than what ought to be happening that agriculture occupies only one chapter here.)

Even before the droughts of 1970–4 brought grave disruption of the rural economy in certain countries such as Ethiopia, Niger, and Upper Volta, including real famine conditions for large groups of people, the extent of agricultural development which had taken place in recent years differed greatly from one tropical African country to another, as also had the nature of the development. One estimate of the rate of growth in these countries is reproduced in Map 2.8, although since it covers many crops for which no data are collected the figures must be taken as only very approximate.

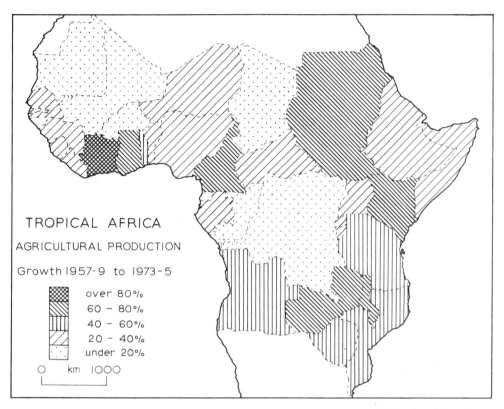

MAP 2.8. An estimate of change in agricultural production in tropical Africa (1957–9 and 1973–5 averages) based on United States Department of Agriculture and FAO data.

The country which has experienced the most rapid expansion of agricultural activity in recent years is Ivory Coast, and this growth has provided the basis for a rapid advance in all sectors of the country's economy. The production of each of its major export crops has increased greatly, while at the same time some measure of diversification has been achieved; and, according to returns submitted to the FAO, even the production of many basic food crops doubled during the 1960's. In part this reflects the low level of development in relation to resources before independence, and it might be argued that Ivory Coast differs from Ghana only in that the burst of growth has occurred rather later; but if comparison is made with other countries such as Liberia and Sierra Leone, rather than with Ghana, more positive factors favouring this development in Ivory Coast must be sought. One of the most important has been the continuing close ties with France which has provided guaranteed markets for Ivory Coast produce and an uninterrupted flow of aid in the form of government funds and personnel. The guaranteed markets have ended as EEC decisions have been fully implemented; but the EEC as a whole now provides a large market for the main export crops even if at lower prices, and is also providing much financial aid. The rapid agricultural advance in Ivory Coast perhaps results from the combination of willingness to remain dependent on these external ties, possession of unused high-potential land, and absence of other resources such as minerals to deflect attention from agriculture.

Over a twenty-five year period considerable expansion of agricultural production has also taken place in a number of other countries such as Ghana, Kenya, and Sudan, although in each of these the growth rate was higher in the late 1950's than in the 1960's. In each, the share of agriculture in the national income has fallen substantially, but this is in part the result of industrial development based upon the internal market that a relatively prosperous agricultural sector has provided. In a larger number of countries, including some of the largest, such as Nigeria and Ethiopia, agricultural output has expanded only a little faster than the population, so that the standard of living of the great majority of the rural dwellers has risen very little. An even more static picture is presented by Sierra Leone, Liberia, Upper Volta, and Benin, where the production of crops probably expanded more slowly during the 1960's than the population. In Sierra Leone and Liberia, as also in Gabon, agriculture has tended to be neglected as attention has been focused on minerals. This has meant that most of the increase in national income has been enjoyed by only a small group, and the conditions of life for most people in most parts of each country have hardly improved in any way. In Upper Volta and Benin agriculture still dominates the economy, and so stagnation in this sector has meant inevitably that these countries have lagged ever further behind their more prosperous neighbours in every aspect of development.

In Zaire, Rwanda, and Guinea there was an absolute decline in the production of cash crops, and possibly food crops also, during the 1960's. In Zaire political unrest led many people to move from rural areas to the towns in search of security, while others who remained on their farms found that marketing facilities had disappeared. In Rwanda, too, civil strife and consequent massive migrations have contributed to this situation. There has been no comparable strife in Guinea, but political factors have been important there too— the abrupt break with France bringing disorganization in such fields as the extension service and marketing arrangements. Fortunately, these set-backs may only be temporary, and future prospects for agriculture are probably better in Guinea than in many other countries. The early 1970's brought further absolute declines in agricultural production, in this case in the desert margin states from Mauritania to Chad, and as a result of drought rather than politics. Again there is some hope that there declines will be only temporary, and Chad is one country which showed signs of recovery by 1976.

Amongst the countries in which considerable agricultural development has taken place in recent years, there are marked differences in its character. In some countries it has taken the form almost entirely of an expansion of the commercial element in small-scale farming, but in others—including Ivory Coast—an important plantation element has been present. In a few territories, notably Liberia and Angola, large-scale farming of various types has remained more important than small-scale farming in terms of cash crop production, and in Rhodesia the former has forged ahead while the latter has stagnated. The greatest change in the character of commercial agriculture has certainly taken place in Kenya, where the small-farm sector now accounts for over half the total value of farm sales compared with only 15–20% in the mid-1950's.

In part the change in Kenya represents new structures in fixed locations as European farmers are replaced by African smallholders, but it also involves some geographical dispersal of cash cropping and commercialized livestock farming. Even there, however, the extent of the dispersal is very limited—as it is in most other countries. Indeed, while there has been some diffusion of agricultural innovation (and especially of cash cropping) in such countries as Sudan, Senegal, Ivory Coast, and Ghana, most development has taken place in the districts which were already most advanced agriculturally twenty years ago. The general trend in agriculture, as in other sectors of the economy, seems to be for the spatial differences within most countries to increase rather than to diminish.

The discussion of individual cash crops indicated that the same trend is apparent on an international scale. The distribution of certain crops, such as sugar, has been widening, but more often—as in the case of cocoa, coffee, or tea—most new planting has taken place within the countries which were already the main producers in the early 1950's. The geographical patterns that were visible then have therefore been intensified rather than altered.

Agriculture still plays a dominant role in the economy of most tropical African countries, and must continue to do so for the foreseeable future. In particular, it must continue to provide a livelihood for the great majority of the people, for the current increase of employment in other activities is little faster than the general increase of the population. It is therefore extremely unfortunate that the general rate of agricultural growth over the past two decades has been so much slower than in the early 1950's. Most of the new African governments have attempted to increase the rate, but they have often had little success. This is partly because one of the fundamental problems is the level of world prices for their export crops, which lies largely outside their control, and partly because both physical and social factors make specific policy decisions much harder to implement in the realm of agriculture than in, say, mining, industry, or transport. This is especially so in the case of small-scale agriculture where the decision-making process ultimately rests in the hands of a vast number of individuals.

However, there are certain hopeful exceptions to this general pattern of relative stagnation in African agriculture. In Ivory Coast rapid growth has taken place on many fronts without any major changes in the structure of the rural economy or society; in Kenya some major structural changes were inevitable, and these have benefited some groups in particular need, while a more privileged rural sector has also prospered; in Tanzania there has been great emphasis on structural change by a government more genuinely committed than most to rural development, but as yet the benefits must be sought in terms of social welfare rather than greater agricultural productivity. Some means must be found of combining the experience of such countries, and of combining external assistance and organization with the farmers' knowledge of their own diverse environments and capacity for self-improvement, to bring broadly based development across rural Africa. Only if agriculture advances along with other sectors, and if the very limited areas of relative agricultural prosperity can be greatly widened, will African economic development directly benefit the majority of the population.

SELECTED READING

Agriculture is discussed at length in all the general works on the geography and the economic development of tropical Africa noted in Chapter 1. It receives special attention in:
  FAO, *Africa Survey* (Rome, 1962).
The fullest account of traditional African agriculture is:
  W. ALLAN, *The African Husbandman* (Edinburgh, 1965).

A thorough discussion of recent change is:
FAO/ECA, *African Agricultural Development* (New York, 1966).

Written by the same hand, and more emphatic in its criticism of much of the change is:
R. DUMONT, *False Start in Africa* (London, 1966).

A valuable review, with a supplementary volume of case studies, is:
J. C. DE WILDE *et al.*, *Experiences with Agricultural Development in Tropical Africa* (Baltimore, 1967).

A useful series of local studies for one country is:
H. RUTHENBERG (ed.), *Smallholder Farming and Development in Tanzania* (Munich, 1968).

Further insights into the processes of agricultural change are provided by:
P. HILL, *Studies of Rural Capitalism in West Africa* (London, 1970);
C. G. KNIGHT, *Ecology and Change* (New York, 1974);
A. I. RICHARDS *et al.*, *Subsistence to Commercial Farming in Present-day Buganda* (London, 1973).

A detailed study of change during the colonial period in one country is:
J. A. HELLEN, *Rural Economic Development in Zambia 1890–1964* (Munich, 1968).

Geographical discussions of developments elsewhere include:
J. T. COPPOCK, Agricultural developments in Nigeria, *Journal of Tropical Geography* 23, 1–18 (1966);
D. N. McMASTER, East Africa: influences and trends in land use, in R. M. PROTHERO (ed.), *A Geography of Africa* (London, 1969), pp. 204–63.

Other work undertaken by geographers on African agriculture is exemplified in:
M. F. THOMAS and G. W. WHITTINGTON (ed.), *Environment and Land Use in Africa* (London, 1969).

The contrasting experiences of two countries in the 1960's are discussed in:
J. M. DUE, Agricultural development in the Ivory Coast and Ghana, *Journal of Modern African Studies* 7, 637–60 (1969).

For what is almost a case study in recent rural non-development in Gambia, see:
M. R. HASWELL, *The Nature of Poverty* (London, 1975).

Among the many development plans, one devoted specifically to agriculture is:
FAO, *Agricultural Development in Nigeria 1965–1980* (Rome, 1966).

Many recent agricultural projects in Africa are discussed in:
G. HUNTER *et al.*, *Policy and Practice in Rural Development* (London, 1976);
U. LELE, *The Design of Rural Development: Lessons from Africa* (Baltimore, 1975).

Resettlement schemes are assessed in:
R. CHAMBERS, *Settlement Schemes in Tropical Africa* (London, 1969);
B. FLOYD and M. ADINDE, Farm settlements in Eastern Nigeria, *Economic Geography* 43, 189–230 (1967).

Accounts of the Tanzanian resettlement programme include:
J. CONNELL, The evolution of Tanzanian rural development, *Journal of Tropical Geography* 38, 7–18 (1974);
G. HUIZER, The Ujamaa Village program in Tanzania, *Studies in Comparative International Development* 8, 183–207 (1973);
G. HYDEN, Ujamaa, villagization and rural development in Tanzania, *ODI Review* 1, 53–72 (1975).

Resettlement from areas flooded by new dams is examined in:
D. BROKENSHA and T. SCUDDER, Resettlement, in N. RUBIN and W. M. WARREN (eds.), *Dams in Africa* (London, 1968), pp. 20–62.

The Gezira irrigation scheme is described in:
A. GAITSKELL, *Gezira* (London, 1959);
W. A. HANCE, *African Economic Development* (New York, 1967), ch. 2.

The expansion and contraction of European mixed farming in Kenya is discussed in:
R. S. ODINGO, *The Kenya Highlands: Land Use and Agricultural Development* (Nairobi, 1971).

For more detailed maps of crop distribution, and other relevant maps also, see:
H. R. J. DAVIES, *Tropical Africa: Atlas for Rural Development* (Cardiff, 1973).

Useful economic case studies on individual crops may be found in:
S. R. PEARSON and J. COWNIE (eds.), *Commodity Exports and African Economic Development* (Lexington, 1974).

Sugar production is discussed more fully in:
A. M. O'CONNOR, Sugar in tropical Africa, *Geography* 60, 24–30 (1975).

Many interesting questions on the role of livestock in African development are raised in:
T. MONOD (ed.), *Pastoralism in Tropical Africa* (London, 1975).

3

FISHING AND FORESTRY

AT ONE time, hunting and gathering provided the main sources of livelihood over much of tropical Africa, but in most areas they gave way long ago to farming. They are still of vital importance to some very small groups, and a subsidiary source of food and other require-ments over wide areas, but their relative importance continues to decline. Yet a specialized form of each makes an increasingly valuable contribution to the economy of the region, since fishing takes place both along the coasts and in the lakes and rivers, and the forests are tapped for fuel and for timber.

The role of fishing and forestry as sources of income is very small in comparison with that of agriculture over tropical Africa as a whole. This is not true of every individual country, however, and within certain countries there are districts in which either fishing or forestry is the most important form of economic activity. Furthermore, these activities are of particular interest in relation to African economic development because they have been expanding rapidly in many areas in recent years. In some countries either fishing or timber production has grown more rapidly than any other sector of the economy during the past decade, and in the region as a whole progress has been much faster than in agriculture. Without doubt there is scope for much more development in the future in terms of both an increased tempo of economic activity and the improvement of the quality of life for people in this region.

FISHING

Tropical Africa has large stocks of fish in its rivers and lakes and also around its shores, but as yet they are not very fully exploited, and the region accounts for only about 4% of the world's total catch. However, fish is a popular item of diet for most people, and provided it is available at sufficiently low prices it is much in demand. The number of fish caught is therefore steadily rising as more people take up fishing as a source of livelihood, and especially as improved techniques bring increased productivity. According to FAO esti-mates, total landings in tropical Africa have risen from about 1 million tons in the mid-1950's to over $2\frac{1}{2}$ million tons by 1975.

Roughly two-thirds of the catch is taken from coastal waters and one-third from inland waters, and the general rate of development has been similar in each case. River and lake fishing is still almost entirely a small-scale enterprise, undertaken from canoes by fishermen working in small groups. Some of the marine fishing is also of this nature, but in some of the countries bordering the Atlantic Ocean, notably Angola, the post-war period also witnessed the development of a large-scale fishing industry financed by foreign capital. Both the small canoes and the large trawlers have contributed to the increase in the volume of fish landed during the past two decades. Some of the fish are consumed by the fishermen and their families, and some are marketed locally in fresh form, but most are in some way processed near the landing places since they are a highly perishable commodity. The greater part of the catch from rivers and lakes is smoked, and then distributed by small-scale traders, often over long distances. Some of the marine catch is treated in the same way, but some is processed on a factory scale into such products as canned fish and fish meal, partly for export overseas.

The Distribution of Fishing

Although the volume of fish landed has risen at a comparable rate in both inland and marine waters, there have been marked differences between one country and another in each case (Table 3.1). Throughout the past two decades the largest catch has been taken in

TABLE 3.1. FISHING IN TROPICAL AFRICA

	Catch in 000 tons		
	Average 1955–7	Average 1964–6	Average 1973–5
Angola	370	310	380
Zaire	100	80	130
Senegal	70	130	340
Tanzania	60	100	170
Chad	50	100	110
Uganda	40	80	170
Ghana	30	70	230
Nigeria	?	?	620

Sources: FAO, *Yearbook of Fishery Statistics;* and national sources.
Note: The fact that the estimate for Nigeria was raised in 1973–4 from 150,000 tons to 600,000 tons indicates the unreliability of some of these figures.

Angola, but after reaching 400,000 tons in 1956 and 1957 it fell sharply, and it remained around 300,000 tons until 1972. In that year it inexplicably doubled, before falling back to 450,000 tons in 1973, and then dropping much further as a result of the political upheavals of 1975. The country benefits from the presence of the cool Benguela current, which provides very favourable conditions for fish, but after 1957 there was a little-understood fall in the number of fish found in these waters. Most of the catch is landed in the south, notably at Mocamedes, and is processed into dried fish, oil, and meal. Exports of these products were worth about $15 million a year in the 1960's, which was less than in the mid-1950's, but they had risen to $53 million by 1973.

In contrast to the situation in Angola, fishing is of rapidly increasing importance in Senegal, which also feels the effects of a cool offshore current providing a favourable environment for fish. The total catch in 1966 was double that ten years earlier, and although smaller in volume than landings in Angola it was of higher value. Most of the development took place in the late 1950's, but there was a notable improvement around 1965–6. The increase in the catch at that time was largely the result of more fishing from canoes and of the use of improved techniques, both along the coast and on the Senegal River; but there has also been a notable development of large-scale offshore sardine fishing, and an attempt to participate in the tunny fishing now undertaken far outside territorial waters by vessels of many nationalities. Several French companies invested in boats and processing facilities in the late 1950's, and although these have been less active recently, Senegal is now building up its own fleet and establishing more freezing and canning plants with both French and Soviet aid. The catch reached 320,000 tons in 1973, when it was valued at $91 million.

Other major west coast producers of fish are Ghana and Ivory Coast, and this is one of the few fields in which progress in the former during the past decade has been even greater than in the latter. The traditional canoe fishing, practised all along the Ghana coast, has brought in increasing quantities of fish especially as more and more outboard motors have been fitted; and a new large-scale fishing industry has developed even more rapidly than in Senegal. The establishment of a fishing fleet was one of the more successful results of the period of government participation in economic activities, but further development is now being encouraged in the private sector. Japanese enterprise is playing an important part in the industry by the provision of both technical knowledge and capital equipment, and is committed to assisting in its further development. The growing importance of large-scale fishing in Ghana is clearly reflected in the provision of a large fishing harbour as an integral part of the new port of Tema.

The people who live near the coast in Ivory Coast have never taken as much interest in fishing as those in Ghana, and much of the small-scale fishing that is practised is in the hands of migrants from that country. To an even greater extent than in either Senegal or Ghana, therefore, the recent increase in the Ivory Coast catch results from the establishment of a large-scale fishing industry. A new harbour was opened at Abidjan in 1964, and this provides the base for a steadily expanding fleet of sardine and tuna boats, most of which are owned by French firms. Here too, several new freezing and canning plants have been opened, and their relative importance is greater than in Ghana since existing marketing arrangements are less well developed.

A complete contrast to Ivory Coast is provided by Benin, where there is a well-established tradition of fishing, especially on the lagoons behind the coast, but where no significant new development has occurred in recent years. Little information is available on the catch in Nigeria, and although it is probably large in absolute terms, fishing is certainly less important in relation to the size of the country and its population than in either Senegal or Ghana. There is also no evidence that its importance is currently increasing. The coastal waters are much less rich in fish than those further west, and most of the catch comes from the Niger River and its tributaries and from the extensive lagoons and swamps just behind the coast. Until the 1972–3 drought the main prospect for fishery development seemed to be on Lake Chad, where efforts had been made to improve traditional techniques and to provide better road access to the main landing places. At present, the lake catch is normally greater in the Chad Republic but the drought must have cut the catch greatly as the lake shrank to a quarter of its usual extent.

Much fuller records exist for the catch on the lakes of East Africa, which has roughly trebled over the past fifteen years. In this area, fishing is still entirely a small-scale enterprise, but there has been some increase in the numbers of fishermen and a great increase in productivity per man following the widespread adoption of nylon nets and of outboard

69

motors on the canoes. Some stretches of water, such as the Kenya portion of Lake Victoria and Lake George in Uganda, have been fished to capacity for some time; but elsewhere new fishing grounds have been tapped, sometimes with the help of new access roads. There has been a similar increase of fishing activity further south, on Lake Malawi, and also on the Kafue Flats in Zambia.

Fishing Prospects

The prospects for further development in many parts of tropical Africa are very bright, for the region has large untapped resources and there is a huge potential market especially in view of the serious shortage of protein in the diet of most people. Furthermore, there are opportunities for making use of those species which are not suitable as food either as fish meal, which provides excellent fodder for livestock, or as fertilizer, which is urgently needed in many areas. From this viewpoint it is perhaps regrettable that much of the Angola and Senegal catch is exported.

Among the ocean waters which could be tapped more fully are those off Mauritania, which are at present exploited almost entirely by vessels working from Europe. Like those further south, off Senegal, these cold-current waters are very rich in fish; and in Mauritania the lack of agricultural resources provides an added incentive to make use of this source of food and income. Fishing was in fact one of the few forms of commercial activity in Mauritania before iron came to dominate the economy; now the revenues obtained from iron mining may provide the capital for a great expansion of fishing.

Sierra Leone, Guinea, and Liberia are among the other West African countries in which fishing is at present of some importance and could be developed much further. Along the east coast prospects are generally poorer, but even there some little-touched resources exist, and plans for the establishment of large-scale fishing industry have been made, for example, in Somalia, which has the longest coastline of all tropical African countries.

Many of the rivers and lakes of the region are already very intensively fished, but on others the catch could be greatly increased. Two examples are provided by the many channels and swamps of the White Nile basin in Sudan, and the waters away from the shoreline in Lake Victoria. New opportunities have been provided by the lakes created behind the great dams built mainly for power generation, and the development of fishing forms an integral part of the Kariba, Volta, and Kainji projects. As yet the annual catch from these new lakes is small, for it has not always proved possible to persuade farmers whose land has been flooded to take up fishing, but it is notable that many Ewe fishermen are now migrating to the resettlement villages near the shores of Lake Volta.

A prospect of great potential importance is fish-farming on small artificial ponds. Considerable efforts were made by the colonial governments to develop this, and although the total achievement was small, there are some countries such as Rwanda where fishponds do provide a valuable food in certain overcrowded areas far from other sources of fish. A vast amount of further effort will be required if fish farming is to become of major importance in tropical Africa, but in many countries it is still government policy to do everything possible to encourage it.

In many different ways, therefore, fishing has a valuable contribution to make to African development—not only as a large-scale commercial enterprise earning foreign exchange, but more importantly as a source of income spread widely among the thousands engaged in fishing on a smaller scale, as a basis for further small-scale enterprise in distribution and marketing, and as a source of food for the population as a whole.

FORESTRY

One feature of tropical Africa that is in a state of constant change is its vegetation cover, although this type of change normally takes place only slowly. A general trend has been towards a reduction in the extent of forest, as it has been cut and burnt in order to clear the land for cultivation. This still continues on a massive scale in countries such as Zaire where shifting cultivation remains widespread. Yet large tracts of land are still forest-clad, and this forest represents a very valuable natural resource, especially in terms of potential timber production. In addition, some forests play an important role in the conservation of water and the protection of soils, particularly in highland areas.

Increasing use is being made of these timber resources, and at the same time efforts are being made to control exploitation in such a way that the forests will eventually be renewed in an equally, or even more, valuable form. In most African countries certain zones have been designated forest reserves, and in a few places afforestation of land of low agricultural potential is now being undertaken, sometimes using softwoods which yield timber much more quickly than the hardwoods of most natural African forests. Such planting, which has progressed furthest in Kenya and Rhodesia, where natural forests are not extensive, has recently been taking place at the rate of about 30,000 hectares a year.

The area of tropical Africa covered in savanna woodland is even larger than that covered in forest, but this yields wood of much lower commercial value. Nevertheless, like wood from the forests, it is very widely used in the round for building poles, and also for fuel. In fact by far the largest part of the wood cut in tropical Africa is used for fuel; but in contrast to felling for timber, there is no evidence that cutting for fuel expanded rapidly over the past twenty years as a whole, except where increasing quantities were used for such activities as curing tobacco or smoking fish. Indeed, as economic development proceeds it is normal for other sources of fuel to displace wood even for domestic purposes, as they have already in such enterprises as the railways. However, population increase alone has led to some expansion of wood cutting in many areas, while even cutting at a steady rate can create pressure on resources where this is faster than the rate of regeneration. In addition, the increased oil prices of the 1970's have reversed the general trend away from wood fuel by making alternatives such as kerosene more expensive. Undoubtedly development policies in Africa must acknowledge that most people will depend on wood fuel for many years to come, and must tackle the problems arising from its increasing scarcity in some areas. At present all too little is known about fuelwood supplies and consumption, which is why attention is focused on timber felling for the remainder of this chapter.

The total volume of logs felled for timber in tropical Africa is thought to have risen from about 10 million cubic metres (m^3) in 1956 to over 30 million m^3 in 1973. Part of the expansion has been a response to growing markets within the region, but much has been in the production of timber for export overseas. In contrast to those for most primary products, timber prices remained fairly steady for many years, so that the increase in the volume of exports of logs and sawn timber from 3 million m^3 in 1956 to $8\frac{1}{2}$ million m^3 in 1972 brought a rise in earnings from $100 million to $330 million; and rising prices have since increased the figure substantially. Much of the felling is undertaken by Europe-based firms, and nearly all the exports are to Europe, so this provides a clear example of the continuance of what is often termed the "colonial" type of economic activity.

71

The Distribution of Timber Felling

The recent expansion of timber felling has been by no means evenly spread over the forest areas of tropical Africa, and therefore the pattern of log production has changed considerably (Table 3.2). The coastal zone of West Africa is by far the most important area of production, and in this as in many other fields the greatest expansion within this area since the mid-1950's has taken place in Ivory Coast. At that time it was a relatively minor timber producer, for no more than ½ million m³ were cut each year; but in 1973 over 5½ million m³ were felled—considerably more than in any other tropical African country. The value of log and timber exports from Ivory Coast increased twelvefold between 1956 and 1971, and in the latter year was twice as high as in any other country; and it has since risen still further. Several large logging companies from France and other EEC countries have been attracted by the favourable terms offered both before and after independence, and these have extended felling from the accessible areas near Abidjan to districts such as Dabou, Gagnoa, and Guiglo far to the west. In 1966 new legislation tightened control over the character of forest exploitation, but timber cutting in Ivory Coast is still a very profitable business for the companies concerned, and it continues to expand.

TABLE 3.2. TROPICAL AFRICA: TIMBER FELLING AND EXPORT

	Volume of industrial timber felled (000 m³)		Value of logs exported ($ m.)		Value of sawn timber exported ($ m.)	
	1956	1973	1956	1973	1956	1973
TROPICAL AFRICA	10,000	31,000	70	520	22	90
Zaire	1,700	1,900	4	3	2	4
Ghana	1,600	2,500	15	69	12	33
Gabon	1,400	2,400	22	88	0	1
Nigeria	1,300	3,200	8	14	3	3
Ivory Coast	750	5,700	7	240	1	32
Uganda	750	1,100	0	0	0	1
Cameroon	700	1,400	3	46	1	5
Ethiopia	600	1,200	0	0	0	0
Tanzania	550	1,200	0	0	0	1
Angola	500	1,200	2	9	0	2
Congo	350	700	8	18	0	3

Sources: FAO, *Yearbook of Forest Products* and *World Forest Products Statistics 1954–63*.
Notes: Total wood removals are far higher in volume, but no reliable estimates of these can be made. By 1973 veneer and plywood exports earned a further $65 million (Gabon 17 m., Congo 13 m., Ivory Coast 10 m.).

Until the outbreak of the civil war there was a steady increase in timber felling in Nigeria, though at a much slower pace than in Ivory Coast. It was shared between the extensive forest areas of Bendel State, from which much timber is exported, and the more scattered forests elsewhere which are exploited mainly to supply local needs. By contrast, timber production in Ghana, which developed extremely rapidly in the early post-war years, expanded only slightly in the late 1950's, and has since fallen somewhat. The resources have been depleted to a much greater extent than in Ivory Coast, and partly because of this cutting and marketing have been so strictly controlled that conditions have not been attractive for private foreign investment.

The leading timber exporter in tropical Africa in the mid-1950's was Gabon, and okoumé cutting dominated that country's cash economy at that time. So much felling took place, however, that the most accessible forests were seriously depleted, and it has recently been possible to do little more than maintain production and exports at a roughly constant level. Rather than pressing for expansion of this industry, the Gabon government has focused attention on mining developments which have successfully diversified the economy. The geography of the Gabon timber industry has not remained static, however, for in order to maintain production it has been necessary to shift the location of operations. Until recently, felling was confined to areas near to the coast or to rivers down which the logs could be floated, but now it extends further inland despite the higher transport costs which result. Meanwhile, in some of the areas where felling has ceased a major reafforestation programme has begun which will eventually permit a greatly increased rate of extraction.

Production of timber has increased rather more in Cameroon, and in neighbouring Equatorial Guinea it expanded rapidly before independence to supply widening markets in Spain, coming to play a role in the economy comparable to that which it played in the past in Gabon. Equally rapid development has taken place in Congo, where logs and sawn wood together provided more than half the total value of overseas exports until oil production began. New sources there have been tapped—first far inland along the Ubangui River, and more recently beside the new Comilog railway.

In other parts of tropical Africa timber is cut mainly to supply local markets, and there is little surplus for export. In Zaire timber cutting was affected, like most other industries, by the disturbances following independence, but it has, in general, recovered quickly, and the level of production is now similar to that reached in the 1950's. The industry is very widely distributed, although the most intensively worked forests are those in the Mayumbe area between Kinshasa and the sea. The neighbouring Cabinda enclave, north of the Zaire River, provides the richest source of timber in Angola, and accounts for most of the substantial increase of commercial production over the past fifteen years in that country.

Most countries in eastern Africa, from Ethiopia to Mozambique, have sufficient forest resources to satisfy most local needs but not to support large-scale felling for export. In many of these countries the local needs are still mainly for building poles, often cut by rural dwellers for their own use, but in some the growth of internal markets has contributed to a steady increase in commercial timber production over the past two decades. In Uganda, on the other hand, the local market for timber was slack throughout the 1960's, and therefore the rate of cutting increased very little.

Sawmilling

The greater part of the wood felled for export is still shipped overseas in the form of logs, but the value of the timber industry to the exporting countries is much increased if the wood is sawn before shipment. The governments of the countries concerned have therefore been making great efforts to encourage the expansion of local milling. The interests of the importing countries prevent this occurring as rapidly as the African governments would wish, however, and while exports of sawn timber from tropical Africa have risen rapidly, their share in total timber exports has changed little over the past twenty years (Table 3.2).

It is in Ivory Coast that the greatest development of sawmilling has taken place. Before 1960 very little timber was exported ready-sawn, and milling was confined to very small concerns supplying local needs; but since independence several of the logging firms have been persuaded to establish large mills, although even now only one-eighth of the timber which they cut is sawn before export. Ghana had built up an export trade in sawn wood equal in value to that in logs in the early 1950's, but it has not succeeded in expanding it since then. Some growth in the Ghana sawmilling industry has occurred, however, as the local market has expanded. Similar development has taken place in Nigeria, and there it has been much more widely distributed over the country than in Ghana.

In all the countries in which timber is felled mainly for local use, the fortunes of the sawmilling industry naturally reflect closely the expansion or contraction of felling. Thus over tropical Africa as a whole about 2 million m³ of sawn wood were probably produced in 1973 for local use, in addition to 1 million m³ for export, roughly treble the figures estimated by FAO for 1956. On a local scale the relationship between felling and milling is less close, for the sawmills are sometimes located in the cities a long way from the forests. In East Africa this trend towards location close to the market has increased in recent years, although there are other countries in which a dispersal of milling has taken place as new sources of timber have been tapped.

Timber Prospects

While the value of the timber industry to tropical Africa has increased considerably over the past decade, there is still scope for it to increase much further. The region accounts for only 1% of the world's timber output, even though it has 15% of the world's forest area. There are some localities in which the forest resources have been greatly depleted, but there are many others where they have hardly been touched. In some of these, exploitation is now beginning; in others it awaits new transport facilities to permit the evacuation of timber at reasonable cost, the persuasion of customers to accept a wider variety of species, or the expansion of local markets. One country in which there is a good prospect of improved transport facilities is Gabon, where the first stage of the Trans-Gabon railway is being built to primarily assist the tapping of areas with a high timber potential. One prospect for new outlets for timber production in the future may be the development of the pulp and paper industry with intropical Africa. The early 1970's witnessed the establishment of this industry in Kenya and large-scale afforestation in Malawi for the same purpose.

Increased production for export, of course, depends on world market conditions, but these appear to be more favourable for timber than for most primary products. Consumption in the industrially advanced countries is rising steadily, and their own resources are limited. The value of exports will, however, be greatly increased if a larger proportion of the timber can be exported sawn rather than as logs. In many ways this seems a rational development especially as transport costs would be much reduced, but it is naturally resisted by the existing sawmilling interests in the importing countries. Even more valuable, but even more difficult, would be the development of large-scale exports of more highly processed wood products, including pulp and paper.

Markets within tropical Africa will undoubtedly expand in the future, and should permit an increase of timber felling and sawmilling in many parts of the region. However, it would be unfortunate if the division of the region into many small countries encouraged each to aim for self-sufficiency in forest products, when some are much better endowed in this respect than others. Forestry is undoubtedly one field in which greater economic integration within tropical Africa could be beneficial, for even on the basis of existing markets there are many opportunities for more trade in timber between those countries which produce a surplus and those which at present import large quantities from overseas.

The recent trend has certainly been towards an increasing dispersal of timber production within tropical Africa, as it has begun to develop in countries where it was formerly of
little importance while remaining almost static in such countries as Ghana and Gabon. This
trend is encouraged by the afforestation being undertaken in some countries such as Rhodesia, which do not have sufficient natural stands to supply all local needs. In the long term,
however, the distribution of production may again become more concentrated, especially
if plans for massive reafforestation programmes in the rainforests of Equatorial and West
Africa are implemented. As a result of the replacement of a vast number of species, most of
little value, by pure stands of the most useful species, it should be possible to cut a far
greater value of timber from each hectare than has been possible in the past. In these
circumstances, such countries as Gabon and Ivory Coast might take their place among the
world's chief sources of timber towards the end of the century. Development of this nature
making the most of local resources and based on clear comparative advantage, especially if
combined with local processing, would certainly be of benefit to tropical Africa provided
that it did not divert attention from the task of ensuring that Africa's forests and woodlands
also meet the needs of its own people both for building materials and for fuel.

SELECTED READING

A clear account of the pattern of fishing and forestry in the 1950's is provided in:
  G. H. T. KIMBLE, *Tropical Africa* (New York, 1960), chs. 6 and 8.

The potential contribution of these activities to African development is discussed in:
  UNITED NATIONS, *African Agricultural Development* (New York, 1966), chs. 9 and 10.

The marine fisheries of several countries in addition to Zaire are discussed in:
  M. DORMONT, *Pêche Maritime au Congo* (Paris, 1970).

Another useful case study is:
  R. M. LAWSON, The growth of the fishing industry of Ghana, *Economic Bulletin of Ghana* **11**, (4), 3–24
  (1967).

A thorough study of the African timber industry is:
  FAO, *Timber Trends and Prospects in Africa* (Rome, 1967).

Timber exports from Africa are discussed in:
  J. J. MACGREGOR, The development of African primary products and the international trade in timber, in
  I. G. STEWART and H. W. ORD, *African Primary Products and International Trade* (Edinburgh, 1965).

A detailed study of one country's timber industry is:
  S. K. ADEYOJU, *Forestry and the Nigerian Economy* (Ibadan, 1975).

For a critical discussion of forestry in West Africa, see:
  M. GAZEL, Le Développement de l'exploitation forestière en Afrique de l'ouest, *Présence Africaine* **86**,
  38–67 (1973).

4

MINING

MINING has played an extremely important part in the economic development of tropical Africa over the past sixty years, and its contribution in the period since 1956 has been as great as in any previous period. Over the region as a whole it is, of course, of less fundamental importance than agriculture as it directly affects far fewer people and is more often undertaken by foreign companies primarily for their own benefit, but in certain areas it has provided the chief basis for economic advance. Precisely because it is markedly localized, mineral exploitation must receive close attention in a study of the geographical pattern of African development.

All African states are anxious to encourage mining activity, for there is probably no other form of development which can increase the prosperity of a country so rapidly. Indeed, the only way in which any country has doubled its national income within a few years is through the exploitation of new mineral resources. Throughout the continent the ranks of prospecting companies have swelled greatly in the past twenty years, with new techniques such as airborne geophysical survey supplementing the older techniques of exploration; but this prospecting has not everywhere brought the same degree of success, for mineral resources appear to be distributed very unevenly.

Africa's mineral resources have been described in great detail by geologists such as De Kun and Pelletier. The most valuable known at present lie in South Africa, but there are other highly mineralized zones in Rhodesia and on the borders of Zambia and Zaire. Parts of West Africa are also relatively well endowed, and oil has lately transformed the development prospects of Nigeria. On the other hand, over most of eastern Africa the position is much less favourable: a wide range of minerals have been found, and some maps of mineral deposits there suggest at first glance a great wealth of resources, but most of the deposits are too small and scattered to be of great value.

It is not only the size of each deposit which is significant, but also its grade and the ease with which it can be worked. In addition, such issues as labour and power supplies, mining legislation and its effects on the attraction of capital, and accessibility in relation to markets, are often factors of vital importance. Thus the distribution of mining is very much more localized than that of known mineral resources.

Even so, recent years have witnessed not only a great expansion of mining activity in tropical Africa but also a substantial widening of its distribution. The total value of mineral production in the region in 1956 (a year of high prices for many minerals) was just under $1000 million, whereas by 1966 it had reached $2000 million. The number of countries contributing more than $25 million to the total rose during this period from four to eleven. By 1972 the total value had risen above $3000 million, and in 1974 high prices, especially for oil, brought a dramatic rise to over $15,000 million. The geographical pattern of this development is shown in Map 4.1.

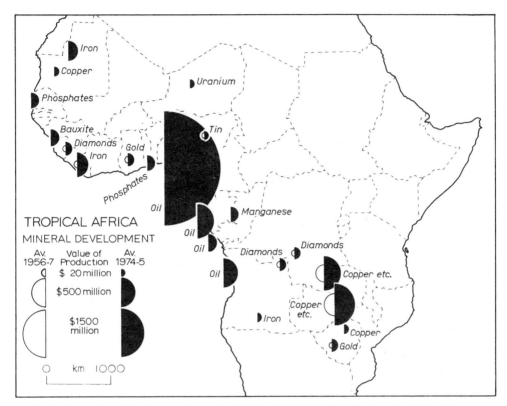

MAP 4.1. Mineral development in tropical Africa; 1956–7, 1974–5. The locations included are those yielding minerals worth over US $25 million per year by 1975.

THE MAJOR MINERALS WORKED

Mining is not a single industry but a collection of many, all of which have experienced different patterns of growth in recent years (Table 4.1).

OIL

One of the most striking features in the changing face of several developing countries is the forest of drilling rigs which has sprung up where oil has been exploited (Plate 9), and the role which oil has played in transforming the economies of these territories is even more impressive. There is nothing in tropical Africa to match Kuwait or Saudi Arabia, but oil production increased rapidly during the 1960's in certain countries (Table 4.2), bringing a great boost to the national economy, and its importance as a source of income has been

77

TABLE 4.1. VALUE OF MINERAL PRODUCTION IN
TROPICAL AFRICA

	Value in $m.		
	Average 1956–7	Average 1972–3	1974
Oil	1	2,600	10,200
Copper	460	1,430	2,250
Iron	40	360	450
Diamonds	100	270	280
Phosphates	0	60	260

Cobalt, gold manganese, tin, and zinc were each mined to a value of between $40m. and $120m. in all three periods.

Sources of data for Tables 4.1–4.5: United Nations, *Statistical Yearbook* and *Yearbook of International Trade Statistics;* United States, *Minerals Yearbook;* and national sources.

TABLE 4.2. OIL IN TROPICAL AFRICA

	1956	1957	1958	1966	1973	1974	1975
Production (000 tons)							
Nigeria	0	1	260	21,110	101,800	111,600	88,100
Gabon	0	173	505	1,450	7,600	10,200	11,600
Angola	9	10	51	630	8,200	8,700	8,400
Congo	0	0	0	0	2,100	2,500	1,800
Export value ($m.)							
Nigeria	0	0	3	258	2,880	8,510	7,520
Gabon	0	3	7	16	120	670	750
Angola	0	0	0	0	250	510	
Congo	0	0	0	0	30	160	130

greatly increased by the sharp price rises of 1973–4, achieved through the actions of OPEC of which Nigeria and Gabon are members.

In 1955 no oil was produced on a commercial scale in tropical Africa, but exploration teams were at work in many countries, and a few discoveries had already been made. One of these was in Angola, where a search began in 1952 on the coastal plain south of Luanda and where the first shipment was made in 1956. Production expanded rapidly after 1961, reaching a peak of 900,000 tons in 1964; following a setback in 1965–9 it then rose sharply again. New and much larger fields have been developed both off- and on-shore in the Cabinda enclave, north of the Zaire River, mainly by the US firm Gulf Oil, and these brought the annual production to 8¾ million tons by 1974. Apart from a brief suspension of operations in 1976, the ending of Portuguese rule and establishment of a government hostile to the United States has not had any immediate impact on this industry; but its concentration in Cabinda poses a problem for the new government since it has given encouragement to the separatist movement there.

Further to the north geological conditions are quite similar, and oilfields were found in 1953 near Port Gentil in Gabon. Production there began in 1956 and quickly surpassed that in Angola. Initially the industry benefited from the location of these fields close to the second town and port of the country, but after 1966 mining extended to richer fields further south, notably around Gamba. As a result, production expanded even more rapidly, while the spatial impact of mining was widened. By 1972 the main focus had again shifted north towards Port Gentil as a consequence of new off-shore finds, and of the 11½ million tons produced in 1975 well over half was from off-shore. By that time well over $500 million had been invested in the industry by French oil companies, encouraged by Gabon's close attachment both to France and to private enterprise.

Rather less-favourable attitudes have not prevented the same companies from prospecting off the shore of neighbouring Congo. This brought rapid success, and production there began in 1971, rising to 2½ million tons in 1974 but falling off a little in 1975. In that year production also began off Zaire, and almost ⅓ million tons was brought ashore in 1976, but that country's share of Atlantic waters is so small that it can aim at little more than self-sufficiency.

Nigeria joined the ranks of the oil producers at the end of 1957, and there the industry has expanded far more than in Angola and Gabon. Beneath the sedimentary rocks of the Niger delta and neighbouring coastal plains, vast reserves of oil have been found, and these have attracted several of the major international oil companies to the area. The most important up to the present has been Shell–BP, which spent $70 million on exploration before production began and a further $500 million between 1958 and 1967. Further drilling has led to discoveries off-shore also. These fields present few serious geological problems, but the swampy nature of much of the land, the dense population wherever there is firm ground, the torrential rains of the wet season, and the high incidence of disease in the swampy areas all hinder development. It was in part the Suez crisis which stimulated production only a year after the first discovery, but as new finds followed, exploitation soon became very worth while on all grounds. One factor of increasing significance in a pollution-conscious age is a sulphur content far lower than in Middle Eastern oil.

The first production was from Oloibiri, 75 km west of Port Harcourt, but soon other wells nearer that town were also yielding oil (Map 4.2). Total Nigerian production rose from ¼ million tons in 1958 to 3 million tons in 1962 and 20 million tons in 1966, by which time oil exports were worth $258 million and Nigeria had become one of the major oil-producing countries of the world. An extensive system of pipelines had been laid, and a major oil port established at Bonny. Large quantities of natural gas were also being produced for local use. The greater part of the total oil production then still came from Shell–BP wells in the former Eastern Region; but in 1964 it had begun also at Ughelli and Kokori in the Mid-West, and in 1965 at a point 11 km off the coast even further to the west, where Gulf Oil had the concession. This distinction between areas east and west of the Niger River became of great significance when civil war broke out in 1967. This war drastically cut oil exports for many months as the eastern fields were affected by fighting and blockades, but by 1969 they were rising rapidly again as development west of the Niger was accelerated. From a new base at Warri several new fields were opened up around Ughelli, and a new pipeline was laid from these to Forcados. Since the war ended Shell–BP have again been very active east of the Niger, while still expanding their production to the west. At the same time several other companies have made large investments, notably Agip/Phillips, tapping the area around the borders of Rivers and Imo States and shipping out oil by a new pipeline to Brass, and Mobil, winning oil from a series of rich fields off Eket in Cross River State.

By 1973 there were over 850 wells in production, spread over eighty fields, while seven companies were still drilling. Production in that year just topped 100 million tons (of which the local refinery used a mere 2½ million tons), for the first time matching that in Libya, and export earnings reached $2750 million. In terms of the new states which were created in 1967

79

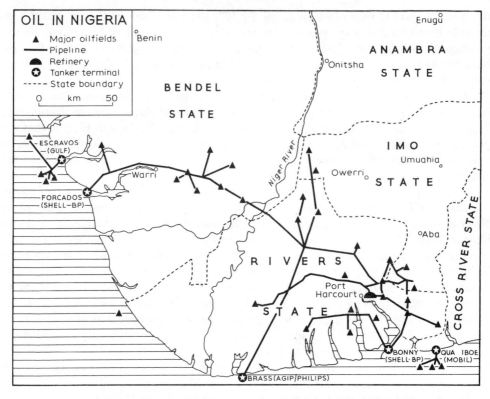

MAP 4.2. Major oilfields and installations in Nigeria.

much the most important producers were Mid-western (now Bendel) and Rivers, both East-central (now Imo) and South-eastern (now Cross River) following well behind. These together accounted for about two-thirds of the production, while the remainder was won from the off-shore fields. Production rose further to 113 million tons in 1974, while huge price rises brought export earnings to $8500 million. The rate of extraction dropped in 1975 as the worldwide demand for oil slackened, but partially recovered in 1976 so that production for that year was 102 million tons. It is probable that it will remain around that level for some while, but there are plans for making much more use of the associated natural gas, most of which now goes to waste. Even now some 400 million m^3 is used annually, notably in thermal electricity generation, but the proposal is to direct 20,000 million m^3 annually to a huge and sophisticated liquefied gas plant at Bonny for export overseas. The project involved long negotiations between Shell-BP and the Nigerian government before final agreement was reached in 1976, for the estimated cost is around $1000 million for the plant alone, while a further $2000 million may be needed for the pipelines and ships required.

COAL

Coal deposits exist in several countries of tropical Africa, but the coal is rarely of high grade, the local market is generally small, and there has never been much prospect of export overseas. It is often said than an expansion of coal mining must await the development of larger local markets, but in the two countries where it has been mined for many years the demand has recently fallen following the development of hydroelectricity and also a swing to oil by such consumers as the railways. In Rhodesia, production at Wankie was about 4 million tons a year in the late 1950's, but has been only about 3 million tons since 1961. In Nigeria, output from the mines near Enugu reached almost 1 million tons in 1958, but then fell to ¾ million tons a year even before the civil war brought complete disruption. Mozambique is a minor producer whose output has remained almost static.

The demand for coal from Wankie came until 1966 not only from Rhodesia but also from Zambia. Rhodesia's UDI interrupted this trade and stimulated interest in Zambia's own coal deposits at Maamba in the Gwembe valley. Development there proceeded very rapidly despite problems of inaccessibility, and production reached ½ million tons in 1968 and almost 1 million tons in 1972; but costs are so high that this must be seen as a solution to a short-term problem rather than a major step in Zambia's economic development.

Although a generally static situation has characterized the coal industry in tropical Africa as in most parts of the world in recent years, there are prospects for expansion now that oil prices have risen, especially since coal is required for the production of steel from iron ore. The importance of coal mining in Rhodesia is in part related to the existence there of this industry, which is likely to expand at some future date. A similar development in Nigeria could give new life to the mines there, while an iron and steel industry may eventually provide a demand for the coal of southern Tanzania.

COPPER

Copper is the mineral which has been of greatest commercial value to tropical Africa during most of this century. Even in 1956 production amounted to 650,000 tons (metal content of ore), which was 22% of the world total, and which was worth over $500 million at that time of high prices (Table 4.1). During the following decade the industry expanded

TABLE 4.3. COPPER IN TROPICAL AFRICA

	Production in 000 tons copper content of ore				
	1956	1961	1966	1971	1974
Zambia	404	575	623	651	830
Zaire	250	295	317	406	507
Rhodesia	2	14	17	23	32
Uganda	0	16	16	16	12
Mauritania	0	0	0	4	17

considerably, and since 1967 annual production has exceeded 1 million tons—still just over one-fifth of the world total and worth over $1000 million every year. Its value rose above $2000 million in 1974, but economic recession in the industrialized countries brought a fall in demand and prices in 1975. While the earlier growth in production did not radically alter the character or distribution of copper mining, and is therefore perhaps less striking than such entirely new ventures as oil in Nigeria, it contributed more than any other mineral development to increasing income in tropical Africa until the 1970's.

By far the most important deposits known are those in a zone 300 km long and 50 km wide on the borders of Zambia and Zaire, generally referred to in Zambia at least as the Copperbelt (Map 4.3). These two countries have for many years accounted for all but a

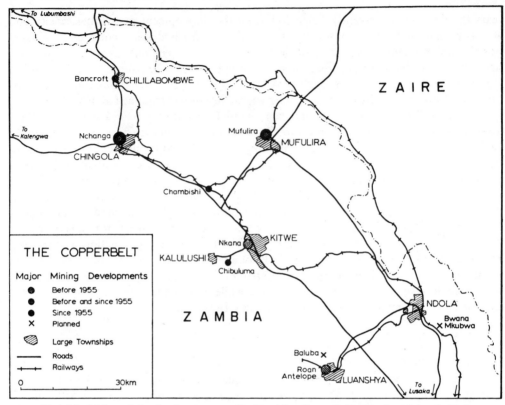

MAP 4.3. Major mining developments on the Zambian Copperbelt. The size of the circles is proportional to 1969 copper output.

small fraction of the copper production of tropical Africa. The very sparse population of the area, its lack of local power resources, and especially its distance from any port, presented great problems when efforts to exploit the deposits were first made in the 1920's: and although the high grade of the ore and the ease of working it provided sufficient incentive to overcome these problems, their influence is still felt today.

Most of the individual Zambian mines have expanded their scale of operations in recent years and some new mines have been opened, so that production rose from 400,000 tons in 1953 to 700,000 tons in 1965. Total new investment during this period amounted to at least $250 million. Transport and power problems resulting from strained relations with Rhodesia then led to a slight drop in production accentuated in 1970 by a major mine disaster, but it again rose above 700,000 tons in 1972, and remained at that level through 1973 and 1974. Nchanga mine, owned by Anglo-American until all the mines were 51% nationalized in 1969, has the largest reserve of high-grade ore, including much which can be worked opencast, and this has now become the largest producer of all: but the rival Rhodesian Selection Trust also undertook substantial new investments at its Mufulira mine in the early 1960's, and there are plans for further development there. Even at the oldest mines, Roan Antelope and Nkana, new shafts have been sunk. RST opened a completely new mine in 1955 at Chibuluma, where the deposit is small but of exceptionally high grade and yields cobalt as a byproduct, and then established another in 1965 at Chambishi. Meanwhile, after a period of problems, the new Anglo-American mine at Bancroft came into full production in 1959. Subsequent discoveries further afield have led to the development in 1969 of a mine far to the west at Kalengwa despite a long road haul to the smelters. Meanwhile within the Copperbelt mining has extended to sites where the grade of ore is rather lower than elsewhere, notably Bwana Mkubwa, where an old mine closed for many years was re-opened in 1971, and Baluba, where production began in 1973. The extension of mining to some of these relatively low-grade deposits of refractory ore has been made possible by the successful development of a new treatment process usually termed TORCO.

In the Shaba region of Zaire there had been some expansion in the early 1950's, and this area would undoubtedly have shared in the later growth if political problems had not intervened. In the event, the maintenance of production there at an almost constant level of 250,000–300,000 tons throughout the decade from 1956 to 1966 despite the political strife, represented a remarkable achievement. The main change during this period was the nationalization of the industry, formerly controlled by the Belgian company Union Minière, but this had little impact on production. Since the late 1960's production has increased each year to reach just $\frac{1}{2}$ million tons in 1974. So far this has been mainly the result of expansion at existing mines, the largest of which is at Kamoto near Kolwezi at the western end of the mining zone; but there has also been investment in new mines owned jointly by the government and Japanese firms, the first of which, at Musoshi, south of Lubumbashi, began production in 1973. Another, the Tenke-Fungurume mine situated near Likasi, is due to be yielding 100,000 tons a year by 1979 provided that power from the Inga hydroelectricity scheme can be supplied to the Shaba region in sufficient quantities by then.

Copper mining began on a very small scale in Rhodesia around 1948, and expanded in 1957–60 as new mines were opened north-west of Salisbury, though only to about 15,000 tons a year. Since 1966 export markets have still been found; and further expansion has taken place notably in Mangula while other small mines have been opened. In Uganda a copper mine was opened in 1956 in the Ruwenzori foothills, and production there quickly reached 15,000 tons a year: but the reserves seem to be very limited in extent, and there has been no opportunity for further development. Indeed, it is not possible to anticipate a life of more than a few more years for the mine. More promising is a new development in Mauritania, where there is a deposit containing at least 500,000 tons of copper metal at Akjoujt, 270 km inland from Nouakchott. Production there by an international consortium began in 1970 after an investment of $60 million. Even this ore-body, however, is equivalent to less than a single year's production in Zambia, and it is still in that country and in Zaire that the greatest prospects exist for increased earnings from copper.

Minerals often found associated with copper are zinc and cobalt. Tropical Africa makes only a small contribution to world zinc production, but it provides the greater part of the world's cobalt. The demand for cobalt was very slack throughout the 1960's, however, and while it has continued to be worked in both Zaire and Zambia as a byproduct of copper there has been no significant expansion. The market for zinc was rather more favourable between 1960 and 1965, and although production has been very static in Zaire, there has been some development at the Kabwe (Broken Hill) mine in Zambia. A slight increase in lead production has also taken place there, although the past two decades have witnessed the closing down of the only other important lead mines in tropical Africa.

IRON ORE

The most important new development in the field of metal mining in tropical Africa in recent years has been a great expansion of iron-ore working. In 1956 production of iron in

TABLE 4.4. IRON ORE IN TROPICAL AFRICA

	Production in 000 tons iron ccntent				
	1956	1961	1966	1971	1974
Liberia	1,460	2,140	11,540	16,080	24,460
Sierra Leone	820	1,030	1,380	1,530	1,500
Guinea	430	270	300	0	0
Rhodesia	60	240	830	320	310
Angola	0	470	500	3,820	3,100
Mauritania	0	0	4,640	5,620	7,580

ore amounted to only $2\frac{3}{4}$ million tons, but by 1961 it had reached 5 million tons and by 1974 it exceeded 37 million tons. Mining began in Sierra Leone in 1933 and in Rhodesia in 1943, and between 1951 and 1957 it extended to Liberia, Guinea, and Angola; but the following decade brought considerable change as production rose much more rapidly in some countries than in others, and took place for the first time in Mauritania (Table 4.4).

The largest contribution to the expansion has been made by Liberia, where the development of iron mining has transformed the economy. A deposit in the Bomi Hills, about 70 km north of Monrovia, has been worked since 1951, another 60 km further north-west at Mano River since 1961, and a third in the Bong Range, 80 km north-east of Monrovia, since 1965 (Map 4.4). Much the most important working, however, is that in the Nimba Mountains near the borders with Guinea and Ivory Coast. This lies 270 km from the coast, but the deposit is huge and easily worked, and it contains 67% iron with very little silica or phosphorus. Production there began only in 1963, yet by 1968 it reached 7 million tons, just half the total Liberian output in that year. Production at each of the mines continued to expand into the 1970's.

All the workings have incurred considerable costs, such as those caused by the need to build a railway to each mine, but the richness of the ore bodies, the existence of large markets in North America and Europe, and the relative proximity of Liberia to these have made the investments worth while. In the case of the Nimba Mountains operation these have amounted to over $200 million, including the cost of the railway and port built by the mining company. One other favourable factor has been the fact that the Liberian government has been very well disposed towards foreign private investment, and has offered very attractive terms to the entrepreneurs.

In the late 1950's both Sierra Leone and Guinea rivalled Liberia as iron-ore producers, but operations have now ceased in both countries. In Sierra Leone a $25 million expansion programme in the early 1960's had assisted a 50% increase in production; but the richest of the ores at Marampa are now approaching exhaustion, and the mine was closed down in 1976. Although large reserves of lower grade ore remain there, and high-grade ore has been found elsewhere, neither appears sufficiently attractive to bring further investment. The deposit worked in Guinea was unusually accessible, lying only 10 km from Conakry, and reserves remain there. The decline in production must be attributed largely to political problems, especially attitudes towards foreign capital and the difficulties in replacing French technicians. The same factors, together with the problem of inaccessibility, for some years discouraged development of the even richer deposits on the Guinea side of the Nimba Mountains, but in the early 1970's plans were being made for the exploitation of these by an international consortium, including several African governments as well as foreign companies.

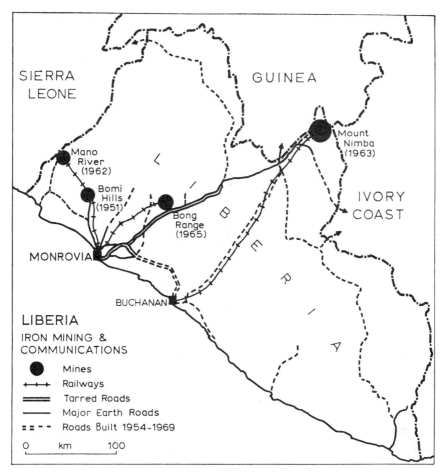

MAP 4.4. Iron mines, roads, and railways in Liberia.

Angola has several large deposits of iron ore, and Portugal became very interested in these after the loss of Goa from which it used to obtain its supplies. The first mining took place in 1956, but much expansion followed, initially at Cuima, south of Nova Lisboa. Between 1966 and 1969 work proceeded on the development on an even larger scale of the deposits at Cassinga, further to the south. $100 million was invested, in this case largely by West German concerns which were seeking new sources of ore, and as a result total Angolan production rose from ¾ million tons in 1967 to nearly 4 million tons in 1970 and 1971. However, the Cassinga mines were closed down and severely damaged by the 1975 conflict.

One of the most remarkable new mining enterprises in Africa is that which is now producing iron ore from the Kedia d'Idjil Range which rises from the Sahara in Mauritania. The deposits were found in 1935, and an international combine, MIFERMA, was established in 1952 to develop them. Although they lie far inland in largely uninhabited country, they contained at least 110 million tons of 64% ore lying at the surface, and were sufficiently attractive to draw a capital investment of almost $200 million for the mine, railway to the coast, port facilities, and new townships. France, West Germany, Italy, and Britain all contributed to the investment, and each is now taking a share of the ore. Production began in 1963, and by 1965 it had reached 4 million tons. In that year production from the original working at Tazadit was supplemented by that from a new working at F'Derik, so that the total has risen to over 7 million tons a year. Mauritania therefore now stands second only to Liberia among African producers of iron ore.

One feature common to all the workings so far mentioned is that all the ore is sent to markets overseas. The value of iron mining to African countries would be far greater if the ore could be used as the basis of local steel manufacture, but as yet this takes place only in Rhodesia. There iron ore has been mined to supply the Redcliff iron and steel works since the 1940's, and the enlargement of its operations provided the main justification of an expansion of iron in ore production from 70,000 tons in 1956 to 820,000 tons in 1965, although some direct export of ore to Japan had also begun by then.

The next decade may witness many further changes in the distribution of iron production, for while there are plans for expansion at many existing mines iron ore exists in most other African countries and there are various plans for entirely new developments. Among these are the projected exploitation of the Belinga ore deposits of north-east Gabon, the Bangolo deposits in the west of Ivory Coast, and the Mirrote deposits of northern Mozambique. Such developments will depend, among other things, upon a growth in world markets for iron ore, which were rather depressed in the late 1960's and early 1970's.

BAUXITE

Bauxite, which is of increasing importance as the source of aluminium, is widely found in tropical Africa. Some reports indicate that this region has over one-quarter of all known reserves in the world. In the early 1950's production was confined to small-scale operations in Ghana and Guinea, but the extent of the reserves was already clear and a great development of bauxite mining seemed to be in prospect. This has not come as rapidly as was hoped, mainly because the chief aluminium companies of North America and Europe have found cheaper sources of ore elsewhere, notably in Australia and in the Caribbean area; but there has been a substantial growth, and there will probably be much more within the next twenty years.

The main development has taken place in Guinea, where there are several workable deposits. Those of the highly accessible Los Islands were first exploited in 1952; but after 1960 production there was overshadowed by the operations of a company jointly owned by American and French firms and the Guinea government, known originally as Fria and now as Friguia, at a mine 150 km north of Conakry. Over $2\frac{1}{2}$ million tons is extracted there annually, and this is transformed into alumina before export. More recently another consortium, including the government and American firms, has developed the less accessible but even larger Sangaredi deposit in the Boké region further north at a cost of almost $250 million. Production began in 1973 and should quickly reach 5 million tons a year, rising to 9 million tons in the 1980's. Yet another mine, developed with Soviet assistance at Débélé near Kindia, 100 km inland from Conakry, began production in 1974 at the rate of $2\frac{1}{2}$ million tons a year.

Agreements to establish other bauxite mines were made in 1971 with Yugoslavia and with a Swiss firm, while during 1976 Guinea was negotiating for Arab finance for a $1500 million project at Ayekoyé in the Boké region, designed to produce 2 million tons of alumina annually from 9 million tons of bauxite, and later to involve aluminium smelting. Even by 1975 Guinea had reached third place among the world's bauxite producers, and if all current plans are implemented it may become the leading producer in the 1980's.

In Ghana, bauxite mining began near Awaso in 1941, but expansion there during the past decade has been only slight, and the contribution of bauxite mining to the country's economy is very small. The situation is likely to change only when ore from other richer local sources is used in the Tema smelter, probably in the 1980's. Sierra Leone became the third tropical African producer of bauxite in 1963, when a mine was opened in the Mokanji Hills in the south, production there surpassing that in Ghana by 1968 and reaching 700,000 tons by 1972.

MANGANESE

Manganese has made some contribution to the mineral earnings of tropical Africa throughout the post-war period, and although the two main producers of the 1950's, Ghana and Zaire, have failed to expand their output, there has been an important development of the industry in Gabon.

The deposits at Nsuta near Tarkwa in Ghana are not rich enough to attract new large-scale investment, and production there has remained between 200,000 and 300,000 tons a year (metal content) for twenty years. At Kolwezi in Zaire there was some growth between 1956 and 1959, but production then fell somewhat and has remained static ever since. The deposit at Moanda in south-east Gabon is much richer; indeed, it is among the best in the world, with over 200 million tons of 50% ore which can be worked opencast. Development there was for some years hindered by extreme inaccessibility, but after the completion of a cable railway across the border into Congo production began in 1962. It rose rapidly to reach 630,000 tons in 1965, about 8% of the world total, and while low world prices have discouraged much further growth since then, there are plans for substantial expansion in the late 1970's.

TIN

Tin is comparable to manganese in terms of its value to tropical Africa today, but it differs in that there has been no new development anywhere in recent years. Indeed, while the production in Nigeria remained almost constant throughout the 1960's and its value rose somewhat, partly through the establishment of local smelting, there has been a substantial fall in output from Zaire, the only other major producer. Some of the best deposits there are approaching exhaustion, and while others could be developed, disturbed political conditions and uncertain markets have together discouraged this. In Rwanda, too, production is now rather lower than in the 1950's.

GOLD

Gold was the first mineral to be worked on a large scale in tropical Africa, but nowhere has it attained an importance remotely comparable with that in South Africa. In 1956 it was being mined in many countries, although it was an important element in the economy only in Rhodesia and Ghana, but since that time the general trend has been towards smaller production. In several countries, such as Tanzania, it ceased altogether as costs rose above the pegged price of gold. Even in Rhodesia and Ghana, where geological conditions permit lower costs than elsewhere, production has remained almost static throughout this period, although in Ghana its distribution has changed, with some expansion at Obuasi but closure of most other mines.

DIAMONDS

Diamonds provide a sharp contrast with gold, for there has been a great increase in the value of tropical African production, although the fortunes of the industry have differed from one country to another (Table 4.5). In terms of quantity the leading producer is East Kasai province of Zaire, but no more diamonds are won there now than in the mid-1950's, a modest growth before 1960 having been offset by a decline during subsequent political disturbances. In terms of value also, Zaire was the most important in the 1950's, but in this respect its relative position has dropped sharply as the production of gem stones at Tshikapa has virtually ceased and the industrial stones mined at Bakwanga fetch much lower prices than gems.

TABLE 4.5. DIAMONDS IN TROPICAL AFRICA

	Average 1956–7	Average 1966–7	Average 1973–4
Production (000 carats)			
Zaire	14,828	12,791	13,354
Ghana	2,832	2,678	2,445
Angola	802	1,280	2,108
Sierra Leone	756	1,431	1,537
Tanzania	375	967	525
CAE	126	531	410
Export value ($m.)			
Zaire	30	25	60
Ghana	24	15	12
Angola	14	41	83
Sierra Leone	14	40	85
Tanzania	9	28	21
CAE	3	15	11

Diamond mining is now of greatest value in Sierra Leone, where most of the stones are of gem quality; although there has been little growth there since the mid-1960's. Mining by the Sierra Leone Selection Trust began at Yengema in the 1930's, but digging elsewhere was officially opened to individual Africans only in 1956. It was this which contributed most to the rapid growth of production from 650,000 carats in that year to 1½ million carats in 1965. The value of these stones rose from $10 million to $47 million as the proportion of gems increased, and diamonds now dominate the country's exports. The situation in Ghana is very different, for small-scale digging in the south-west has almost ceased, leaving only the large Ghana Consolidated Diamonds Ltd. which operates in the Birim area further east and which has maintained a fairly constant level of production. The large mines at Dundo in north-east Angola and Mwadui in northern Tanzania increased their production substantially in the 1960's but production was cut back at Mwadui in the early 1970's as the deposits appeared to be approaching exhaustion, while it fell sharply at Dundo with the departure of the Portuguese in 1975. Diamonds also became important to the Central African Empire in the 1960's, produced mainly by numerous small-scale operators, while some digging also takes place in Liberia, although some of its exports are diamonds smuggled out of Sierra Leone.

PHOSPHATES

The list of minerals won in tropical Africa was lengthened in the 1960's by the establishment for the first time of large-scale mining of phosphates. Phosphates have long been of great importance to north Africa, but until 1960 there was only one minor working south of the Sahara, at Pallo in Senegal. Production of phosphates there expanded slightly during the 1960's, but it has been far surpassed in importance by a new development at Taiba, 130 km north-east of Dakar. Another rich deposit was found in Togo in 1952, and production there began in 1961, the mineral being railed a mere 20 km to a new pier at Kpémé. In each country exports had risen by 1971 to over 1½ million tons a year, worth $15 to $20 million.

Production was then further expanded, to reach 2½ million tons in Togo and 2 million tons in Senegal by 1974, but the importance of phosphates to these countries increased far more as a result of a huge rise in world prices in 1974. In that year they brought $145 million to Togo, six times more than any other export, while phosphates in crude and processed form together brought $125 million to Senegal, just matching earnings from groundnut products.

Uganda has a rich phosphate deposit near Tororo, but the long haul to the coast has prevented its exploitation other than on a very small scale for a local fertilizer factory. A larger development of this nature has taken place in Rhodesia, at Dorowa, and it is to be hoped that various deposits known elsewhere might soon be used in this way, thus making a direct contribution to both the manufacturing and the agricultural sectors of the economy.

THE ROLE OF MINING IN THE NATIONAL ECONOMIES

In many countries of tropical Africa the role of mining in the economy has not changed markedly in recent years. In several its importance has increased substantially in absolute terms but has fallen somewhat in relation to other sectors of the economy, notably manufacturing and services. In Zambia, mining assumed a position of dominance early in this century and has maintained it ever since; and it is increased copper production which provides the basis for the country's current rapid development. Yet although minerals still account for over 95% of its exports (Table 4.6), the contribution of mining to the national income has fallen from rather more than 50% during most of the 1950's to about 35% today. In Zaire the share of minerals in total exports has risen above the level of 60% which was maintained during the 1950's, since mining survived the political troubles better than some other activities, but even there its share of the national income is thought to have fallen somewhat.

TABLE 4.6. THE ROLE OF MINING IN SELECTED AFRICAN ECONOMIES

	Mining as % of GDP		Minerals as % of exports		Value of Mineral exports ($ US)	
	1972	1974	1972	1974	1972	1974
Gabon	30	49	64	80	140	680
Liberia	30	36	78	73	190	290
Mauritania	29	36	82	86	100	170
Zambia	25	34	98	97	740	1370
Nigeria	16	45	84	93	1820	8550
Sierra Leone	16	15	78	74	90	90
Zaire	15	22	80	83	550	1150
Angola	8		44	60	230	630

Sources: United Nations, *Yearbook of National Accounts Statistics* and *Yearbook of International Trade Statistics;* and national sources.

A similar pattern is repeated in Rhodesia, where asbestos, chrome, coal, and gold mining have all remained static, but copper, nickel, and iron production have risen: mining has decreased its share of the national income from 8% to 6%. In Ghana, too, the gold, diamond, and manganese industries have all tended to stagnate, causing the share of mining in both exports and national income to decline, and no great change is likely until the country's bauxite deposits can be developed. In many other countries, such as Sudan, Ethiopia, Chad, and Malawi, mining has remained of little or no importance.

There are some outstanding exceptions to this generally stable pattern, however, as the examination of individual minerals may have indicated. In Mauritania the national economy has been completely transformed by the development of iron mining, even if this transformation has not yet impinged upon the way of life of most of the population. In 1962 the exports of the country were worth only $3 million; yet by 1964 they were worth $46 million of which iron ore accounted for $43 million compared with $2 million for the second export commodity, fish. There is little prospect of any substantial reduction of this overwhelming importance of minerals in the near future, for other opportunities for economic growth in the country are very limited.

In Liberia the change in the economy has been only a little less remarkable than in Mauritania, although it has been spread over a longer period and is rather less confined geographically. Although iron mining began in 1951 it still contributed only 16% of Liberian exports in 1955. By 1961, however, iron ore had taken the lead from rubber, and by 1965 it accounted for 73% of all export earnings. Iron mining has played the major role in changing Liberia from one of the poorest countries in tropical Africa to one with an income per head well above the average for the region, and if the revenues accruing from it are wisely used it could now provide the basis for rapid economic development.

Gabon also has a relatively high national income per head largely as a result of the mineral developments of recent years. There was no mining of any significance in the country before 1957, yet by 1967 minerals accounted for almost two-thirds of its exports and a quarter of its national income. They enabled Gabon to balance its budget, and put it in a position of some strength in its negotiations with other members of the Equatorial Customs Union, none of which are so well endowed in this respect.

The importance of mining in the economy of Gabon became even greater in 1974 as a result of much higher export prices, especially for oil (Table 4.6). It is these which have now made Gabon the most prosperous country in tropical Africa in terms of export earnings, and even national income, per head of the population.

In Nigeria, mining long played a small role in the economy, but the picture there has been transformed by the rise of the oil industry, which has grown sufficiently to assume a position of great importance even in such a large and diverse economy. Minerals accounted for only 5% of the value of exports in 1961, but by 1966 the proportion was 40%. Until the civil war intervened there seemed every prospect that revenues accruing from the oil industry would allow a phase of unusually rapid economic development to come to Nigeria, and perhaps this may now occur. In the early 1970's expanding oil sales contrasted with stagnation in other exports, so that the share of oil in total exports reached 84% by 1972; and it was then playing a vital part in providing funds for post-war reconstruction as well as in ensuring a healthy balance of trade. Since oil has become so important to Nigeria, the sharp rise in world prices in 1973–4 (reflected in an increase of the Nigerian posted price from $4 to $15 per barrel) has dramatically altered the economic situation of the country, causing its total export earnings to rise from $2300 million in 1972 to $9500 million in 1974.

Other countries in which the importance of mining in the economy has increased include Guinea and Sierra Leone, where minerals now provide the leading exports, and Angola, where they still ranked behind coffee in the 1960's but far surpassed it as oil prices rose. Even a minor mineral development may be of great significance for a small and poor country. The newly opened phosphate deposit now provides the leading export of Togo, for example, accounting for 40% of all foreign exchange earnings in 1972 and 72% of much increased earnings in 1974. Similarly, in the Central African Empire other commercial activities are so limited that diamonds are the leading export in some years, even disregarding those that are smuggled out through Zaire and Congo. In Congo itself mining was of no importance until 1969 when the potash deposits at Holle, 45 km inland from Pointe Noire, were first worked. The ½ million tons exported in 1971 were worth $16 million, second only to timber; but by 1974 their value was far surpassed by that of oil, which has more than doubled the total value of exports. A uranium mine opened at Mounana in 1961 is only a minor element in the Gabonese economy; but a mine only a little larger at Arlit in Niger opened in 1971 is of great significance for that country's economy, providing half its export income in 1974 and two-thirds in 1975.

The importance of mining in the economic development of each country cannot be assessed only in terms of its direct contribution to the national income and to exports. Most successful mining enterprises pay large sums in royalties and taxes to the governments, thus providing much-needed funds for their development programmes. The establishment of a mining industry may contribute directly to an expansion of transport facilities, power production, manufacturing, and internal trade. The most outstanding example of the role of mining in encouraging other forms of economic activity over a period of several decades is provided by Zambia: the most interesting cases in the period since 1950 are perhaps Liberia and Nigeria.

The establishment of iron mining in Liberia has provided the justification for construction of three new railways, two running inland from Monrovia and one extending for 267 km from Buchanan to Mount Nimba (Map 4.4). While the first two handle only traffic to and from the mines, the Nimba line is open to other traffic since this was a stipulation of the mining concession imposed by the Liberian government, and it is carrying a little timber. In Uganda the development of Kilembe copper mine required a 333 km extension of the railway which previously terminated at Kampala; and in Congo a 283 km line from Dolisie has been built to handle the manganese now worked in Gabon. Several important mineral lines have been built elsewhere, but in some cases, as in Mauritania, they are owned and operated by the mining company, and there is little prospect of their ever carrying anything other than mineral traffic.

Road transport is not widely used for the haulage of minerals, but mines normally need some road access. In several cases equipment has had to be moved to the mine by road prior to the opening of a railway. Thus in Liberia each of the mining companies has undertaken a substantial amount of road building, and many short new roads have been built around the Nigerian oilfields. The development of copper mining in Mauritania has required the investment of $10 million by the mining company on the reconstruction of the road to the coast, and this is available for whatever traffic that desert environment can provide.

Since most of the newly worked minerals are exported overseas, substantial improvements in port facilities have had to be made. Several existing ports have been much enlarged, examples including Monrovia and Moçamedes, while some completely new ports have been built, including Buchanan in Liberia and Bonny in Nigeria. In some cases the new facilities are designed to serve only the needs of the mining industry, but in others they are available for other goods also. Expansion of port facilities has also been necessary to meet the needs arising from the increased production of many older mining enterprises. As copper exports from Zambia rose, the need for extra berths at Beira and Maputo was accentuated: with changed political circumstances the impact is now being felt on Dar es Salaam.

Thus, as in Zaire, Zambia, and elsewhere in pre-war years, the expansion of mining in several African countries in the past decade has created new patterns of transport, and also required the provision of new facilities, some of which are available to serve other sectors of the economy. The clearest example of this is undoubtedly provided by Liberia, which had a particularly slender transport system in 1956, and which now has one comparable with those in most other tropical African countries.

Mining has also played an important part in stimulating the construction of some of the large dams and power stations examined in Chapter 6. The rising demands of the copper industry of Zambia provided the main justification for the Kariba power project and more recently for the Kafue scheme. Similarly, in Zaire it is the power requirements of copper smelting and refining which explain the early development of the power resources of the head-waters of the Zaire River and its tributaries, while the much greater potential of the lower river remained unexploited until the 1970's.

In Liberia the iron mining companies have established their own thermal power plants both at the mines and at the ports. The capacity of these had reached 140 MW by 1965, and it has since been increased further. Although this electricity is essentially for the mining companies' own needs, some surplus has been provided to make up deficiencies in public supplies in Monrovia. In Mauritania the iron mining company has established 11 MW thermal plants both near the mines and at Nouadhibou, and these together generated 34 million kWh in 1967. This may be compared with the total capacity of 2.5 MW and production of 4 million kWh of the other power stations in the country. Many smaller mining concerns in other countries have had to establish power stations, but usually these are designed only to meet their own needs, and have little impact beyond the mine.

Some of the new developments in the mining industry have provided the basis for new forms of manufacturing, and have therefore played an especially important part in assisting African countries in their economic aims. In certain cases the minerals have provided the raw material or the source of power: in others, manufacturing industries have been established to satisfy some demand provided by the mining industry or by the wage earners employed in it.

There is no sharp distinction between mineral processing that is essentially part of the mining industry and that which can properly be regarded as manufacturing; but there are several examples in tropical Africa of new plants which process a mineral beyond the stage in which it is generally exported. Thus oil refineries have been established on the oilfields of Nigeria and Gabon, although nearly all the oil produced is still exported unrefined. The value of iron mining to Liberia has been substantially increased by the installation at Buchanan of the largest ore washing and pelletizing plant outside the United States: and at Fria in Guinea bauxite is transformed into alumina before export, although the next stage of local aluminium refining has been postponed. Meanwhile in some of the older mining areas the extent of processing has been increased. For instance, on the Copperbelt refining as well as smelting capacity has been enlarged, notably by the opening of an important new refinery at Ndola in 1958.

The close association between mining and manufacturing in countries such as Britain, the United States, and the USSR depends in part on the use of coal, and to a lesser extent oil and gas, as a source of power. While no such close association can be seen emerging in tropical Africa, cases may be found where the availability of fuel has assisted the development of manufacturing. Coal from Wankie, for example, has assisted some forms of industrial growth in both Rhodesia and Zambia. In Nigeria coal will become more important when an iron and steel industry is established, but here natural gas could be particularly valuable, and has already attracted a few industries to Port Harcourt, Aba, and Ughelli. Both natural gas and oil are now also used for the generation of electricity, which further assists industrial development there.

Minerals are proving more important for new African manufacturing industries as raw materials than as fuels. For some years limestone used for cement manufacture was the only important example of this, and it is still the most widespread, but now local phosphates are being used for fertilizer production in several countries, and a copper wire and cable plant has been established at Luanshya in Zambia. For the future, several countries hope to use local bauxite for aluminium production, local iron ore for steel, and local oil for a sophisticated petro-chemicals industry.

New mining enterprises have also contributed to industrial growth through the market which they provide for manufactured goods. In Port Harcourt several factories have been built to supply goods for the Nigerian oil industry, and in Liberia two large sawmills and plants producing explosives and oxygen have been built to satisfy some of the needs of the iron mines. In addition, in both these countries the substantial incomes earned in the mining activities have widened the market for consumer goods, and thus played a part in making various new manufacturing concerns viable. The same process has been at work on a small scale in Gabon. On a much larger scale the expansion of the copper industry has been of fundamental importance in the recent growth of manufacturing in Zambia, both directly in the case of such new plants as those producing explosives at Mufulira and oxygen at Kitwe, and indirectly through its contribution to rising incomes.

Mining has also assisted the development of manufacturing through the capital which its profits have made available for investment. Some of the older-established mining enterprises preferred to diversify their activities rather than to invest in further expansion of mining. Thus capital for new manufacturing industries in Zambia was provided out of the profits of the copper companies, even before partial nationalization accelerated the process.

The profits obtained from mining have also been used in some cases to improve social conditions. Thus both the major Zambian copper companies contributed substantially in the 1960's to the school-building programme on the Copperbelt. The indirect contribution of mining to other forms of development through government revenues must also be noted. It is not usually possible to point to individual forms of government expenditure as being covered by mining royalties or taxes. However, these provide more than half the total revenue in some African countries, and thus it is fair to say that it is the extent of the funds accruing from mining that has permitted Zambia to spend large sums on its new university, and to expand very rapidly its medical services.

In Liberia, where total government revenues amount to only $100 million a year, the direct contribution of the iron mining industry is at least $15 million, while it makes further indirect contributions in ways such as port dues and taxes on oil and other imports.

In Nigeria the oil industry already made a direct contribution of over $100 million to the economy even by 1965, partly in the form of local purchases and wages, but mainly in payments to the government. By 1971–2, however, it accounted for $1100 million of the total federal government revenues of $2100 million, while increased oil prices and direct government participation in the industry raised its contribution to over $5000 million by 1974–5. Oil still has not made Nigeria a rich country, but it has sharply reduced its dependence on foreign aid, and should ensure that lack of finance is not a major hindrance to rapid economic development in the late 1970's and the 1980's. It certainly enabled the country to prepare an extremely ambitious development plan for the period 1975–80, proposed government expenditure over this period being 20,000 million Naira ($32,000 million) compared with 3000 million Naira under the 1970–4 plan.

Despite these undoubted benefits of new mining developments, it must, of course, be remembered that most are undertaken primarily for the profit of the foreign companies undertaking them, and much of the export revenue which they yield is remitted overseas. Furthermore, while the contribution of these developments to the economy of several African countries has certainly been impressive, they have usually had no perceptible impact on the majority of the population. A thriving modern sector has arisen within the economy of Liberia and Gabon, but although their national income per head may now be relatively high, most people in both countries are still extremely poor. It is this situation which caused the authors of an economic survey of Liberia to entitle their report *Growth without Development*. Recent studies of the operations of MIFERMA in Mauritania and FRIA in Guinea have shown how these form only tiny enclaves of modernization within economies which in many respects are changing very little. This situation is clearly reflected in the very limited geographical extent of most of the changes resulting from recent mineral developments.

THE AREAL EXTENT OF THE IMPACT OF MINING

There are only two countries in tropical Africa in which the location of mining enterprises has profoundly influenced the spatial of other economic activities. Fifty years ago the Copperbelt became the economic focus of Zambia. In 1920 this area was very sparsely populated, but it has drawn so many people to it that it now houses 15 % of the total population of the country and 70 % of the urban population. Towns have grown up there in which manufacturing and service industries are much more important in terms of employment and income than copper mining itself. As the copper industry has expanded in recent years, so has the relative importance of the Copperbelt in the whole national economy, though the capital, Lusaka, is now providing a strong countervailing force. The situation is to some extent similar in Zaire, where the economic strength of Shaba (formerly Katanga) was reflected by its great importance in the political developments of the 1960's though there is still the capital, far away to the west, which forms the dominant economic focus of the country.

It was possible in the mid-1960's to see signs of a situation parallel to that in Zaire emerging in Nigeria, where the oil industry was bringing a new prosperity to the south-east. (As in the case of Shaba a few years earlier, mining provided sufficient economic strength to enable the former Eastern Region to declare itself an independent state, though no doubt the motives in the two cases were different.) However, the role of the mining area as a focal point in the whole space economy showed little sign of challenging that of the national capital: and the civil war served only to increase the greater attraction of the latter for most forms of economic activity. As a result of the development of the oilfield, the delta area in Bendel and Rivers states has become an important focus of economic life in Nigeria, but it certainly does not dominate the spatial organization of the country in the way that the oil sector now dominates the national economy.

The direct spatial impact of the oil industry in terms of employment or related activities is far outweighed by its indirect impact through the allocation of government revenues amongst the nineteen states. This constitutes one of the most important spatial decisions that has to be made by any African government, and the formula applied in the early 1970's represented a compromise between allowing the states with oil to reap all the benefits and redistributing all the revenues throughout the Federation. The royalties from on-shore oil went largely to the states of origin, though some went into a pool for redistribution; but royalties from off-shore oil and all taxes went to the federal government, and could be used anywhere in the country.

The local impact of iron ore mining in Liberia has been discussed by both Hance and Swindell as well as in the economic survey mentioned above. There, economic activity on the orefields is largely confined to the mining operations, the benefication of the ores to decrease the costs of transporting them, and the generation of electricity to meet the mining companies' own requirements. The main exceptions are the sawmills, notably that at Mount Nimba. Hance observes that rather than diverting economic development away from Monrovia, the establishment of large-scale mining has contributed much to the recent growth of that city. It has also produced a small pocket of commercial activity at the port of Buchanan.

A very full discussion of the limited local impact of the bauxite mine at Fria in Guinea has been provided by Suret-Canale. He notes that while during the period of construction employment exceeded 10,000, now that the mine and processing plant are in full operation, less than 1500 people work there. Life in nearby villages seems to have been hardly affected at all. The situation is similar around the copper mine in Uganda and the phosphate working in Togo. The iron ore deposits of Mauritania lie in such a barren desert zone that it is not surprising that no economic activities have been attracted there other than those directly serving the mines.

The expansion of diamond digging by individuals in Sierra Leone has probably done more to spread income than have most of the mining developments. It has certainly made some contribution to redressing the balance between the relatively affluent Creoles of the Freetown area and the poorer people of some interior areas. It provides at least seasonal employment for more than 50,000 people, far more than are employed by any large-scale enterprise in Africa producing a comparable value of minerals, although most obtain very little income, and the structure of the industry may mean merely that earnings go through private dealers to Swiss banks rather than out as company profits. It has also brought many problems, since much illicit mining and trading takes place, creating an atmosphere of mutual suspicion among the local Kono people, immigrant African groups, Lebanese dealers, the large-scale mining company and the government, and since the search for diamonds draws people out of food production.

A combination of many factors seems to be limiting the local impact of most of the new mining developments. The minerals are generally produced primarily for export rather than local use, and much of the equipment used for their extraction is imported rather than produced locally. The mining companies are often largely self-sufficient in all forms of supplies, and also in services such as education and health. The demand for food and certain services for the mine workers generally has some impact on the local economy, but this would often be much greater if these workers had their families with them.

Those activities which depend on government initiative, including local administration, have usually been established, at least on a skeletal basis, before the mining development takes place. When this is so they tend to expand in the places where they have been established rather than to shift to the new mining area, unless the new mining enterprise is exceptionally large, or has exceptionally good prospects for a long life, or unless it comes at least partly under government control.

CONCLUSIONS

Mining activity has increased substantially in tropical Africa in recent years, and has made a valuable contribution to the economic development of certain parts of the region.

During the 1960's the outstanding importance of the Copperbelt was further reinforced, and production expanded in various other old-established mining areas; but certain new elements in the spatial pattern of mineral exploitation also rose to importance, notably the oilfields of Nigeria and the iron ore fields of Liberia. Around 1966–9 the rate of expansion slowed, as strained relations between Zambia and Rhodesia, the civil war in Nigeria and saturated markets for iron ore all provided setbacks, but it is accelerating again, and there are good prospects for further development. Again, these include the probable expansion of existing mining activities as well as the establishment of new ones. The latter include both new developments in countries where mining is already important such as the exploitation of iron ore in Gabon and further bauxite deposits in Guinea, and also developments which would be smaller in scale but which may provide poor countries with mineral revenues for the first time such as the working of bauxite in Malawi and manganese in Upper Volta.

The structural pattern of mining in tropical Africa has not changed fundamentally, and still consists largely of foreign companies extracting minerals for export overseas. These concerns are contributing substantially to the economic growth of the countries in which they operate and are providing funds for many forms of development; but the mines themselves rarely constitute the spatial foci of such development or have much direct impact on the lives of most people even in the districts in which they lie. As a result of new mining developments the economic dualism that Zambia has experienced for decades is now a feature of Gabon and Mauritania also. In many cases even the extent of basic processing before export is far less than it might be. In terms of its geographical impact the pattern of mining which has often been described as "colonial" continues today, and is characteristic even of most of the new developments which have taken place since independence. The situation in which minerals are used locally as fuels and raw materials for industrial development, and in which mineral deposits form the basis of industrial regions, remains very largely a goal for the future.

The position of most new mining enterprises as isolated islands of modernization in a sea of underdevelopment is sometimes attributed to the fact that most of them are still foreign concerns. Undoubtedly, this is a contributory factor, in part because a large share of the profits are remitted overseas, but probably also because alien mining companies often do not identify themselves with national development. However, the situation might be little different if the enterprises were owned by African companies or governments, unless active steps were undertaken to integrate mining developments into the pattern of

PLATE 9. Oil drilling in eastern Nigeria: the most important new mineral development of the past two decades within tropical Africa.

PLATE 10. The oil industry has now extended west of the Niger river, and this has involved the laying of long pipelines, sometimes through virgin forestland.

PLATE 11. Nkana mine on the Zambian Copperbelt. Mining on the Copperbelt of Zambia and Congo continues to expand, and this is still the only area in tropical Africa where it forms the basis for a major urban-industrial complex.

PLATE 12. Resource-based manufacturing in a rural setting: a cement plant in Uganda. Most other industries are more clearly market-orientated in their location, and are found in the main urban centres.

PLATE 13. Kariba Dam, extending across the Zambezi from Rhodesia (*left*), where the existing power station is located, to Zambia (*right*), where another is planned.

PLATE 14. Volta Dam, which has transformed the landscape of eastern Ghana and is permitting the generation of vast quantities of electricity in the power station on the extreme left of the picture.

PLATE 15. All the major dams in tropical Africa have involved the flooding of some settled areas. The building of the Kainji Dam in Nigeria has caused the abandonment of settlements such as Bussa, of which part is shown here.

PLATE 16. New Bussa, built to provide a new home for the people of Bussa, shows how in the midst of change there may be continuity, for many features of the old settlement are retained including its compact nature and the pre-eminence of the chief's home (*foreground*).

other economic activities. Conversely, with effective regional economic planning it may prove possible in the future to use new mining ventures as spearheads for development in some poor regions even if they are undertaken by European, American, or Japanese concerns.

Even mining developments financed by foreign capital and supplying markets overseas can radically change the whole pattern of economic activity in an African country, as the example of Zambia clearly shows. None of the new developments of the 1950's and 1960's in fact had this result. In Mauritania, Liberia and Gabon one factor limiting the impact of mining is probably the small size of the national economy and the consequent limited opportunity for industrial development based on national markets. In Nigeria this problem is much less serious, and there the initial growth of oil mining might had had great repercussions if the civil war had not intervened. Now that peace has returned to Nigeria, and if greater economic integration among the small nations is achieved, mining may yet provide the catalyst for rapid and broad-based economic development in these parts of Africa. In so far as this was based on mineral exports it would still be dependent development, but in a situation of increasing global scarcity of minerals, and especially if African countries were supplying these to the more industrialized countries in processed form, it might come closer towards development based on interdependence.

SELECTED READING

The role of mining in African development is discussed from different viewpoints in:
R. C. HOWARD-GOLDSMITH, The role of minerals in African development, in G. WOLSTENHOLME, *Man and Africa* (London, 1965);
A. M. KAMARCK, *The Economics of African Development* (New York, 1971), ch. 6;
S. A. OCHOLA, *Minerals in African Underdevelopment* (London, 1975).

Through surveys of the pattern of mining in the 1950s are:
LORD HAILEY, *An African Survey* (London, 1957), ch. 22;
G. H. T. KIMBLE, *Tropical Africa* (New York, 1960), ch. 9.

Detailed studies of African mineral resources are:
N. DE KUN, *The Mineral Resources of Africa* (Amsterdam, 1965);
R. A. PELLETIER, *Mineral Resources of South-central Africa* (Cape Town, 1964).

The only recent development in coal mining is described in:
I. L. GRIFFITHS, Zambian coal: an example of strategic resource development, *Geographical Review* 538–51 (1968).

Different stages in the evolution of the Nigerian oil industry are discussed in:
A. MELAMID, The geography of the Nigerian petroleum industry, *Economic Geography* **44**, 37–56 (1968);
L. H. SCHATZL, *Petroleum in Nigeria* (Ibadan, 1969);
S. R. PEARSON, *Petroleum and the Nigerian Economy* (Stanford, 1970);
J. O. ABIODUN, Locational effects of the civil war on the Nigerian petroleum industry. *Geographical Review* **64**, 253–63 (1974);
S. A. MADUJIBEYA, Oil and Nigeria's economic development, *African Affairs* **75**, 284–316 (1976).

The oil industry of Gabon is examined in:
G. DAVERAT, Un producteur africain de pétrole, le Gabon, *Cahiers d'Outre Mer* 117, 31–56 (1977).

On the development of iron mining, see:
W. A. HANCE, *African Economic Development* (New York, 1967), ch. 3;
V. MARBEAU, Les Mines de fer de Mauritanie, *Annales de Geographie* **74**, 175–94 (1965);
K. SWINDELL, Iron ore mining in West Africa, *Economic Geography* **43**, 333–46 (1967).

Two stages in the growth of bauxite mining in Guinea are discussed in:
J. SURET-CANALE, Fria, un exemple d'industrialisation africaine, *Annales de Géographie* **73**, 172–88 (1964);
P. Y. DENIS, Réalisations récentes et perspectives de développement en Guinée, *Cahiers d'Outre Mer* **116**, 321–47 (1976).

The major recent change in diamond mining is examined in:

K. SWINDELL, Diamond mining in Sierra Leone, *Tijdschrift voor Economische en Sociale Geografie* **57**, 96–104 (1966).

The most useful studies of the impact of new mining developments are those by Hance, Marbeau, and Suret-Canale noted above, and also:

R. W. CLOWER *et al.*, *Growth without Development: an Economic Survey of Liberia* (Evanston, 1966).

The role of copper mining in contemporary Zambian development is a major theme of:

R. L. SKLAR, *Corporate Power in an African State* (Berkeley, 1975).

5

INDUSTRIAL DEVELOPMENT

LARGE-SCALE manufacturing is a very recent addition to the tropical African scene, and most parts of the region are still untouched by it. In almost every country some industrial development has taken place in recent years, but often it has had very little impact on most of the population, especially since in many industries increasing efforts have been made to economize on labour. Total employment in manufacturing in tropical Africa has, in fact, risen remarkably little during the past twenty years. Nevertheless, in a few places the rate of industrial growth during the 1960's and early 1970's has been most impressive, even in terms of employment; and in others it has been sufficient to bring a substantial local rise in income levels as improved productivity has permitted the payment of higher wages.

Every African government is anxious to encourage new forms of industrial activity, and most are making strenuous efforts to increase its share in the national economy since there seems to be a close association throughout the world between industrial development and high standards of living. As indicated in an earlier chapter, there are serious limitations to the possibilities of economic growth based primarily on agriculture, especially as world markets for most agricultural products seem to be expanding more slowly than those for most industrial products. Some forms of manufacturing can raise the value of the exports on which African countries depend so heavily, while others can save foreign exchange by replacing imports with locally produced goods. Industrial growth, therefore, plays an important part in the development plans that are now being implemented in most of the countries of tropical Africa.

In certain countries there is a well-established tradition of craft industry. In Nigeria and in Sudan, for example, there have been people engaged in such activities as spinning, weaving, pottery, and leather working for centuries. These activities are still extremely important today in some places, and indeed their significance in the economy can easily be underestimated. However, they do not receive much attention here because there is little evidence of great change in recent years. In many areas the importance of traditional crafts has even declined, as the makers of such things as shoes and cooking pots have faced increasing competition from factory-made goods whether imported or local. This is the continuation of a process that has been in operation throughout this century, partially justifying the view of underdevelopment itself as an active process rather than just a condition. However, there has simultaneously been an expansion in every country of new crafts or small-scale industries such as tailoring, furniture making, and bicycle repairing. Old vehicle tyres are even providing the raw material for a new generation of shoemakers.

Such activity is generally very small in scale, often involving self-employed individuals with little capital or equipment, and although its existence as part of "the informal sector" is increasingly recognized by governments, most is entirely unrecorded in surveys of industry or employment. It is therefore quite impossible to say whether it has been growing faster in Kenya or in Tanzania, in Ghana or in Zaire, and whether its relative importance is greater in capital cities, provincial towns, or even rural areas. The indications are that such small-scale industry is remarkably widespread, mainly producing very basic requirements for very local markets, but that it is now expanding fastest in the booming cities such as Abidjan and Nairobi.

Another distinctive feature of this form of activity is that it depends upon local initiative rather than either alien enterprise or government planning.

The attempts which have been made by some African governments to encourage the spread of small-scale cottage industry have generally met with little success, though it does not follow that further attempts should not be made. Indeed, it is often suggested that far more attention should be given to development in this field and that success might follow from redirected efforts to evolve and apply an "intermediate" technology. The particular merit of this is that it might ensure that the benefits of an enlarged manufacturing sector are spread as widely as possible among the whole population.

Large-scale manufacturing dates entirely from the arrival of the Europeans with their relatively advanced technology. The transfer of this technology to the African situation is probably easier in the case of industry than agriculture, especially since initiative need not be so widely dispersed, but even so there are many problems which limit the rate at which development can take place. Unskilled labour is generally available wherever there is much prospect of industrial growth, but everywhere there is a scarcity of people with technical and managerial skills. Capital is often available from overseas for large profitable ventures, but in such cases much of the income goes overseas, while capital is not so readily available for the more modest type of enterprise which is sometimes more appropriate.

There is little doubt that the chief limitation for large-scale industrial development in tropical Africa is the size of the markets to be supplied. First Europe, then America, and finally parts of Asia have developed industry partly on the basis of overseas markets: but there are no large overseas markets left for Africa to exploit. Apart from the further processing of raw materials before export, industrialization must depend mainly on the markets provided by the people of this continent themselves. Unfortunately, in most African countries the domestic market is extremely small, because of both the small size of the population and the general low level of income. Future industrial development must therefore form part of a broad programme of economic development which will raise incomes in many ways simultaneously; and it will be greatly assisted if markets can be widened by increasing economic integration between neighbouring countries.

INDUSTRIAL DEVELOPMENT UP TO 1956

As soon as cash cropping and commercial mineral production were established in tropical Africa, small factories had to be built to prepare the crops and minerals for export. There were, for example, many cotton ginneries in operation within the first few years of this century. Establishments such as railway repair shops also had to be set up during this period. The first real manufacturing industries followed in the 1920's, using local raw materials to supply products for which a local market quickly developed. Examples included a cigarette factory in Kenya, textile mills in Ivory Coast and Zaire, and a variety of small industries in Rhodesia. A few more factories were built in the early 1930's, such as a brewery in Senegal and cigarette plants in Nigeria and Uganda, but the depression and World War II then discouraged much further development until the early 1950's.

Manufacturing in tropical Africa in the mid-1950's was therefore still very limited in both its character and its distribution. Many agricultural and mineral products had to be processed to some extent before export, but generally only the minimum of processing was undertaken. The main exceptions were the refining of some of the copper mined in Zaire and Zambia, and the milling of some of the groundnuts grown in Senegal. Most industries used local raw materials to produce the types of consumer goods that are in large demand and are costly to import because they are bulky, fragile, or perishable. These included furniture, bricks, soap, bread, and beer, which were produced in many countries; and cement, flour, and various metal products, which were produced in a few. The large local demand had also permitted the establishment of cigarette manufacture in eight territories by 1956, while there were a number of small textile and clothing factories. In some countries the industries providing most employment were those concerned with repairs and servicing rather than manufacturing, notably railway and motor-vehicle workshops.

A substantial industrial complex had developed only in Rhodesia, but a number of lesser foci had appeared by this time. These included two in Zaire—one based on metallurgy in Shaba and one based on consumer goods in Kinshasa; one in and around Nairobi in Kenya; and one in Dakar in Senegal. To some extent these coincided with areas of relative prosperity, but they coincided much more closely with the distribution of Europeans, who then provided the chief market for many goods as well as the chief source of capital and enterprise.

THE CHARACTER OF RECENT INDUSTRIAL DEVELOPMENT

The industrial development which has taken place since independence has been very diverse in nature, but certain patterns tend to be repeated from one part of tropical Africa to another. Each of the broad types of manufacturing existing in the mid-1950's has expanded, but the growth of consumer goods industries to replace imports has been especially rapid. Within each broad type there are many industries which have been established for the first time during this period, in some cases roughly simultaneously in several places within tropical Africa.

Export Processing Industries

The processing of primary products before export has been further developed to increase the value of these exports in terms of both local employment opportunities and foreign exchange earnings, even if not as extensively as might be desired. For instance, several mills have been built to transform palm kernels into oil before export, first in Zaire in the 1950's and then in Benin, Nigeria, and Sierra Leone around 1965-6. Similarly, the proportion of West African groundnuts crushed locally to produce oil for export rose sharply in the late 1950's as new oil mills were built in both Senegal and northern Nigeria (Table 5.1). It rose even further in the early 1970's when drought hit the groundnut crop, for nut exports fell much more steeply than oil exports. By 1975 oil exports were higher than ever in Senegal, but they had disappeared in Nigeria as a result of greatly increased local consumption.

101

TABLE 5.1. THE EVOLUTION OF AN EXPORT PROCESSING INDUSTRY (000 tons)

	Production of groundnut oil			Exports of groundnut oil			Exports of groundnuts		
	Average 1956–7	Average 1966–7	1975	Average 1956–7	Average 1966–7	1975	Average 1956–7	Average 1966–7	1975
Senegal	100	185	215	97	146	209	237	230	17
Nigeria	40	104	40	38	85	0	381	562	2
Niger	2	9	27	2	9	21	71	160	0
Gambia	0	21	15	0	21	14	45	36	51

Sources: United Nations, *Yearbook of Industrial Statistics;* FAO, *Trade Yearbook.*

Groundnut crushing before export developed in Niger and Gambia also in the 1960's, and the lack of other industries enhances its importance to those countries: but in Sudan, where groundnuts have more recently become a major export crop, oil mills still serve only the local market.

Most cocoa and coffee is still exported in the same form as ever, but there are now small instant-coffee factories in Ivory Coast and Tanzania, while the four major cocoa producers all process a small part of the crop. Unfortunately, neither of these commodities is well suited to processing before export, since each is more perishable in manufactured forms. There may be greater scope for processing cotton before export if customers can be found for yarn or even finished textiles rather than lint. As yet, little has been achieved in this field, but the Lomé Convention has encouraged efforts, especially in francophone West Africa, to produce cotton textiles for sale within the EEC. Forms of processing of agricultural exports which are of minor significance for Africa as a whole, but have become important locally, include the preparation of pyrethrum extract in Kenya and Tanzania, decorticated cashew nuts in Tanzania and Mozambique, and sisal products in all three countries.

Some primary products which are too perishable to be exported in their natural state can be sold abroad if canned, and new canning industries have become important to several African countries. Pineapples are now exported in this form from Kenya and Ivory Coast and both countries aim to expand fruit canning rapidly. Similarly, fish canneries have been established in several West African countries, while new meat packing industries in Kenya and elsewhere have also been set up partly to supply overseas markets.

Mineral processing was already very important by the mid-1950's, but it, too, has continued to expand since then. Copper is normally smelted in the mining area into a product which is 99% pure, and smelting has expanded along with mining; but, in addition, an increasing proportion of the smelted metal has been further refined. In Zambia, production of electrolytic refined copper exceeded that of crude blister copper for the first time in 1955, and by 1973 refined copper accounted for 639,000 of the total of 707,000 tons of metal produced. To make this development possible the older refinery at Kitwe was supplemented by another at Ndola in 1959. In Zaire also the production of refined copper has increased year by year, from 126,000 tons in 1956 to 224,000 tons in 1973, although it still accounts for only half of total copper production.

A development similar in nature, although much smaller in scale, has taken place in Nigeria, where the value of the almost static tin production has been increased by the establishment in 1961 of a local smelting industry. All the tin mined is now exported as metal rather than as ore concentrates. A third example of processing before export is provided by the iron ore washing and pelletizing plant at Buchanan in Liberia, opened in

1968, which represents an investment of $52 million. It makes a valuable contribution to the Liberian economy, even though it forms part of the alien enclave and does not have much direct impact on the people of the country.

There would seem to be great opportunities in tropical Africa for the aluminium smelting industry, using the ample hydroelectric power resources of the region to process its large deposits of bauxite: but it has not yet been possible to tie together large-scale bauxite mining and a major power project within a single country. It is sometimes suggested that this is deliberate policy on the part of the great aluminium companies, and certainly the present pattern of the industry cannot be adequately explained in terms of ore and power resources alone. The ore mined in Guinea is transformed in alumina before export, but aluminium metal production there awaits the implementation of the Konkouré power scheme. Yet large aluminium smelters have been established in both Cameroon and Ghana, in each case dependent on imported alumina. This includes some from Guinea in the case of the plant in Cameroon. This, the first aluminium smelter in any tropical country, was opened in 1957 alongside the Edéa power station. That in Ghana, built at Tema between 1964 and 1966 at a cost of $128 million, is the chief consumer of electricity from the Volta scheme. Production at Edéa is 50,000 tons a year, while at Tema it has reached 150,000 tons since extensions were completed in 1972 and is due to be increased to 22,000 tons in 1976. These smelters have been built with a view to the eventual use of local bauxite, for both Cameroon and Ghana have large deposits; but in each case mining will require heavy investment, including new railway construction, and the necessary finance has not yet been forthcoming.

Potentially there is scope for much more mineral processing, such as the refining of the oil exported from Nigeria rather than merely the tiny proportion used locally. However, this is not necessarily in the interests of the mining companies, especially when they have processing capacity in the importing countries, and it may well not take place whatever inducements are offered by the African countries in their efforts to industrialize. The transforming of iron ore into steel before export would be especially attractive to these countries, but for the foreseeable future the competition of the established steel industries elsewhere probably rules out this activity other than to supply markets within Africa.

Local Materials Processed for Local Markets

The greater part of the industrial development that has taken place in tropical Africa in recent years has been dependent primarily upon local markets, and has taken the form of import substitution. In some cases this has made manufactured goods available in larger quantities and at lower prices. In others this has not been achieved, and the new industries have had to be protected by high tariffs and import quotas; but even so new employment and sources of income have been provided and foreign exchange has been saved. Wherever possible these industries have made use of local raw materials, and sometimes they have stimulated new forms of primary production.

There has been a widespread if not dramatic expansion of such characteristically small-scale activities as maize milling and woodworking, as the local demand for maize flour and for furniture has increased. On a larger scale, new cigarette factories have been built during the past two decades in almost half the countries of the region, either supplementing earlier plants as in Rhodesia in 1961, or for the first time as in Sierra Leone in 1960 (Table 5.2). The manufacture of vegetable oils and of soap for local use has increased both by the

TABLE 5.2. THE GROWTH OF TWO INDUSTRIES USING MAINLY LOCAL RAW MATERIALS

	Cigarette production (00 million)			Cement production (000 tons)	
	Average 1956–7	Average 1973–4		Average 1956–7	Average 1973–4
Zaire	36	50	Rhodesia	486	714
Nigeria	24	83	Zaire	462	557
Kenya	18	33	Kenya	197	824
Uganda	16	19	Mozambique	159	538
Senegal	11	20	Senegal	152	294
Mozambique	9	27	Zambia	144	412
Angola	8	24	Angola	108	768
Ethiopia	3	17	Uganda	74	148
Tanzania	0	36	Sudan	64	254
Ivory Coast	0	27	Ethiopia	25	206
Cameroon	0	14	Nigeria	0	1214
Congo	0	12	Ivory Coast	0	648
Sierra Leone	0	10	Ghana	0	436
Malawi	0	5	Tanzania	0	380
Chad	0	3	Cameroon	0	197
Gabon	0	3	Togo	0	123
Rhodesia	?	40	Liberia	0	88
Ghana	?	17	Malawi	0	86
Zambia	?	12	Gabon	0	72
Sudan	?	6	Congo	0	52
			Mali	0	47
			Niger	0	33

Source: United Nations, *Statistical Yearbook* and *Yearbook of Industrial Statistics.*

establishment of numerous small oil mills, as in Tanzania, and by the opening of large enterprises such as that which went into operation in Zambia in 1965.

Among the major industries which are now expanding rapidly the most widespread is the manufacture of textiles (Map 5.1). Various types of cloth are now much in demand in most African countries, and many of these produce some cotton from which to manufacture them: yet few had a textile industry operating on a factory scale until very recently. Since the mid-1950's the small industries then existing in such countries as Sudan, Ethiopia, Ivory Coast, Angola, and Rhodesia have greatly expanded, and mills have been established for the first time in many others, including Uganda, Kenya, Tanzania, Mali, Nigeria, and Ghana. In several of these countries this industry now employs more people than any other: by 1972 employment in textile manufacture had reached 13,000 in both Tanzania and Uganda, and 37,000 in Nigeria. Since 1965 even such small and poor states as Niger and Malawi have opened their first textile factories, spinning and weaving locally grown cotton; and, indeed, there are now very few countries which do not have some form of textile industry even if it only involves the printing of plain imported cloth.

There has also been rapid development in many branches of the clothing industry, sometimes using local textiles, but sometimes depending on imported materials. This is one of the many industries which is now particularly far advanced in Rhodesia, but some type of new clothing factory has opened in recent years in almost every territory. Small shoe-makers can be found throughout tropical Africa, but shoes are now produced on a factory scale in many countries. The Bata company, for example, has during the past two decades opened large factories in Sudan, Zambia, Nigeria, Ivory Coast, and Cameroon, and smaller plants in several other states.

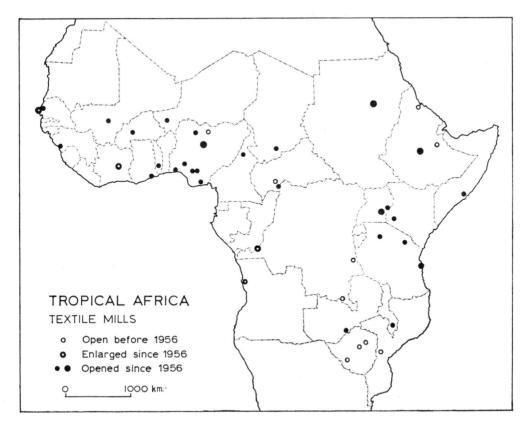

MAP 5.1. Cotton textile mills in tropical Africa. No data are available to permit a distinction according to size, but centres with two or more mills are indicated by a larger circle.

An industry which is of particular importance to developing countries is cement manufacture. This is such a bulky product that local production brings a great saving in transport costs; and the availability of cement at lower prices assists many other forms of development. In some countries, such as Zaire, Rhodesia, and Senegal, which have had cement plants for many years, little expansion of production has taken place (Table 5.2), for the demand has continued at a steady rather than accelerating rate. Elsewhere the demand has increased sharply, and Kenya, Zambia, and Sudan have each added a second plant to one built in the early post-war period, while (at a surprisingly late stage) plants have been built for the first time in Malawi, Tanzania, and several parts of Nigeria (Map 5.2). Since 1965 the industry has extended even to countries which can provide only a very small market, such as Niger, Mali, and Congo. The importance of this industry is such that countries such as Ghana and Ivory Coast, with a substantial market but no suitable or accessible limestone, have built plants using imported clinker.

An industry which has developed much more recently than cement manufacture, but which is also particularly important because of its potential role in other forms of economic development, is fertilizer production. Local phosphates have been used for this purpose in Uganda since 1963, in Rhodesia since 1965, and in Senegal since 1968; and on the basis of imported raw materials a substantial fertilizer complex was established in Mozambique in

105

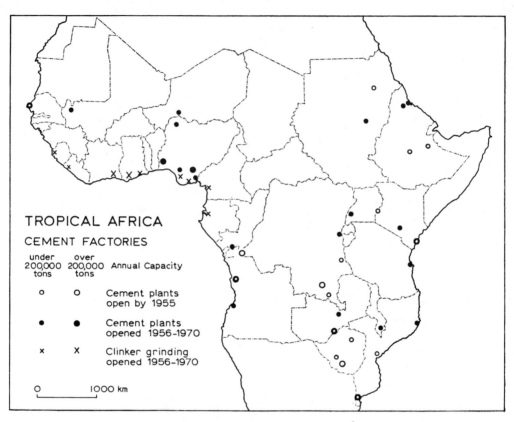

MAP 5.2. Cement factories in tropical Africa. Plants at which capacity has been increased to over 200,000 tons are indicated by a small white circle within a large black circle.

1968. The manufacture of nitrogenous fertilizer is very attractive to most African countries, since this is the type most generally needed and since the main requirement is large quantities of electricity. Plants have therefore recently been built in Ivory Coast, Tanzania, and Zambia, and on a larger scale in Rhodesia; while others were under construction in 1976 in Cameroon, Congo, Kenya, and Zaire, and on a very large scale at Port Harcourt in Nigeria. However, this is an industry in which economies of scale are strongly felt, and in which the need for co-operation between African states to permit large-scale production and international marketing is especially great.

The industry which has generally played the largest part in the rise of powerful industrial nations is steel manufacture. Many African countries possess the basic raw material for this—iron ore—but few have been able to consider establishing the industry because of the very large scale on which it would have to operate if it were to produce steel at prices comparable to that of imports. As yet the only plant making steel from iron ore is that in Rhodesia, which dates from the 1940's but which has expanded its production substantially. Even there the domestic market is not large enough to support a really efficient industry. However, it is practicable to establish small rolling mills using scrap as raw material, and these also have the advantage of being well suited to the use of electric power rather than a carbon fuel. Such mills have therefore been built in several countries, including Nigeria,

Ghana, Uganda, Zaire, and Ethiopia. As the market for steel expands, and provided that international agreements are reached, the prospects for large integrated iron and steel works based on local ore should improve; and plans for these in Liberia, Nigeria, and Tanzania may come to fruition during the 1980's.

Imported Materials Processed for Local Markets

A range of industries poorly represented up to the mid-1950's were those producing goods for the local market largely from imported raw materials. The main exceptions were the milling of wheat flour and the brewing of malt beer. The latter industry has expanded greatly in some countries, especially Nigeria, although not in Senegal and Sudan where the influence of Islam seems stronger, and new breweries have been opened in all but the smallest countries of the region (Table 5.3). The demand for wheat flour has increased more slowly, and although new flour mills have been built in several countries, such as Ivory Coast, Ghana, Nigeria, Cameroon, and Tanzania, there are other territories in which the increase in production has been small. These include Kenya and Senegal where the Europeans who provided the largest market have declined in numbers and where sales to neighbouring countries have fallen as these have established their own mills.

It would be impracticable to list all the industries of this type which have become important in tropical Africa for the first time in recent years, but it might be noted that they range from paint manufacture, which is now found in many countries, through glass manufacture and radio assembly, which had been established in several by 1970, to motor-

TABLE 5.3. THE GROWTH OF TWO INDUSTRIES USING MAINLY IMPORTED RAW MATERIALS

	Whear flour production (000 tons)			Beer production (000 hl)	
	Average 1956–7	Average 1973–4		Average 1956–7	Average 1973–4
Kenya	77	131	Zaire	1306	5198
Senegal	69	81	Kenya	384	1485
Ethiopia	22	59	Senegal	126	116
Mozambique	19	87	Cameroon	125	900
Nigeria	0	280	Nigeria	105	4014
Sudan	0	240	Uganda	88	446
Ivory Coast	0	87	Angola	56	1196
Tanzania	0	48	Tanzania	53	696
Congo	0	27	Mozambique	52	790
Cameroon	0	25	Ghana	44	392
Sierra Leone	0	25	Ethiopia	42	357
Uganda	0	22	Sudan	42	71
			CAE	12	158
Angola	?	82	Malawi	0	294
Zambia	?	70			
Ghana	?	40	Zambia	?	2670
Rhodesia	?	?	Ivory Coast	?	602
			Rhodesia	?	?
			Production has now also begun in Benin, Burundi, Chad, Congo, Gabon, Rwanda, Sierra Leone, Togo, and Upper Volta.		

Sources: United Nations, *Statistical Yearbook* and *Yearbook of Industrial Statistics.*

TABLE 5.4. OIL REFINERIES IN TROPICAL AFRICA

Country	Site	Opened	1975 capacity (m. tons)
Angola	Luanda	1958	1.7
Ethiopia	Assab	1966	1.0
Gabon	Port Gentil	1967	1.2
Ghana	Tema	1963	1.5
Ivory Coast	Abidjan	1966	1.8
Kenya	Mombasa	1963	3.0
Liberia	Monrovia	1968	0.5
Mozambique	Maputo	1961	2.5
Nigeria	Port Harcourt	1965	2.8
Rhodesia	Umtali	1965	1.0
Senegal	Dakar	1964	1.5
Sierra Leone	Freetown	1968	0.7
Sudan	Port Sudan	1965	1.0
Tanzania	Dar es Salaam	1966	0.8
Zaire	Moanda	1967	0.8
Zambia	Ndola	1973	1.1

Sources: Diverse.

car assembly, which in 1976 was as yet confined to Rhodesia, Zambia, Nigeria, and Ivory Coast.

One of the most striking developments of the 1960's was a proliferation of new oil refineries. There were none in tropical Africa until one was built in Angola in 1958, yet by 1967 there were fifteen in operation (Table 5.4). Those in Angola, Zaire, Gabon, and Nigeria now use local oil, but all the rest depend on imported supplies, and with the exception of those in Rhodesia and Zambia all are located at ports. It would probably have been advantageous if fewer larger refineries had been built, for some are too small to be truly efficient, while others are unable to operate at full capacity. The present dispersed pattern of the industry must be seen in terms of both the wish of each country to have its own plant and also the vigourous competition between the international oil companies which have undertaken this development. The period from 1968 to 1972 was one of consolidation, with some increase of capacity at several existing plants, but a new refinery was opened in Zambia in 1973 and a second burst of construction began in 1975. The absurd situation in which Nigeria has suffered severe shortages of refined products is being rectified by the building of two additional refineries, while by 1976 new refineries were under construction in Cameroon, Congo, Mauritania, and Togo, and planned in Guinea and Somalia.

THE DISTRIBUTION OF INDUSTRIAL DEVELOPMENT

West Africa

Some industrialization has taken place in every West African country over the past two decades, but they differ greatly one from another in the extent of this development (Map 5.3). Most has occurred in the coastal states which provide the largest markets, especially Nigeria on account of its size, and Ghana and Ivory Coast on account of their relative prosperity. In the poorer inland states such as Upper Volta and Niger, manufacturing still plays a very small part in the economy, but at least a start has been made even there.

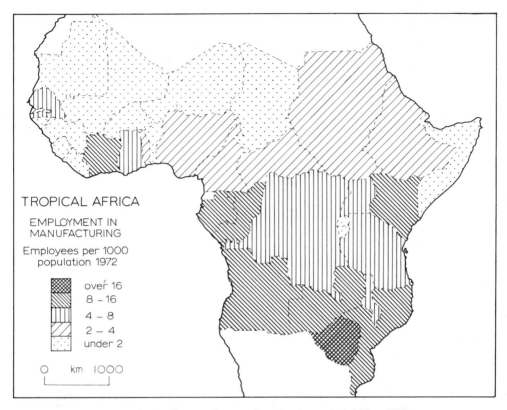

MAP 5.3. Employment in manufacturing in tropical Africa, 1972.

Nigeria is well placed for industrial development in comparison with most other African countries, for it has a wide range of local raw materials; it has coal, oil, and hydroelectric power; it has a domestic market of over 70 million people, and since 1974 high oil revenues have both stimulated local demand for many manufacturers and provided government with capital for investment. The greatest concentration of factories is in and around Lagos, where they range from palm-kernel and cocoa-processing plants to breweries, flour mills, textile, clothing and shoe factories, and many types of engineering works. However, partly as a result of the pressure of the former regional and now state governments and partly as a result of the wide spread of the national market, new factories have also been opened in many other parts of the country (Map 5.4). Thus the groundnut oil-milling industry is focused on Kano; new textile mills have been built at Kaduna and Gusau in the north, and Aba and Onitsha in the east, and cement plants have been established near Abeokuta in the west, Enugu and Calabar in the east, and Sokoto in the north. Port Harcourt was chosen as the location for the country's first oil refinery, and the planned locations for the second and third are Warri and Kaduna rather than Lagos.

Although there has been a substantial expansion of manufacturing since independence there is scope for considerable further development. With far-reaching economic planning, and provided that political stability is maintained, more could be achieved even on the basis of the national market alone, while the relatively large plants which this could support should be competitive in other West African markets. There are, for instance, good prospects

109

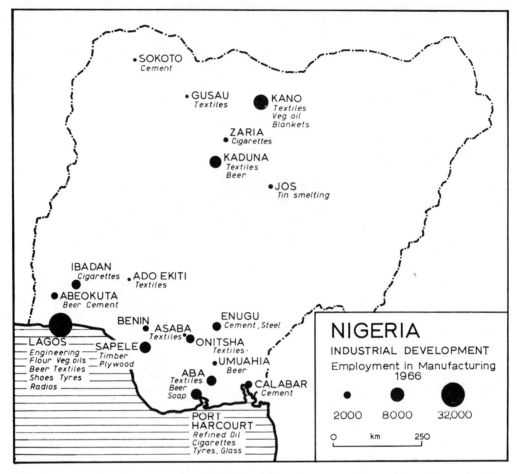

MAP 5.4. Industrial development in Nigeria: centres with more than 1,000 employees in manufacturing, 1966.

for an iron and steel industry using local ore and coal, and after much heated debate a location at Ajaokuta in Kwara State has been proposed for this; and also for chemical industries based on oil and on natural gas, much of which now goes to waste.

The role of manufacturing in the economy of Ghana in 1956 was greater than in that of Nigeria, although it is notable that several industries normally established at an early stage in developing countries, such as cement and textiles, were not represented. These have now been developed, along with many other consumer goods industries, notably in the fields of clothing and metal products. Among the many new oil refineries in Africa one of the first was that opened at Tema in 1963. The largest industrial enterprise is the aluminium smelter which forms an integral part of the Volta scheme, and which has greatly increased the contribution of manufacturing to the economy. The distribution of industry within Ghana has changed little, for most is still found in Accra or in the new town of Tema which lies only 30 km away. A few factories have been built in Takoradi and Kumasi, but none of national importance have yet been established in the north.

Even before World War II there was a substantial development of manufacturing in Dakar, which was the commercial as well as administrative capital of the whole of French West Africa. Now that it has lost this role its attractions as a location for industry have decreased, and therefore it has experienced relatively little growth over the past decade. A few new enterprises have been established, including a large oil refinery and a fertilizer plant using local phosphates; but the production of commodities such as beer, textiles, and cement remained almost static between 1960 and 1970, and the index of total manufacturing production in Senegal has risen more slowly than in most African countries.

In contrast to the situation in Senegal, there has been an extremely rapid development of manufacturing in Ivory Coast, which has taken on the role of pacemaker among the French-speaking states in so many ways. The rate of growth has been particularly striking since it began from virtually nothing in the early 1950's. Even between 1960 and 1964 employment more than doubled in the food, textile, chemical, and metal-processing industries; and the growth has continued since with the establishment of such concerns as an oil refinery, new textile mills, and a vehicle assembly plant. It seems likely that this growth represents in part the making up of lost ground, and in part a response to the expansion of the cash crop economy which is unlikely to continue at the same pace as in the recent past. It is also related to the political stability of the country and the favourable conditions for foreign private investment. It is possible that the impetus will carry industrial development even further in the future, but a critical factor will probably be the degree of access which Ivory Coast enjoys to markets beyond its borders. This industrial growth has been very heavily concentrated in Abidjan, which accounted for just half of all employment in manufacturing in 1975, and a much higher proportion if industries such as sawmilling are excluded.

Sierra Leone and Guinea still contribute only a very small part of the total production of manufacturers in West Africa, but in each the extent of development in 1956 was so slight that the subsequent rate of growth has been relatively rapid. Developments in Sierra Leone during the 1960's included industries such as beer and cigarette production, which were established in many African countries at an earlier date, and also oil refining, but between 1968 and 1975 no major new industries were established.

In Guinea, small plants have been established both to increase the value of exports and to supply local markets, examples being fruit-canning factories and textile mills; and the large FRIA enterprise transforms its bauxite into alumina before it is exported. But although the political reorientation of the country brought some Soviet aid for industrial development, this has been outweighed by the unwillingness of Western countries to invest in Guinea, and progress has been much slower than was hoped. Plans for a complete aluminium industry, for example, which depend on the development of hydroelectric power, have had to be shelved at least temporarily.

In the other countries formerly administered by France, there was very little manufacturing industry indeed at the time of independence, but in all some progress has been made during the 1960's. The countries of the interior have the largest internal markets, and industries producing bulky goods are there to some extent protected by high transport costs on imports. In Mali, cigarette, textile, and cement plants have been built with assistance from China and the Soviet Union. A shoe factory opened in Upper Volta in 1963, followed by a cigarette plant in 1967 and a textile mill in 1969; and in Niger a small cement plant opened in 1966 has been followed by a brewery and a textile factory. In some respects the prospects are poorer in the small coastal states of Benin and Togo, but the former has increased the processing of its palm-product exports and established a mill designed to produce cotton textiles for export, while in the latter both a brewery and a textile mill were opened in 1966. The only country where virtually no manufacturing has yet begun is Mauritania.

Equatorial Africa

In respect of industrial development, as in most other ways, the situation in Zaire was greatly affected by the political turmoil following independence. A substantial amount had taken place there before World War II, and by 1956 manufacturing contributed over 10% of the GDP. A number of new factories were built in the following three years, ranging from additional copper refineries to shoe factories, but even during that period the index of industrial production remained stationary. After 1959 it fell sharply, and although the impact of the political conflict varied greatly from one industry to another, there were few in which any significant expansion occurred until the opening of an oil refinery on the coast in 1967. By the early 1970's, however, political stability and the relatively large domestic market were encouraging a high level of industrial investment. Among the enterprises established during this period have been the $120 million Maluku steel mill, a $50 million cement plant near Matadi, the country's first large flour mill also at Matadi, three new breweries, and a new textile mill, a tyre factory and a commercial vehicle assembly plant. It is notable that the great majority of the larger new industries have been located in the Bas-Zaire region, within 200 km of Kinshasa, although the new textile mill is at Kisangani, near the main cotton-growing area, and one of the breweries is at Mbandaka.

In the states to the north of the Zaire River, some industrial development has taken place although not at a very rapid rate. In the Congo Republic the situation is similar to that in Senegal in so far as this period has brought some deterioration in the prospects for industries serving more than the small domestic market, despite the establishment of the Equatorial Customs Union. However, industrial activity there was in 1956 far more limited than in Senegal, and there have been opportunities for new forms of development to serve the local market in fields such as beer brewing and textile manufacture. The development which has taken place has been largely concentrated in the city of Brazzaville, though a few plants have been built at the port of Pointe Noire.

Among the states of former French Equatorial Africa there is no equivalent to Ivory Coast in West Africa as far as manufacturing is concerned. The Central African Empire and Chad both have plans for much industrial development, but as yet it is very limited. However, one should differentiate between the CAE, in which the production of soap, beer, and shoes has begun at Bangui and a large textile mill was opened at Bouali as early as 1953, and Chad, where industry is still largely confined to agricultural processing. Gabon has recently emerged as the most prosperous of the former French equatorial countries, but this has not yet provided the basis for much industrial development, for the market which its small population provides is not a sufficient attraction. However, to the large plywood factory built in 1948 there has now been added an oil refinery at Port Gentil, also using a local primary product but in this case to supply the Equatorial Customs Union.

The Equatorial Customs Union also includes Cameroon, and there industrial activity is rather greater than in any of the other member states. Most of this activity has begun since the mid-1950's, when manufacturing was largely confined to agricultural processing and beer and cigarette production. The most important development was the opening of the large aluminium plant which consumes most of the power produced at Edéa. This is exceptional among industries established in tropical Africa in the 1950's in being power-orientated, as has been noted above. Certainly all the other enterprises recently established in Cameroon are based upon the needs of the local market. They include flour milling, textile, shoe, cement, match, paint, and insecticide manufacture. Most are located at Douala, which is the commercial capital as well as the main port, but a few are at the administrative capital, Yaoundé.

Eastern Africa

In the north-eastern part of tropical Africa many forms of craft industry are very well established in both Ethiopia and Sudan: but in both countries these have been supplemented by an increasing amount of factory industry in recent years. In Sudan employment in large-scale manufacturing rose from 9500 in 1956 to 19,700 in 1962 and 43,000 in 1971. The flour and oil mills, which were the most important industries in 1956, have expanded, but the main growth has been in textiles and shoes, metal fabricating, cement, and oil refining. The textile mill established at Khartoum in 1962 is the largest in tropical Africa. The greater part of the industrial growth has taken place in the capital, which accounted for 65% of all industrial employment in 1971, but there are important exceptions such as the cigarette factory at Wad Medani, the oil refinery at Port Sudan, and the cement plants at Atbara and Kosti.

In Ethiopia the rate of industrial development has been comparable, employment in manufacturing having risen from 16,000 in 1955 to 53,000 in 1972, and the value added having risen at a similar rate. There also the food industries have grown slowly while various others have expanded rapidly from almost nothing. The most striking growth has been in textiles (Table 5.5), and among the important new industries is the oil refinery opened in 1966. Since other major developments have been in brewing, cement production, and metal fabricating, the parallel with Sudan is close in the structure as well as the rate of industrial growth. Here also most factories are in the capital, Addis Ababa, but there are some in Asmara, as well as a few older plants at Dire Dawa and the oil refinery at Assab.

In Kenya, Tanzania, and Uganda, there is no tradition of craft industry comparable to that in Sudan and Ethiopia, but during the post-war period, and especially since 1956, large-scale industry has developed equally rapidly in these three countries. The extent of manufacturing is particularly impressive in Kenya and especially in the city of Nairobi and its immediate neighbourhood (Map 5.5). A substantial nucleus of industry existed in Kenya even in 1956, but the contribution of manufacturing to the GDP rose from $50 million in that year to $220 million in 1972. Like so many other countries, Kenya has its new oil refinery, opened near Mombasa in 1963; and more recently large textile mills have been built at Thika, Kisumu, Nanyuki, and Eldoret. Most of the other new industries are rather smaller in scale, and it is these which are heavily concentrated in and around the capital city.

In the early post-war period Kenya offered all the advantages to a potential industrial investor in East Africa. Capital and labour were more readily available, and transport facilities were better than in Tanzania or Uganda; but the greatest attractions of a site in Kenya, and especially one near Nairobi, were proximity to the largest markets for manufactured goods and the best accessibility to the whole East African market. This can reasonably be considered as a single market because of the customs union that has long existed between the three countries, and this has undoubtedly been one factor favouring industrial development in East Africa.

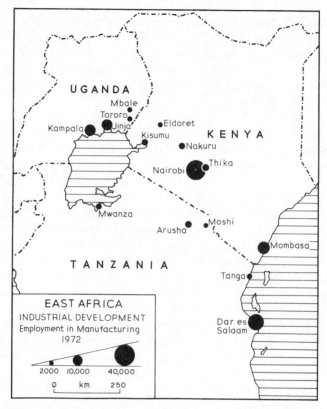

MAP 5.5. Industrial development in East Africa: centres with more than 2000 employees in manufacturing, 1972.

In recent years first Uganda and then Tanzania have made considerable efforts to catch up with Kenya, and while they do not yet match it, the rate of industrial growth has in fact been faster in both countries in certain periods. In the late 1950's some industries were attracted to Uganda through the efforts of the Uganda Development Corporation, which had been set up in 1952, and by offers of power from Owen Falls at low rates for large consumers. These included a textile mill opened in 1956 and a steel-rolling mill opened in 1962, both located at Jínja. Later in the 1960's further textile mills were built and many small industries sprang up in Kampala, but more recently industrial growth has been checked, especially by the expulsion of the Asians who had been active entrepreneurs.

In Tanzania industry made little progress until the 1960's, but there a big impetus was given by independence and by a policy of encouraging self-sufficiency instead of heavy reliance on imports from Kenya. After remaining static for some years the contribution of manufacturing to the GDP rose from $17 million in 1960 to $140 million in 1972. In 1966 both a cement plant and an oil refinery were opened near Dar es Salaam, while between 1966 and 1969 four large textile mills were built. Tanzania is one of many African countries in which most new industries have been located in or near the capital city, but the Government is aiming at greater dispersal, and among the new textile mills two are in provincial centres (Map 5.1).

114

South-central Africa

Probably the most impressive expansion of manufacturing has taken place in south-central Africa. Rhodesia already had in 1956 a substantial range of industries, which included a small iron and steel works, and which together contributed 13% of the GDP. Upon this basis much further growth took place, as Southern Rhodesia assumed the role of supplier of manufactured goods to the whole Federation of Rhodesia and Nyasaland. With the break-up of the federation there was a pause in the growth, and in several industries production fell in the 1960's. However, the unused capacity which this left proved a great asset to Rhodesia after UDI, when international trade sanctions provided some measure of added protection for locally produced goods. In many fields production has risen again to replace imports; in other cases factories have been converted to produce new commodities. By 1975 contribution of manufacturing to the GDP had risen to 24%, and this sector provided employment for 160,000 people.

As in most other countries, the capital city has the greatest share of this manufacturing, but it is rivalled by Bulawayo, while there are important industries in several smaller towns. In 1972, Salisbury accounted for 44% of all manufacturing employment, Bulawayo for 32%, and Gatooma, Gwelo, Que Que/Redcliff, and Umtali for 4% to 5% each. This distribution pattern has changed remarkably little, for the respective shares were very similar ten years previously.

In the period during which Rhodesia was experiencing an industrial boom, its federal partners were starved of new industries; but since the dissolution of the federation much has been done to make up this lost ground. In Malawi the domestic market is too small to support a wide range of manufacturing concerns, but the period since 1960 has witnessed the establishment of factories producing soft drinks and beer, textiles and clothing, and cement. This development has been assisted by the establishment of the Malawi Development Corporation in 1964 and by the opening of the Nkula Falls hydroelectric power station. Almost all has taken place in and around the chief city, Blantyre, for any other location would be less satisfactory in terms of markets, but some industries may be attracted to the new capital city at Lilongwe, while a pulp and paper factory is planned for the north, near its raw material.

Important as recent industrial development has been for Malawi, it is far outstripped by the growth which has taken place in Zambia. There the stimulus given first by the break-up of the federation, and then by the Rhodesian crisis, has been even greater than in Malawi, for Zambia was much more heavily dependent upon imports from Rhodesia. The high level of income generated on the Copperbelt, the availability of power from Kariba, and an internal political climate favourable to foreign investment have all contributed to this growth. Among the items now produced are beer, textiles, shoes, matches, tyres, and fertilizers, while additions in 1973 included an oil refinery and a car assembly plant. There has also been a substantial increase in the local refining of copper before export and in the manufacture of supplies for the mines. This industrial growth has largely been divided between Lusaka-Kafue and the Copperbelt towns, and it would be interesting to know what factors have affected the choice of location for each plant.

Both Angola and Mozambique have a remarkably wide range of industries in relation to their general levels of income, for the large numbers of Portuguese settlers provided a substantial market for manufactured goods. Some of these industries are now long-established, several in Mozambique dating from before World War II; but others are quite new,

115

since these countries have shared in the general expansion of manufacturing in tropical Africa over the past two decades.

In Angola the production of beer, flour, cement, and cotton textiles has increased between three- and tenfold since 1956, and new industries include oil refining, begun in 1958 and expanded in 1967, tyre manufacture, and numerous small-scale consumer industries. In Mozambique the general increase in prosperity has been less than in Angola, and the expansion of beer, flour, cement, and textile production has been more modest. But there, too, an oil refinery has been established, and it has formed the basis for an industrial complex which now includes the manufacture of three types of fertilizers and also sulphuric acid.

In both countries manufacturing has always been heavily concentrated around the capital, and the developments of the past decade have tended to consolidate this situation rather than to counteract it. A change is envisaged, however, as a result of the inauguration of the Cabora Bassa hydroelectric scheme in Mozambique. This offers the greatest promise for future industrial development in either country, perhaps including aluminium smelting; and if this promise is realized it could greatly change the distribution of industry within Mozambique.

CONCLUSIONS

Much progress has been made in industrial development during the past two decades in many parts of tropical Africa. Yet much more remains to be done if the region is to move towards the income levels now enjoyed by Europe and North America, or even that of other areas still generally regarded as underdeveloped, such as most of Latin America. Table 5.5 indicates the small extent of employment in manufacturing even in the larger countries. It also shows the general similarity of industrial structure.

Some of the development that has occurred has taken the form of increased processing of primary products before export, often located near the source of these products. It may be possible to expand such activities further, although a serious barrier is presented by the tariff structures of most of the importing countries which favour crude materials rather than materials in processed form. One of the best prospects is sawmilling, for a suprisingly large volume of timber is still exported as logs even though these are very costly to transport, while a related export-based industry now planned by several African countries, including Gabon, Ivory Coast, and Malawi, is the manufacture of wood pulp. Other possibilities are the export of refined rather than crude oil, of fertilizers rather than phosphates, and of steel rather than iron ore. Even more attractive from the point of view of employment but probably even more difficult to implement on a large scale would be the export of cloth rather than cotton lint.

The greater part of recent industrial development has consisted of the manufacture of either local or imported raw materials into goods for which there is a local demand. This has sometimes taken place at the point of production or import of the raw materials, or at a source of power, but has more often been established in the best place from which to supply the national market. This is often the capital city, which not only constitutes the largest single concentration of purchasing power, but also has the best transport links with other areas of demand. This is also usually the best location in terms of labour supplies, while the new factories are often built by firms already established in the capital cities as importers of the goods in question.

TABLE 5.5. EMPLOYMENT IN MANUFACTURING IN SELECTED AFRICAN
COUNTRIES, 1972 (000 employees)

	All manufac- turing	Food, drink, and tobacco	Wood and furniture	Textiles, clothing and shoes	Building material, chemicals	Metals and engineering
Nigeria	169	36	14	50	27	26
Rhodesia	136	27	11	31	19	39
Zaire	105	25	15	19	14	10
Mozambique	96	47	12	14	9	11
Kenya	94	23	9	14	12	28
Angola	82	27	4	17	17	6
Tanzania	62	25	4	19	7	5
Ghana	61	11	14	16	7	8
Ethiopia	53	13	4	25	6	3
Zambia	44	13	3	8	7	9
Ivory Coast	40	11	10	8	4	4

Sources: United Nations, *Yearbook of Industrial Statistics;* and national sources.
Note: These figures provide a rough guide only, particularly because of differences in definition and in the degree of limitation to large-scale enterprises. They generally include much employment in crop processing, e.g. sugar mills and sawmilling, not covered in this chapter.

The market has usually been confined to a single country, and this pattern seems likely to continue in the future. Yet in some respects it is not ideal, and efforts are being made to bring about a degree of change. There is scope for much more manufacturing even based on national markets, but in most countries these are too small for many industries, and throughout tropical Africa the restricted size of these markets is a discouragement to greater industrial development. In some cases factories are being built which are too small to be really efficient; more often development is being delayed.

If a greater degree of economic integration could be achieved, either for small groups of countries, or possibly for tropical Africa as a whole, the prospects for the establishment of large efficient industries in such fields as iron and steel, heavy engineering, and chemicals would be greatly improved. Some examples of industries based on markets wider than a single country already exist, such as those established in Rhodesia during the period of the Central African Federation, several in Kenya and a few in Uganda selling their products throughout the East African common market, and the oil refinery in Gabon, located there after much discussion between the members of the Equatorial African Customs Union. In each of these cases serious problems have arisen, and much has to be done to ensure that a more stable pattern of international co-operation exists as a basis for future industrial growth.

The aluminium industry provides the only example of industrial development based on imported materials and export markets, and there is little chance of much further development of this type. Tropical Africa has no comparative advantage over other parts of the world except in power supplies, and there are no other industries which are so clearly power-orientated.

The distribution of manufacturing industry in tropical Africa has in general not changed radically either between or within countries. The greater part of the new development has taken place around existing industrial centres, most of which have expanded and diversified their activities at a rapid rate. However, some such centres have grown more than others and a few new industrial foci have appeared.

117

Thus among the main poles of development existing in the mid-1950's, those in Ghana, Kenya, and Rhodesia have witnessed much expansion, that in Senegal much less, and those in Zaire very little. Countries where manufacturing has increased its role in the economy from a very minor one to one of some importance include Nigeria, Sudan, and Ethiopia, and on a smaller scale but at an even more rapid rate, Ivory Coast, Cameroon, Uganda, and Zambia. In such poorer or smaller countries as Sierra Leone and Malawi, development has proceeded less far; and in countries which are both poor and small in population, such as Gambia, Guinea-Bissau, Upper Volta, Niger, Chad, Rwanda, Burundi, and Somalia, it has only just begun.

Within each country there is clearly a strong tendency for new industries to be located in the same area as those already established, most often in or near the capital city. Thus the largest industrial centre in Nigeria continues to be Lagos, while almost every new enterprise in Ivory Coast has been located in Abidjan. In some cases a site has been chosen at some distance from the capital but still near enough to share the advantages which it offers. The clearest example is Tema, the growth of which is producing a large dual focus for industrial development in Ghana. Another is Thika, 35 km from Nairobi, while a similar pattern is emerging in Zambia, where an industrial centre is being developed at Kafue, 40 km from Lusaka. Attempts have been made in some countries to counter the trend to a concentration of industrial development in a single small zone, but except perhaps in Nigeria they have had very little effect on the general pattern.

The distribution of new industrial development at both the national and the international level indicates a high degree of market orientation. There are cases where raw materials or power supplies have formed the chief attraction, but these are rare. The only rapidly expanding industrial complex whose location appears to be closely related to the location of such resources is that on the Copperbelt; and even there most of the development is not directly dependent on copper mining but is more immediately related to the market which has arisen there. Most industrial development has taken place in those countries which because of their size or their prosperity provide relatively large markets for manufactured goods; and within these most has taken place in the region which provides the largest market or the best access to the whole national market.

There is no reason to suppose that the distribution of manufacturing will change any more in the next decade than in the last. In general the best prospects for growth are still to be found in the areas where most development has already taken place, and progress is likely to remain slow in countries such as those of interior West Africa. Possibly the best prospects for accelerated development, given political stability, are provided by the substantial resources and large domestic markets of Zaire and Nigeria, especially if the Inga as well as Kainji power projects ensure ample low-cost power. On the other hand, it is doubtful whether the rapid rate of growth in Ivory Coast throughout the post independence period and in Zambia in very recent years can be maintained, although undoubtedly many new industries will be established in both countries.

The establishment of closer co-operation between African states may have important implications for the distribution as well as the general rate of industrial development. Unfortunately it is possible that the establishment of new industries based on sub-regional markets may produce an even greater concentration of industrial development within the already prosperous areas, and this may in turn hinder further co-operation. The attraction of location in Lagos or Abidjan and in Kinshasa may be further increased by closer economic integration in western and equatorial Africa; and without a protected position in the national market the prospect of any large industries being located in Upper Volta, Chad, or Rwanda may worsen.

There are some industries which could be located almost anywhere in relation to their markets, and probably almost every country has some advantage to offer as the location of at least one or two industries. The establishment of regional economic planning as well as common markets may assist the realization of these possibilities. Perhaps, for instance, a new area of industrial development will eventually emerge in southern Tanzania based on the deposits of coal and iron there, especially if a market extending throughout East and Central Africa is available. However the freedom of manoeuvre which the economics of industrial location will allow is limited, and in general it must be accepted that some parts of tropical Africa are better placed for industrial development than others largely because of access to markets whether national or international. While greater economic co-operation is likely to lead to a more rapid rate of total industrial development, it is not likely to lead to a more even distribution of this. Indeed, it may be that the recognition of major poles of growth and efforts to co-ordinate and encourage development there will bring greater benefit than efforts to resist the trend towards this pattern.

SELECTED READING

A valuable study of present patterns and future prospects is:
  A. F. EWING, *Industry in Africa* (London, 1968).

Other broad discussions of industrialization in Africa are:
  A. M. KAMARCK, *The Economics of African Development* (New York, 1971), ch. 7;
  A. L. MABOGUNJE, Manufacturing and the geography of development in Africa, *Economic Geography* **49**, 1–20 (1973).

A comprehensive survey of industry in francophone Africa is provided in:
  EDIAFRIC, *L'Industrie Africaine* (Paris, annual).

Industrial development in Nigeria is examined in detail in:
  A. SOKOLSKI, *The Establishment of Manufacturing in Nigeria* (New York, 1965);
  P. KILBY, *Industrialization in an Open Economy: Nigeria 1945–1966* (London, 1969);
  L. SCHATZL, *Industrialization in Nigeria: a Spatial Analysis* (Munich, 1973).

Studies of industrial development in other countries include:
  M. B. K. DARKOH, Manufacturing in Ghana 1957–1967, *Bulletin de l'IFAN* **35**, 813–53 (1973);
  EL SAYED EL BUSHRA, The development of industry in Greater Khartoum, *East African Geographical Review* **10**, 27–50 (1972);
  J. L. LaCROIX, *Industrialisation au Congo* (Hague, 1967) (on Zaire);
  R. B. OGENDO, *Industrial Geography of Kenya* (Nairobi, 1972);
  D. S. PEARSON, *Industrial Development in East Africa* (Nairobi, 1969);
  J. F. RWEYEMAMU, *Underdevelopment and Industrialisation in Tanzania* (Nairobi, 1973).
  A. YOUNG, *Industrial Diversification in Zambia* (New York, 1973).

On the spread of one industry in francophone countries, see:
  M. BATTIAU, Le développement récent de l'industrie textile dans les pays africains, *Cahiers d'Outre Mer* **98**, 121–41 (1972).

The fullest study of small-scale industry yet available is:
  K. SCHADLER, *Crafts, Small-scale Industries and Industrial Education in Tanzania* (Munich, 1968).

On the relationships between industrial development and international economic integration, see:
  K. M. BARBOUR, Industrialisation in West Africa; the need for sub-regional groupings, *Journal of Modern African Studies* **10**, 357–82 (1972);
  R. H. GREEN and A. SEIDMAN, *Unity or Poverty?* (London, 1968);
  F. I. NIXSON, *Economic Integration and Industrial Location: East Africa* (London, 1973).

6

THE SUPPLY OF POWER

AMONG the most impressive symbols of economic change in Africa are the great dams which have been built in recent years primarily to permit the generation of electric power (Plates 13 and 14). The construction of Kariba Dam caught the imagination of the world, while the Volta Dam is now equally renowned. Such engineering works have truly changed the face of Africa, especially since they have created behind them vast new lakes. Some of the dams are the focal points of multi-purpose projects, but in most cases the production of electricity was the main objective.

It is very appropriate that power projects should form such striking symbols of changing Africa, for of all fields of economic activity electricity production is that which is expanding most rapidly. This growth is a worldwide phenomenon, and the share of tropical Africa in the world total has not increased very greatly, remaining well under 1%. Nevertheless, even to have kept pace with the general growth is a substantial achievement, and one which has played an important part in making possible other forms of economic development. At the same time it should be noted that most people remain little affected by these power schemes, and the provision of electricity to limited areas and limited groups is one way in which economic advance is increasing regional and social disparities in Africa.

Before World War II electricity was produced in tropical Africa on only a very small scale, and even in 1948 the total generated amounted to little more than 2000 million kWh. By 1956 the figure had risen to about 6000 million and by 1974 it was 32,000 million. In 1948 the greater part of the production was from thermal stations using coal as fuel, but while thermal production has expanded considerably in some countries, now generally using oil, hydroelectric power has today become more important for tropical Africa as a whole. By 1956 the two types of power stations contributed roughly equal shares, and now hydroelectricity represents more than three-quarters of the total (Table 6.1). In fact, although the amount of thermal power generated has risen substantially over the past twenty years as a whole, in some years there has been a net decrease as old thermal stations have been relegated to stand-by duties only. The huge rise in world oil prices in the 1970s has of course greatly increased the advantages for most countries of using local water power resources rather than importing oil for thermal electricity; and it is likely to encourage increased substitution of electricity for other forms of energy.

The small share of the world production of electric power provided by tropical Africa is in no way related to a lack of physical resources. Fuel for thermal stations is not abundant, although there is sufficient oil in certain countries for a vast expansion of thermal power

TABLE 6.1. ELECTRICITY IN TROPICAL AFRICA

	Installed capacity (MW)		Production (m kWh)		*Per capita* consumption (kWh)
	1956	1974	1956	1974	1974
TROPICAL AFRICA	1,950	8,910	6,000	32,580	140
Thermal	1,180	3,370	3,600	6,870	—
Hydro	770	5,540	2,400	25,710	—
Zaire	549	1,217	1,743	4,000	164
Rhodesia	396	1,192	1,232	5,823	1,106
Zambia	267	1,031	1,282	5,973	1,062
Nigeria	106	860	280	2,828	46
Kenya	81	210	246	800	86
Ghana	80	976	231	3,645	379
Uganda	74	174	95	836	47
Mozambique	56	485	82	747	107
Angola	47	499	77	1,050	169
Senegal	43	120	74	364	92
Tanzania	40	160	129	551	37
Ethiopia	34	315	67	684	25
Cameroon	30	225	40	1,123	180
Sudan	29	120	49	325	23
Guinea	18	125	21	500	120
Congo	16	32	20	99	75
Ivory Coast	14	350	27	855	179
Sierra Leone	14	75	35	219	81
Liberia	8	298	28	860	515
Malawi	8	71	9	230	46
Somalia	8	18	9	42	14
Mali	7	33	8	85	15
Gabon	6	40	9	173	333
Rwanda	6	35	13	132	32
CAE	5	17	5	53	30
Togo	4	25	5	122	56
Gambia	3	9	5	20	39
Benin	2	10	4	52	17
Chad	1	41	3	57	14
Mauritania	1	39	1	95	74
Niger	1	18	3	65	15
Upper Volta	1	17	3	46	8

Sources: United Nations, *Statistical Yearbook* and *World Energy Supplies 1950–1974;* and national sources.

generation; but it is thought that tropical Africa has 30–40% of the world's potential for hydroelectricity production. This high potential reflects several aspects of the configuration of the continent. Much of it is made up of ancient rocks which have experienced several phases of uplift, producing a series of plateaux with sharp breaks of slope between them. Even the largest rivers are broken by falls where they cross these breaks of slope, and it is these which provide the major power sites. In addition, the predominance of ancient hard rocks means that firm foundations for dams are often available, and that many of the rivers carry relatively little silt.

The main problem for water-power generation that is presented by the physical environment is the great seasonal difference in flow of most of the rivers. It is this which has sometimes necessitated the construction of immense dams which not only create a great head of water but also store vast quantities in artificial lakes. However, the factors which contribute

121

most to the low level of power production in tropical Africa are economic rather than physical. The most important are the lack of locally available capital, and especially the small demand for electricity in most parts of the region. It is the provision of capital from overseas, albeit at high interest rates, and especially a belated increase in demand as economic development has taken place, which have made possible the recent growth in production.

THE DISTRIBUTION OF POWER DEVELOPMENTS

The spatial pattern of power developments over recent years shows elements of both concentration and dispersal. Every country has shared in the growth of electricity generation (Map 6.1 and Table 6.1), and supplies have been made available in many areas which had none twenty years ago: yet most of the expansion has taken place in only a few countries, and the Kariba and Volta schemes alone accounted for a large proportion of the new capacity provided in the 1960's (Map 6.2 and Table 6.2).

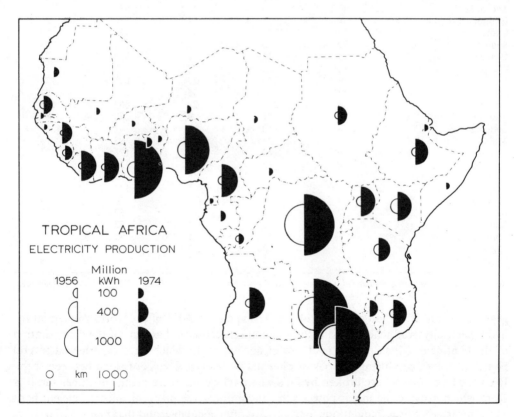

MAP 6.1. Electricity production in tropical Africa: 1956, 1974.

Rhodesia and Zambia

Rhodesia and Zambia together accounted for 40% of all power production in tropical Africa in 1956, and although they have not maintained this share they still occupy a pro-

122

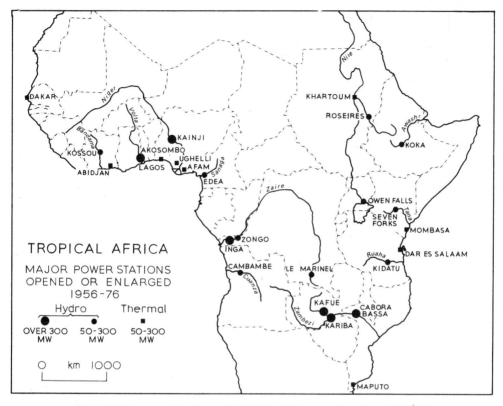

MAP 6.2. Power stations in tropical Africa with a capacity of over 50 MW.

minent position, for production doubled over the subsequent decade. This was due almost entirely to the building of the dam and power station on the Zambezi at Kariba (Map 6.3), the only other developments during the decade being the opening of small thermal stations in a few isolated townships in each country. Indeed, following the opening of Kariba,

TABLE 6.2. MAJOR HYDROELECTRICITY SCHEMES IN TROPICAL AFRICA

	Work begun	First power	First stage complete	Final stage complete	First installed capacity (MW)	Final installed capacity (MW)
Owen Falls	1948	1954	1958	1968	120	150
Le Marinel	—	1956	1956	1956	280	280
Edéa	—	1953	1958	—	160	270
Kariba	1956	1960	1962	—	700	1600
Cambambe	1959	1962	1962	1973	130	260
Volta	1962	1965	1966	1972	600	900
Kainji	1964	1968	1969	—	320	960
Kafue	1968	1971	1972	—	600	900
Inga	1968	1972	1976	—	350	28000
Cabora Bassa	1968	1975	—	—	1200	2200

Sources: Diverse.

Note: Guaranteed capacity is generally lower than installed capacity due to the variability of water levels.

123

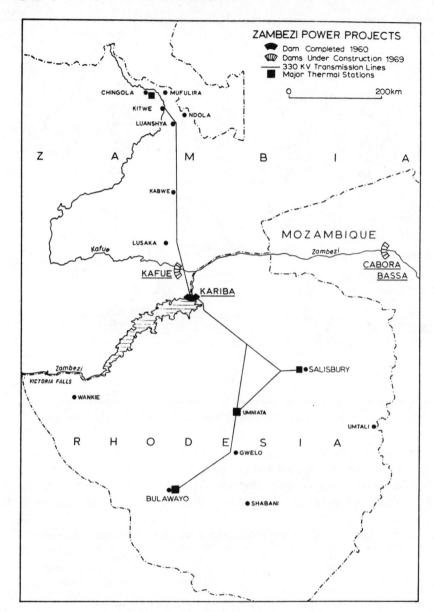

ZAMBEZI POWER PROJECTS

Dam Completed 1960
Dams Under Construction 1969
330 KV Transmission Lines
Major Thermal Stations

0   200km

MAP 6.3. The Zambezi and Kafue river power projects.

several of the existing large thermal plants were closed down. The main stimulus for the expansion of power production, as for the substantial development which had already taken place in 1956, was the demand provided by the relatively prosperous economies of the two countries, and especially by the mines of Zambia and the emerging manufacturing industries of Rhodesia. The necessary physical resources were available in the form of both coal and running water; and financial resources were also greater than in most parts of tropical Africa, even though most of the capital had to be borrowed from overseas. It seems likely that the existence of the Federation of Rhodesia and Nyasaland was also significant both in assisting the obtaining of overseas capital and also in allowing plans to be made on the basis of the large joint market.

Various possibilities for increasing electricity production were considered, including new thermal stations, and hydro stations on the Kafue River and at Victoria Falls, as well as the Kariba scheme. It was decided that in the long term, water power would be more economical than the generation of thermal electricity from coal; and the Kariba site was chosen in preference to the others largely because of the possibility of building a dam there to even out the markedly seasonal flow of the Zambezi and because of its suitable location in relation to the major markets of the Salisbury–Bulawayo axis and the Copperbelt. The Victoria Falls site was less satisfactory in both these respects, and it was also feared that a major power scheme there might reduce the attraction of the falls for tourists. The main factor discouraging the choice of the Kafue site was political, for the Federal and Southern Rhodesian governments preferred a site on the boundary to one wholly within Northern Rhodesia. Kariba also offered a much greater total potential than Kafue, for it was intended that the initial power station on the south bank should be supplemented by another, even larger, on the north bank.

Work on the 130-metre high dam began in 1956, and as the new 280 km lake was gradually forming the first power was transmitted in 1960. The power station had a capacity of 705 MW, and 1500 km of high voltage transmission line carried the electricity to Kitwe, Lusaka, Bulawayo, and Salisbury. The cost of the dam, power station, and transmission lines totalled $240 million, and it will be many years before all the loans which covered this can be paid off.

The effects of the Kariba scheme on the physical landscape are plainly visible, and effects such as the resettlement which was necessary for the 50,000 people who lived on the land that is now flooded are equally obvious. The economic consequences of the availability of greater amounts of electric power are less easily assessed. The region was suffering from power shortages in the years prior to 1960, especially because of inadequate supplies of coal from Wankie and inadequate transport capacity to move it to where it was required; and the establishment of the new source of power permitted developments, especially in the field of manufacturing, which might otherwise have been hindered. On the other hand, the opening of the power station was not followed by any burst of new development.

One reason for this is provided by the break-up of the Federation. The dam was planned while it was in its heyday, but by 1960 the strains were very clear, and political uncertainty had contributed to a substantial fall in the level of investment in new forms of enterprise. Partly because consumption rose more slowly than expected, the cost of power from Kariba could not be reduced in the way that had been planned (from 0.9*d.* per unit in 1961 to 0.4*d.* in 1967, compared with 0.8*d.* for thermal power from Salisbury): and since changes could therefore not be lowered, there was no positive stimulus for new industries.

While power from Kariba is now assisting industrial development in both Rhodesia and Zambia, it is notable that its effect on the location of this development within these countries is negligible. No forms of activity have been drawn to Kariba itself, where the present township is much smaller than that which existed during the period of dam construction: instead, all the power has been taken to the existing foci of economic activity, and the new development has taken place there.

As a consequence of the development at Kariba electricity production within Zambia was lower in 1966 than in 1956, but this situation has subsequently changed greatly. Even after Rhodesia's UDI, Zambia had to continue to obtain most of its power from across the Zambezi, but as a result of development now in progress it will soon be self-sufficient. It was originally intended that as the demands of the Copperbelt rose during the 1970's, the south bank power station at Kariba would be supplemented by another on the north bank; but the strained relations with Rhodesia caused Zambia not only to proceed sooner than expected but also to give first priority to its long-cherished Kafue scheme which did not depend upon Rhodesian co-operation. Work began on a dam across the Kafue in 1968, and this and a 600 MW power station were completed by 1972. In addition to the assured demand from the Copperbelt and Lusaka, and the wish to be independent of supplies from Rhodesia, a further vital factor in this development is the fact that Zambia is sufficiently prosperous to cover much of the $100 million capital cost from its own resources. The Kafue Dam does not entirely overcome the problem of the highly seasonal flow of that river, and therefore construction of a further dam upstream at Itezhitezhi is taking place to permit the capacity to rise to 900 MW.

The plan to build a second power station at Kariba was not abandoned, for Zambia's needs will probably not be satisfied by production at Kafue even when capacity there is raised. Work on it therefore began in 1971, and although delayed by the bankruptcy of the original contractor the first generators were installed in 1976. Since the dam was already built, the capital costs of 600 MW extra generating capacity at Kariba are relatively low. Furthermore, it is to be hoped that the Rhodesia crisis will be resolved before too long, in which case development at Kariba will no longer be a security risk for Zambia, and will be of benefit to both countries.

Ghana

Electricity production in Ghana was until recently much smaller than in Rhodesia or Zambia, but even so it has for many years been higher than in most tropical African countries. There are several small thermal stations, the most important being those in Accra and Tema whose production kept pace until 1965 with the growing demand. Today, however, these are completely overshadowed by the great Volta Dam and power station at Akosombo, which have made Ghana one of the leading African producers of electricity (Map 6.4). As in the case of the dam and first power station at Kariba, they represent an investment of over $200 million if costs such as that of the massive resettlement programme are included.

The development of this great scheme in Ghana is related to the existence of a suitable physical site, to the relative prosperity of the country, and to political considerations. The Volta is not one of the great rivers of Africa, and it suffers from a marked seasonal variation in flow; but its average flow and its gradient in eastern Ghana are sufficient for large-scale power generation, and where it cuts through the Akwapim Hills there were several possible sites for a dam which could even out the flow. The relatively well-developed economy of Ghana encouraged interest of a scheme of this kind both within and outside the country, and provided a steadily increasing demand for power. However, the economic justification for a project of this size rested upon the development of a major power-consuming industry —aluminium production—which was expected to use about half the electricity produced each year. The political factors of greatest significance were the vision and the determination of Nkrumah, who made the Volta scheme the keystone of his economic plans for the country, and the significance of Ghana as one of the first and most influential independent

126

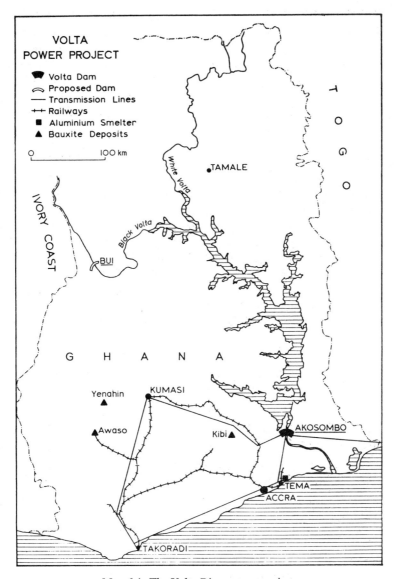

MAP 6.4. The Volta River power project.

African states, which might have turned towards the communist world if American finance had not been forthcoming.

After many years of study, construction of the dam began in 1962 and it was completed in 1965. The first generators were installed in that year, and the power station reached its initial capacity of 589 MW in 1966, the year in which the aluminium smelter came into operation. As a result, electricity production in Ghana as a whole, which had risen from 231 million kWh in 1956 to 527 million kWh in 1965, jumped to 1560 million kWh in 1967. The installed capacity at Akosombo was increased to its final figure of 883 MW in 1972 largely on the basis of an expansion of aluminium smelting.

As in the case of Kariba, the most obvious visible effect of the Volta Dam is the creation of a vast reservoir. This lake, over 350 km in length, has changed the map of Ghana very strikingly, and has had important implications for settlement and communications. Also as at Kariba the effects of the increased supplies of electricity are less clear to see (apart from the opening of the aluminium smelter which was an integral part of the whole project), especially since apart from one textile mill little other development has been attracted to the dam site at Akosombo. Ghana, too, has been passing through a period of political change since the power station was opened, and both for this reason and because of the economic crises left by the Nkrumah regime this has been a period of slackened economic development. Initially, therefore, the provision of the new source of power merely led to the virtual closure of the older thermal plants. But gradually new industries in addition to aluminium smelting are being established, especially in Accra and Tema, and these are consuming more power than the old stations could have supplied.

The implementation of the Volta project was assisted by the location of a suitable dam site so close to the areas of greatest prospective demand, but one unfortunate repercussion is that the electricity generated there is available only to the most prosperous southern part of the country. Transmission lines could be built to the north, but this would represent a possibly unjustified act of faith, for the demand there is at present extremely small. It was originally intended that a complementary 120 MW power station would be built at Bui on the Black Volta towards the north of the country, but as a result of the strained economic situation this project was shelved. By the mid-1970's increasing demand justified firm plans for a second dam and power station, but the circular process of regional development has so concentrated this demand in the south that the dam is to be at Kpong, just downstream from Akosombo, with the Bui project again to follow later.

Nigeria

The demand for electricity per head of the population is much lower in Nigeria than in Ghana, and is even below the average for tropical Africa. Even so, the country is so large that the total market is substantial, and, as elsewhere, it is expanding rapidly. In order to meet this demand the country's generating capacity rose from 106 MW in 1956 to 432 MW in 1966, production increasing during this period from 285 to 1278 million kWh. More recently both capacity and production have risen much further, following the completion of the Kainji Dam. The nature and location of the development that has taken place is of particular interest, since in contrast to most other African countries Nigeria has a variety of power resources and since the market is relatively dispersed.

During the late 1950's coal from Enugu continued to provide the main fuel for power generation, and an important new coal-fired plant was built at Oji River, between that town and Onitsha. Then a gradual shift to oil took place, as the oil deposits of the Niger delta began to be exploited, and the new plant at Lagos uses this fuel. It is there that the greatest demand exists, and by 1967 the city's thermal stations had a capacity of 148 MW, one-third of the Nigerian total. Now a further shift in source and location for thermal generation is occurring, for an important development of the late 1960's was the use of natural gas for electricity generation. New power stations with respective capacities of 55 MW and 72 MW were built on the gasfields at Afam in Imo State, and at Ughelli in Bendel State, playing a role complementary to the Lagos stations in the grid which now extends across southern Nigeria: and there are plans for huge expansion, for instance to 500 MW at Ughelli.

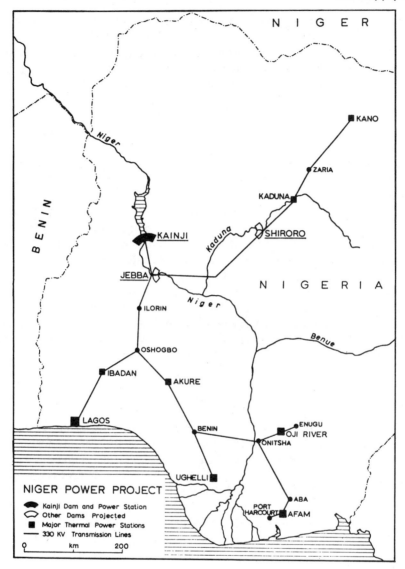

MAP 6.5. The Niger River power project.

As early as the 1920's hydroelectricity was generated on the Jos plateau to supply the tin mines, but this source of power subsequently received little attention since the country had fuel for thermal stations and had few obvious sites for exploiting water power. The River Niger does offer a considerable potential, however, and as the demand for power continued to rise it was decided to use this for the third of the giant power projects of tropical Africa. A dam 400 m long and 70 m high has been built across the river at Kainji, raising the water level by 55 m and creating a 1300 km² lake behind it. The construction work began in 1964, and the first four 80 MW generators were installed in late 1968 and early 1969, by which time investment in the project had reached $250 million. A further eight generators are due to be added by 1980, bringing the total capacity to 960 MW, greater than that at either Kariba or Akosombo at present. In order to meet the even greater demands of the 1980's, plans include a second dam at Jebba, 100 km downstream, where a 500 MW power station could be established, and a third at Shiroro Gorge on the Kaduna River, where there is a potential capacity of 480 MW (Map 6.5). These three schemes are to some extent interdependent since the peak flow occurs at different times on the Niger and Kaduna rivers and Shiroro should be able to take over the base load while the Kainji reservoir is being re-filled in May–August each year.

The decision to proceed with the Kainji project was taken before the full extent of Nigeria's oil and gas resources was known, but it is still considered to be fully justified. It is in fact very well placed in relation to demand, for it lies midway between the greatest consuming area of Lagos–Ibadan in the south-west, and the secondary focus of demand between Kaduna and Kano in the north which lies far from other sources of power. The south-east, from which it is rather remote, can continue to use oil and gas for thermal electricity production, and therefore, in terms of location, the two sources of power that are being developed are suitably complementary. As both have now been connected into a single national grid it should also be possible to co-ordinate them by using hydroelectricity continuously to supply the base load, and thermal electricity to the extent needed to meet the peak load. As elsewhere, a further justification for dam construction was provided by potential benefits in such other fields as irrigation and navigation. The result of these developments of the 1960's has been to change the pattern of power production in Nigeria from one of individual stations meeting local needs to a national system, and to ensure that electricity is available at reasonable cost wherever a substantial demand for it is likely to arise.

Ivory Coast

The rapid growth of the Ivory Coast economy has encouraged the opening of both thermal and hydropower stations there also, even though fuel for the former has to be imported. New oil-fired capacity was installed at Abidjan in 1963–4 and in 1968–70, and a further 150 MW was added there in 1975–6. Meanwhile new hydroelectric plants were opened at Ayamé on the Bia River in 1959 and 1965, and these have been followed by larger projects on the Bandama River. A dam and a 174 MW power station at Kossou were completed in 1973. This scheme, costing $90 million and creating a lake of 1750 km², is in some respects a small-scale version of the Volta project, but it is a reflection of the booming Ivory Coast economy that it does not depend on any single major consumer such as an aluminium smelter.

The parallel with Ghana is extended since a second 210 MW power station is being built further downstream at Taabo, while a further plant of 160 MW is proposed—not for the north but in a hitherto very undeveloped area at Buyo on the Sassandra River. If this goes ahead total generating capacity in Ivory Coast will have risen from 14 MW in 1955 to 102 MW twelve years later and to almost 900 MW after another twelve years, and at a far more steady rate than in most other African countries.

Cameroon

Until the opening of Kariba the largest power station in tropical Africa was that at Edéa on the Sanaga River in Cameroon. Electricity was first produced there in 1953, but the greater part of the 160 MW capacity was installed in 1958. As a result of this, power generated rose from 40 million kWh in 1956 to 840 million kWh in 1959. During the 1960's, however, production remained very stable at around 100 million kWh, falling below this in some years as a result of low water-levels.

The position of Cameroon among the leading African electricity producers does not reflect a generally high level of demand for power there. It depends entirely on the decision of a French company to use the power potential of the Sanaga River to produce aluminium from bauxite mined in Guinea. As now in Ghana also, electricity generation and aluminium smelting are closely interdependent, and the smelter has consumed more than 85% of the power every year.

However, Edéa is well placed to supply the largest town, Douala, only 80 km away, and the capital, Yaoundé, only 180 km to the east, and in these centres demand is now steadily rising. This, together with the limitation which availability of power has placed on aluminium production in years of low water, has now justified further investment. With the aid of a grant from the European Investment Bank, a supplementary storage dam has been built higher up the river at Mbakaou, and capacity at Edéa was increased by 40 MW in 1971. If demand continues to rise, a further 60 MW will be installed there before other sites are developed elsewhere.

Uganda and Kenya

The first major power project in East Africa was the Owen Falls dam and power station at Jinja in Uganda, which harnesses the Nile as it flows out of Lake Victoria. When this was under construction, between 1948 and 1954, it was considered one of the great engineering achievements of tropical Africa; and although it has now been dwarfed by the Kariba and Volta projects, it still provides the chief source of electricity in East Africa. While the dam was completed in 1954, most of the generators have been installed more recently, and the power station reached its full capacity of 150 MW only in 1968. It was hoped that the availability of electricity would draw new industries to Uganda, but although a number of factories such as textile mills, the smelter for Kilembe copper, and a small steel-rolling mill have been established at Jinja, consumption has risen more slowly than was hoped. An essential factor in the success of the scheme has therefore been the opportunity for the sale of surplus power to Kenya. Every year since 1958 over one-third of the electricity generated at Owen Falls has been transmitted there.

Uganda has for some years had plans for building a second dam on the Nile, either at Bujagali Falls, only 8 km downstream from Owen Falls, or at Kaberega Falls in the north of the country, where potential demand is much smaller, but where some stimulus for development is being sought. A decision to proceed at the latter site was made, but Uganda has had difficulty in attracting funds for the project, as Kenya has begun to develop its own power resources more fully and is reducing its imports from Uganda. In 1972 a third site, at the Aru Falls on the much smaller Aswa River was being considered, so that Kaberega Falls might be left as a tourist attraction. Kenya has long produced some thermal and hydroelectricity, and new thermal capacity was brought into being at Mombasa in 1961, 1963, and 1966; but the main new development there is the harnessing of the Tana River at Seven Forks, 170 km north-east of Nairobi. This is taking place in three stages, the first at Kindaruma providing an initial capacity of 40 MW in 1968, later raised to 70 MW. The second at Kamburu provided a further 50 MW in 1974. The third stage at Gitaru, begun in 1975, is more ambitious, and the whole scheme should provide between 270 and 340 MW.

Recent Developments Elsewhere

In every country of tropical Africa there has been some increase of electricity capacity and production since the mid-1950's, and a list of all the new power stations built during this period would be very long. Most of those with a capacity of more than 50 MW are shown on Map 6.2. Zaire was the largest producer of electricity in 1956, the year in which the 276 MW Le Marinel (now Seke) plant was opened, doubling the previous total generating capacity in Shaba, and meeting all the requirements of the copper industry with some to spare for the Zambian Copperbelt. A little further development took place in other parts of Zaire up to 1960, but after that new investment ceased during the years of political instability.

In neighbouring Angola production was extremely small in 1956, but there it has increased greatly. Several new hydroelectric stations have been built, and by 1963 the total capacity had exceeded that of even such a large country as Nigeria. The most important project is the Cambambe dam and power station on the Cuanza River 180 km east of Luanda opened in 1962 with a capacity of 130 MW, and later raised to 260 MW. Smaller dams are those at Matala on the Cunene River, and at Biopio and Lomaum on the Catumbela River. Since the demand for electricity is far smaller than in Nigeria, and since no major consuming industries have been attracted as in Ghana and Cameroon, the power stations have so far operated well below capacity. No industrial development has taken place near Cambambe, and while power availability has assisted some development in Luanda, more is needed before new investment in generating plant is justified.

Other locally important hydroelectric developments have taken place in Ethiopia, where a 54 MW plant was opened in 1960 on the Awash River at Koka, close to the main consuming area, followed in 1966 and 1967 by additional plants nearby with a combined capacity of 64 MW, and in 1973 by one of 100 MW at the Fincha Dam on a tributary of the Blue Nile in Wollega Province. Much larger schemes would be physically possible but would not be justified by the prospective demand at present. The situation is similar in several of the smaller countries such as Malawi, where power stations opened at Nkula and Tedzani falls on the Shire River in 1966 and 1973 have each been of only 20 to 24 MW capacity.

Several countries with a larger demand for power, in addition to Nigeria, Ivory Coast, and Kenya, have established both hydro and thermal stations in recent years. Thus in Tanzania between the opening of the 21 MW Hale plant on the Pangani River in 1964 and the installation of 100 MW capacity at Kidatu on the Great Ruaha River in 1975, new thermal power stations were built both in Dar es Salaam and in several provincial towns. In Liberia much new thermal capacity has been installed both at Monrovia and at the various iron ore mines, as well as a 50 MW hydro plant at Mount Coffee on the St. Paul River. In Sudan new oil-fired plant was installed at Khartoum between the opening of a small hydrostation at the Sennar Dam in 1962 and the building of a larger one, of 90 MW, at the Roseires Dam in 1968–71.

The establishment of thermal power stations in countries which have a substantial hydroelectricity potential but no coal or oil appeared rather anomalous even before the massive rise in oil prices. In part it results from the greater speed at which thermal plants can be built, the lower capital costs involved, and the possibility of locating them exactly at the point of demand. However, it is sometimes suggested that it also results from pressure by the developed countries, since the proportion of capital costs spent on imported equipment is higher for thermal plants, and since firms based in these countries control, and profit from, the supply of fuel. Undoubtedly, if power schemes are planned in advance of demand, and especially if account is taken of the side-benefits of most hydroelectric developments in such fields as water control for irrigation and navigation, the balance of advantage in tropical Africa usually now rests with these rather than with investment in thermal-electric capacity.

THE TWO MAJOR PROJECTS OF THE 1970's

The pattern of power production continues to change as the capacity of existing stations is increased and as new schemes are inaugurated. Thus in 1968 preliminary work began on two extremely important projects in addition to the Kafue Dam discussed above. One is at Cabora Bassa on the Zambezi River in Mozambique, where a dam 150 m high and 300 m long has been built, creating a lake comparable in size with that above Kariba (Map 6.3). The dam is the centre-point of a comprehensive development programme originally costed at $350 million, and it is expected to provide irrigation water and to assist navigation, as well as to permit the establishment of a power station of at least 2000 MW capacity. Existing installations in Mozambique, of which the largest was the Maruzi hydroelectric station, were adequate for local needs, and indeed some surplus was sold to Rhodesia. The justification for building a power station larger than any yet in operation in tropical Africa therefore rested not upon local demand but upon further exports of electricity, in this case primarily to South Africa where consumption is rising rapidly and hydroelectric potential is very limited. That country agreed to take up 7000 MW of the capacity in 1975, when the first generators were installed, and a further 700 MW by 1980. However, production on this scale may provide power cheaply enough to attract new consuming industries within Mozambique, especially in the metallurgical and chemical fields.

The Cabora Bassa project was, of course, not entirely welcome in the context of tropical African development, since it had so many political implications. Not only is South Africa to be the main purchaser of power, but it was also a major source of finance for the project. The dam was also an instrument of Portuguese colonial policy, for the proposed irrigation schemes which it would permit were due to attract many thousands of Portuguese settlers. Some critics argued therefore that any advantage that it might bring to the people of Mozambique was far outweighed by its role in strengthening the solidarity of white control in southern Africa as a whole. The attainment of independence has clearly changed the situation, and it will be the responsibility of the Mozambique government to ensure that this inheritance is an economic asset, but initially it is a political liability in so far as it binds the country to South Africa.

Even this giant scheme may eventually be dwarfed by that at Inga on the Zaire River plans for which were prepared by the Belgians in the 1950's but never implemented because of the subsequent political upheavals. Physical conditions are so favourable that the power potential on the lower Zaire is far greater than on any other stretch of river in Africa—or even in the world—for a river of great volume and exceptionally even flow falls almost 300 m in 300 km below Kinshasa. The area is highly accessible, and is already one of the most highly developed parts of a country which has a great potential for industrial growth and which has increased its generating capacity very little during the past decade. It has been proposed that the eventual capacity at Inga might be 28,000 MW, or more than the present total for the whole continent including South Africa's great coal-fired plants; and a further merit of the site is that this can be attained in easy stages.

Construction work began in 1968 and at the first power station generating capacity of 350 MW was installed in 1972–4. This uses only a small part of the river's flow diverted into the parallel N'kokolo valley, which will supply the immediate needs of Kinshasa and the Bas–Zaire region. Even this involved an expenditure of $130 million, to which Italy and the EEC contributed substantially. This part of the project is due to be brought up to a capacity of 920 MW by 1978, with new transmission lines carrying much of the electricity 1700 km to Shaba Province, and later to 1600 MW, before attention is turned to the main valley for the second and third parts of the "grand design". How soon these further developments take place will, of course, depend on the rate at which demand rises to absorb the power made available in the first stages of the scheme.

CONCLUSIONS

Tropical Africa has exceptionally great water-power resources together with some resources for thermal power production. As yet these have hardly been touched, and the region accounts for only a tiny share of world electricity generation; but even so, power production has increased at an impressive rate over the past decades, and is continuing to rise very rapidly. Some degree of limitation is imposed by shortages of local capital and skilled manpower, but the main factor governing the pace of development seems to be the level of demand for electricity. This clearly indicates the close relationship which exists between power production and other forms of economic activity; and just as the general level of economic development largely determines the amount of electricity produced, so also the availability of electricity has some influence on the general level of development. However, the two are not always closely correlated, and electricity certainly does not provide an infallible key to development, or even to economic growth.

The power resources of tropical Africa are not only ample but also widespread, and so it has been possible for new developments in this field to be widely distributed over the region. Nevertheless, development on a really large scale has been concentrated at only a few points where a number of factors have been particularly favourable. Kariba, Akosombo and Kainji all offered suitable sites for damming a major river to create a great head of water, and at the time that each decision to proceed was taken the Federation of Rhodesia and Nyasaland, Ghana and Nigeria were each relatively strong both economically and politically. Each government was able to contribute part of the capital cost and to obtain the remainder of the necessary finance from overseas. Inga offers an even more suitable physical site, but Zaire did not until recently have the political stability or the economic strength to attract the capital required to proceed with this project.

The level of demand is just as important for the distribution as for the total extent of power development. Zambia and Rhodesia together provided an exceptionally large market for power compared with most parts of tropical Africa, and Nigeria taken as a whole provides sufficient demand to justify a major scheme. The relative prosperity of Ghana creates a market larger than in most countries of its size, but a large aluminium project was also needed to support the Volta scheme. In other countries such as Guinea and Ethiopia the limited demand has inhibited much development of the great hydroelectric potential. From a commercial viewpoint, one of the most promising aspects of the Inga project is its location in an area of substantial potential demand. Not only is the demand for electricity likely to increase greatly in the near future in Zaire as a whole, but also one of the greatest concentrations is sure to be in the Kinshasa–Matadi zone, within which Inga lies.

There are some countries, and especially some cities and mining areas, with only a limited hydroelectric potential near at hand, where the level of demand has justified investment in thermal power stations, generally using imported fuel. Now every effort is being made to avoid this policy wherever possible, except where local oil or gas resources exist. In some cases the need for it may be avoided by greater international co-operation within tropical Africa. This could also help to prevent duplication of expenditure on hydroelectric plants in neighbouring countries, encouraging concentration upon those sites where power can be generated at lowest cost. Until now, except at Kariba, transmission across frontiers has generally taken place only where internal demand has risen more slowly than was hoped, as in the case of sales from Uganda to Kenya, and more recently from Ghana to Togo and Benin. It is, however, basic to the Cabora Bassa development, and could be of great value elsewhere, as at Inga, reducing costs for both the exporting and the importing countries. At the same time, progress is being made on developing the transmission networks within countries to form national grids, which both enable the lowest cost power stations to serve the largest possible areas and reduce the disruptions created when breakdowns occur.

While the provision of electricity is not a sufficient condition for rapid economic development, it can greatly assist the process: and it is certainly a necessary condition for industrial growth. The distribution of power production can therefore be expected to affect the geographical pattern of other forms of development. An examination of the recent growth of electricity production indicates that it has been especially rapid in some of the poorest countries. But this growth has been from very small beginnings, and such countries as Chad, Niger, and Upper Volta still account for only a tiny share of African power generation. In absolute terms most growth has taken place in those countries which were already important producers in the early 1950's, and this is one more aspect of the tendency towards a "widening gap" between African countries. The same trends are apparent within many individual countries. Lomé accounted for over 90% of consumption from public supplies within Togo in 1973, and Abidjan for 72% of consumption within Ivory Coast. Even in Nigeria the capital city accounted for 47% in 1972. As the example of Ghana clearly demonstrates, a chain reaction may often be seen in which relatively well-developed areas offer suitable locations for new power stations, which in turn permit further economic growth; elsewhere the demand for electricity is insufficient to justify its provision, and the consequent lack of power supplies is among the factors discouraging development.

Technical advances in transmission might seem to assist the breaking of the circle, for they are making it possible for electricity to be carried ever further from the point of production. But rather than encouraging a dispersal of new power-using economic activities, this possibility is being used mainly to permit the supply of power to existing foci of development from hydroelectric schemes sited some distance away. Thus where it has not been possible to generate power very close to the existing areas of demand, and a power station has had to be built in a little-developed area—as at Kariba or Kainji—other forms of development have not been drawn to that area.

In many countries concern has been expressed about the need to spread electricity provision more widely, and some progress has been made in extending supplies to areas that formerly lacked them. In addition to the large power plants discussed above many smaller ones have been built, but unfortunately most small schemes have involved proportionately higher costs than the larger ones, and supplies to up-country towns and rural areas often have to be subsidized. There are areas such as southern Uganda and southern Ghana where some of the rural population are supplied with electricity, and there is a need for further study of this aspect of African development in terms of present and potential consumers. It is more practicable to provide electricity to nucleated villages than to dispersed rural settlements, and this is one of the motives for the *ujamaa vijijini* programme in Tanzania. But in most African rural areas the costs of providing electricity to each individual family are at present prohibitive in relation to their capacity to pay for it, so that the towns, and especially industrial concerns, are likely to account for most consumption for the foreseeable future. It might also be mentioned here that the impact of the large hydro-electric schemes on rural areas through spin-offs such as irrigation water have also been very modest as yet.

In general, therefore, the pattern of power development over the past two decades has tended to confirm the existence of islands of prosperity in tropical Africa rather than to assist a wider dispersal of development. With the possible exception of the attraction of major electricity-consuming industries such as aluminium smelters and nitrogenous fertilizer plants to remote power sites, this trend seems likely to continue. And unless governments intervene it can be expected to become even stronger if nuclear power stations become an economic proposition in tropical Africa, since these are not at all tied to the location of physical resources, the only major economic factors in their location being the availability of capital for their construction and the distribution of the demand for the electricity they produce.

SELECTED READING

A valuable inter-disciplinary set of essays on African dams is:
  N. RUBIN and W. M. WARREN (ed.), *Dams in Africa* (London, 1968).
An account of tropical African water power resources and their exploitation up to the 1950's may be found in:
  G. H. T. KIMBLE, *Tropical Africa* (New York, 1960), ch. 7.
Much data on electricity development in African countries up to 1964 is provided in:
  N. B. GUYOL, *The World Electric Power Industry* (Berkeley, 1969).
Useful analyses of the economics of the Volta and Kariba projects may be found in:
  J. A. KING, *Economic Development Projects and their Appraisal* (Baltimore, 1967), pp. 128–55 and 236–68.
On Kariba see also:
  M. M. COLE, The Rhodesian economy in transition and the role of Kariba, *Geography* **47**, 15–40 (1962).
The Volta project is examined in the Rubin and Warren volume, by R. W. Steel, and also in:
  W. A. HANCE, *African Economic Development* (New York, 1967), ch. 4.
A comprehensive account of the project is:
  J. MOXON, *Volta—Man's Greatest Lake* (London, 1969).
The place of Kainji in Nigerian electricity supplies is one theme of:
  E. S. SIMPSON, Electricity production in Nigeria, *Economic Geography* **45**, 239–57 (1969).
The Cabora Bassa scheme is fully described in:
  K. MIDDLEMAS, *Cabora Bassa* (London, 1975).
For a critical view of the scheme, see:
  B. DAVIDSON, Cabora Bassa, *Présence Africaine* **82**, 39–51 (1972).
An intensive study of the Owen Falls scheme and the distribution of electricity in Uganda is:
  G. WILSON, *Owen Falls* (Nairobi, 1968).
A comprehensive discussion of electricity production throughout East Africa, emphasizing its contribution to development, is:
  H. AMANN, *Energy Supply and Economic Development in East Africa* (Munich, 1969).

Discussions of power projects in francophone Africa frequently appear in the journals *Afrique Industries Infrastructures* and *Industries et Travaux d'Outre Mer*.

A useful review of the total energy situation in Africa in the light of the oil crisis is:
   D. Hilling, Alternative energy sources for Africa, *African Affairs* **75**, 359–71 (1976).

7

THE ROLE OF TRANSPORT

TRANSPORT facilities have a vital part to play in the process of economic development. For many people in tropical Africa all movement must still take place on foot, and a vast amount of energy is used up in carrying headloads of produce—and especially water—from place to place. However, modern forms of mechanized transport have now spread over much of the region, and these are greatly assisting the transition from a subsistence to an exchange economy. The building of the first railways at the beginning of this century produced dramatic results in many areas as farmers began to grow cash crops for the first time. The development of motor transport and also the introduction of the bicycle permitted this change to spread much more widely. The process continues today, though much less dramatically now that in most areas mechanized transport facilities are being improved rather than provided for the first time. In some cases agricultural or mining development necessitates such improvements; in others it is stimulated by them, although perhaps less often than some railway and road builders have anticipated. Even where no new facilities have been provided in recent years, economic development has generally brought increased traffic on the transport systems already in existence.

The general expansion has not applied equally to all forms of transport, so that the balance between these has been shifting. In many places there is now severe competition between rail and road transport, and the latter is attracting an increasing share of both passenger and freight traffic. Many railways are still becoming more heavily used year by year, but road traffic is developing much faster. More extreme positions are occupied by air transport and inland navigation. The role of air transport is still restricted by its cost, yet it has been growing very rapidly. The traffic handled on the region's inland waterways, by contrast, has remained almost static. Complementary to these various modes of transport is ocean shipping, which will be considered first.

SEA TRANSPORT

Ocean transport is of particular importance to tropical Africa because of the region's heavy dependence on overseas trade in bulky products. One change for the worse that took place in the 1960's, at least as far as eastern Africa is concerned, was the closure of the Suez Canal. This led to a substantial increase in freight charges between Indian Ocean or Red Sea ports and Europe and its re-opening has been particularly welcomed by Sudan and

Somalia. Most other changes have been for the better, and although they have little direct contribution to make to the growth of the internal exchange economy, they have certainly enabled ever large volumes of cargo to be moved to and from Africa.

Port Traffic

The greatest growth in traffic handled has taken place where new resources have been exploited for export, notably bulky raw materials such as oil, iron ore, or phosphates (Table 7.1). Thus the volume of cargo loaded onto ships in Mauritania, Togo, and Nigeria is now many times greater than it was in the 1950's. Indeed, in simple volume terms all other movements are now dwarfed by oil shipments from Nigeria. Similarly, mineral working in Gabon is responsible for much of the increase in cargo loaded both at its own ports and at Pointe Noire in Congo. In all these cases export-based economic growth has brought an increase in import traffic also, and although this has been of far smaller proportions it has often been considerably more important in terms of port activity as measured, for instance, by employment.

TABLE 7.1. TROPICAL AFRICAN PORT TRAFFIC

	Cargo loaded (000 tons)		Cargo unloaded (000 tons)	
	Average 1956–7	Average 1973–4	Average 1956–7	Average 1973–4
Angola	1,253	15,587	910	1,972
Benin	116	135	136	578
Cameroon	337	936	394	1,211
Congo	261	2,712	198	620
Ethiopia	237	739	177	1,014
Gabon	601	6,140	122	503
Ghana	1,742	2,188	1,337	3,042
Guinea	1,470	(2,500)	210	(570)
Ivory Coast	538	3,956	567	3,542
Kenya	884	2,501	1,790	4,242
Liberia	2,121	25,433	208	1,093
Mauritania	12	(9,600)	10	(360)
Mozambique	3,311	10,900	2,612	4,224
Nigeria	2,094	105,612	2,289	5,000
Senegal	(500)	2,613	2,512	2,219
Sierra Leone	1,519	2,880	537	636
Somalia	85	488	70	444
Sudan	616	884	913	1,910
Tanzania	730	1,112	815	3,083
Togo	46	2,448	56	365
Zaire	849	692	1,206	1,517

Sources: United Nations, *Statistical Yearbook;* and national sources.

Rapid expansion at Abidjan reflects the booming economy of Ivory Coast, and especially the rise in coffee, cocoa, and timber exports. In Ghana exports have grown more slowly in volume, for although more cocoa is being shipped out now than in the 1950's, the same is not true of some bulkier commodities such as logs and manganese ore: but there as in most other countries the volume of imports has more than doubled in fifteen years. The level of traffic at the ports of Mozambique, already exceptionally high by 1956, rose still further as development took place both there and in Zambia, Malawi, Rhodesia, Swaziland, and South Africa: but political events subsequently brought a fall in Rhodesia traffic, while a substantial shift of Zambia traffic from Beira has now occurred, bringing a rapid expansion of port activity at Dar es Salaam instead.

The only major port at which there has been a substantial decline of traffic since the 1950's is Takoradi, which has been replaced by Tema for most of Ghana's imports. Dakar has lost much of its former role as an *entrepôt* for all French-speaking West Africa, but this has been off-set by an increase in local cargoes, notably phosphate exports. At Matadi in Zaire traffic fell sharply during the period of political upheaval, but by 1970 it had returned to pre-independence levels. There are, however, many minor ports at which activity has declined, as a result of what seems to be a universal trend towards ever-greater concentration at larger and better-equipped ports within the same country.

Improved Port Facilities

The increase in traffic to be handled has necessitated investment in improved facilities at most of the major ports of tropical Africa during the past decade. Many have suffered periods of extreme congestion, and at some this problem is still serious despite the provision of new quays and new equipment. In several cases the new equipment has included specialized bulk-handling facilities in addition to more of the traditional cranes and storage sheds for general cargo. Very often port improvement has also involved the dredging of deeper channels to permit the entry of the larger vessels now coming into service, and especially the giant tankers bringing oil from the Middle East and the Caribbean.

At Mombasa five new general cargo berths and a separate jetty for oil imports were brought into operation between 1958 and 1967, at a total cost of about $16 million (Map 7.1 and Plate 17), and more were under construction in the early 1970's. Further south the recurrent problem of congestion at Beira was eased by the construction of four new berths in the early 1960's; while at Maputo (formerly Lourenço Marques) new facilities also include a large sugar terminal and bulk-loading equipment for iron ore from Swaziland. At Lagos a major extension of the Apapa wharves was completed in 1956, yet two more berths had to be opened in 1965, while a further seven were added in 1971–4. Even this did not prevent serious congestion in 1975 when 200 ships were at one stage waiting offshore. Though less diverse than at Lagos, the volume of traffic is now even greater at Monrovia, where the needs of the iron mining companies led to the building of three ore piers and an oil jetty in 1962–3 to supplement the general cargo berths opened in the 1940's.

Many other ports which had only very rudimentary facilities until the 1950's have been required to handle greatly increased traffic. Often this has involved the provision of deep-water berths where lighterage from ships anchored offshore was previously necessary. This took place at Freetown in the early 1950's, but it did not satisfy all the needs of Sierra Leone, and more berths have recently been built there. At Dar es Salaam the first deep-water quay for three vessels was opened in 1956, followed by an oil terminal in 1966. There, too, major extensions have now begun, stimulated in part by the rapid development of Zambian transit traffic. Berths for ocean ships were provided for the first time in 1957 at Moçamedes in Angola and at Nacala in Mozambique, providing each of those countries with a third major port. Until recently Somalia had no ports with deep-water quays, but since 1960 the situation there has changed completely as large sums have been invested in new facilities at Kismayu, Mogadishu, and Berbera.

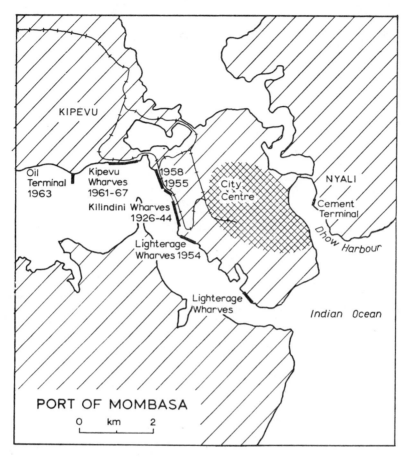

MAP 7.1. The port of Mombasa, Kenya.

New Ports

The most exciting developments are those which have produced modern ports within a few years where nothing but an open beach, or at the most a small fishing harbour, existed before. An outstanding example is Tema, which within four years of its opening in 1962 had overtaken Takoradi as the busiest port of Ghana (Map 7.2 and Plate 18). It had long been clear that Takoradi alone could not adequately serve Ghana's needs, but it was the formulation of plans for the Volta Dam which finally prompted the decision to build a $100 million port at Tema. It lies only 30 km from the capital, Accra, and 80 km from the dam, and is thus well situated to assist in the country's industrial development (Map 6.4). At the same time for the shipment of primary products it is suitably complementary to Takoradi, which lies far to the west. Year by year its effects on spatial patterns of economic activity in Ghana have become more apparent.

A new development which began earlier but still continues is the creation of a great port at Abidjan in Ivory Coast, which became possible only when a canal was successfully cut through the coastal sand bar in 1950 (Map 7.3). Previously all cargoes had to be trans-shipped through Port Bouet, but now ocean vessels can pass into the sheltered waters of the

141

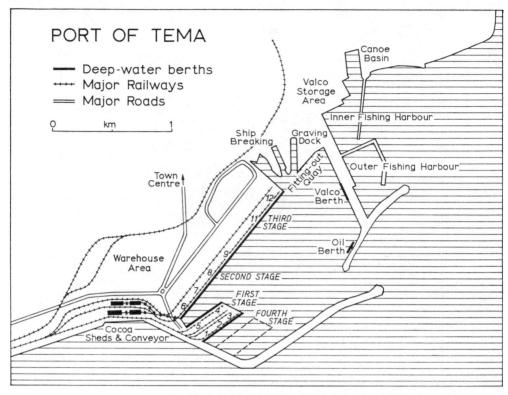

Map 7.2. The port of Tema, Ghana.

lagoon and use one of twelve well-equipped quays. More recently this port has been supplemented by another at San Pedro, 300 km to the west. This was a tiny fishing settlement until a port with six quays was built in 1968–72 at a cost of $45 million. In some ways this development is comparable to that at Tema, although the scale is smaller. However, San Pedro is designed to assist agricultural and forestry development in its hinterland rather than to become an industrial centre; and another notable difference is that whereas port construction at Tema has increased the concentration of economic activity around Ghana's capital city, San Pedro port is intended to have the opposite effect within Ivory Coast.

It is generally agreed that the port of Abidjan has played a vital part in the rapid growth of that city as well as assisting a great increase in Ivory Coast's external trade, and that San Pedro should bring benefits in terms of spreading development to the south-west. There is not such general agreement on the value of recent large investments in new ports in both Benin and Togo (Map 7.4), since these are unlikely to operate to full capacity for many years. In each case a simple lighterage pier has been replaced by a deep-water harbour a short distance away, that at Cotonou being opened in 1964 and that at Lomé in 1967.

Other entirely new ports are those built by mining companies to permit the export of vast quantities of ores, such as at Buchanan in Liberia and near Nouadhibou in Mauritania. At Buchanan the mining company was persuaded to spend an extra $6½ million to provide general purpose quays to supplement those at Monrovia, but as yet each of these ports functions essentially as part of an integrated mining enterprise, and has had little impact on

142

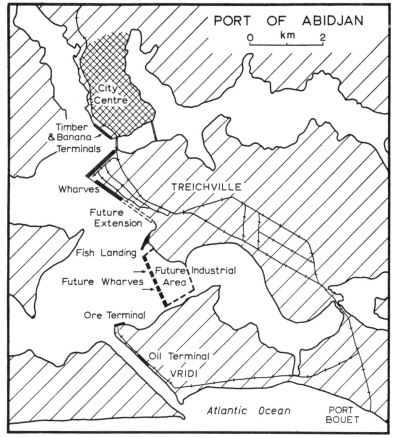

MAP 7.3. The port of Abidjan, Ivory Coast.

other forms of activity. This is equally true of the new oil port opened in 1961 at Bonny in eastern Nigeria (Map 4.2), even though it handles a greater volume of cargo than any other port in tropical Africa. The pier at Kpémé through which Togo's phosphates are shipped

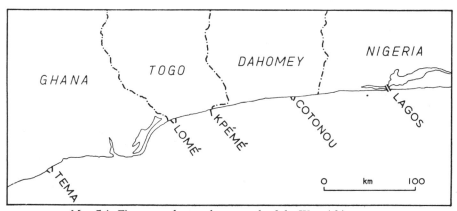

MAP 7.4. Five ports along a short stretch of the West African coast.
(Dahomey has now been re-named Benin.)

143

overseas handles a far greater tonnage than the port at Lomé, yet no other form of development is visible from the road which passes beneath it.

Current Developments

Current port developments include all the types of change noted above. At almost every major port there are plans for expanded and improved facilities, and several such plans were in fact implemented in the early 1970's. The improvements include dredging to permit the entry of larger ships, new storage facilities to ease the promotion of seasonal traffic peaks, and new handling equipment to reduce the length of time that ships have to spend in port. Experiments are being made with container handling and interest is being taken in the idea of ships carrying cargoes in lighters which can be towed to the quayside and unloaded after the ship has left harbour.

Elsewhere, small ports with poor facilities are being replaced by new deep-water harbours nearby. Thus in Gabon the lighterage port of Libreville is now working to its capacity of about 100,000 tons of cargo a year, while 300,000 tons of timber is loaded with difficulty from surrounding roadsteads; and with the aid of a $32 million grant from the EEC a new deep-water port has been built 9 km to the south-east at Owendo. This investment is necessary even to deal with the anticipated increase in the existing forms of traffic, notably timber, to a possible 800,000 tons by 1980, while eventually it should also assist the handling of manganese exports now sent through the Congo port of Pointe Noire, and the exploitation of the Bèlinga iron deposits.

In Guinea, the exploitation of the Boké bauxite deposits has necessitated the building of a new port capable of taking 60,000-ton ships at Kamsar, 17 km up the Nunez River, and this came into operation in 1973. Proposals for other new ports related to mining include one to the north-west of Monrovia if exploitation of the Wologosi iron ore deposits in Liberia became practicable.

In such cases as these investment in new port facilities has an important role to play in assisting development. New ports are of limited value in themselves, and are not economically justified if they merely divert traffic from other ports with adequate capacity. The development of Assab, only 200 km from Djibouti, has sometimes been criticized on this score. It is also possible that major investments at Lagos, Cotonou, Lomé, and Tema represent some duplication of facilities, and that greater international co-operation might have resulted in wiser use of scarce funds. However, port improvements somewhere along this stretch of coast were essential for the economic development that has taken place both in the coastal countries and far inland. The benefits of further investment in ports are likely to be great wherever inadequate facilities are clearly hindering the expansion of economic activity, but in contrast to many other forms of development where perhaps "small is beautiful", the benefits may often be maximised if priority is given to improving large existing ports rather than building new ones.

Shipping

Most African governments are anxious that sea transport should involve not only port development, but also the establishment of Africa-owned merchant marines. As yet this has hardly begun, much the greater part of the continent's overseas trade being carried in ships owned in Europe, North America, and Asia. Liberia appears in some statistics as one of the leading shipping nations of the world, but only because many American companies find it convenient to register their ships there.

In the mid-1950's there were no merchant fleets of any significance operating from tropical African countries, but now at least a start has been made. By 1969 the Black Star Line of Ghana had sixteen ships and the Nigerian National Shipping Line had thirteen ships. Most of these vessels are between 5000 and 7000 tons, and they operate mainly between West Africa and Europe. Smaller companies had also been established in Ivory Coast, Zaire, Ethiopia, and Sudan, each with two to four ships; and an East African shipping line was being formed, involving the governments of the inland countries of Uganda and Zambia as well as Kenya and Tanzania.

It can be argued that the establishment of a merchant marine has a more direct contribution to make to African economies than port development, for rather than improving the infrastructure it widens the range of economic activities undertaken and replaces an "invisible import". However, international shipping is a difficult field to break into, and for the immediate future most investment in sea transport will probably continue to be in new port facilities to be used mainly by foreign-owned ships.

INLAND WATERWAYS

Navigable inland waterways played an important part in shaping the map of Africa during the period of dramatic change around the turn of the century, although the falls which are found on most of the rivers limited their role as routeways even then. Today they are generally of only local importance, and are contributing little to the process of economic growth in most parts of the region. There has been a worldwide tendency in recent years for river transport to handle a decreasing share of both passenger and goods traffic, largely because of its slowness, and tropical Africa is no exception.

Transport on the leading waterway of the continent, the River Zaire, was also greatly affected in the 1960's by disturbed political conditions in Zaire. Cargo traffic handled at the river port of Kinshasa exceeded $1\frac{1}{2}$ million tons in 1959, but in recent years it has reached only half that figure. As new forms of economic development begin, river traffic is likely to increase again, for the extensive system of waterways must remain a major element in the country's transport network for the foreseeable future. But although water transport will continue to be vital in many districts, the Kasai–Zaire River route between Ilebo and Kinshasa may be replaced by a new rail link.

While traffic on the Ubangui and Zaire rivers generated by Congo and the Central African Empire has always been far less than that generated by Zaire, it has been rising steadily. Cargoes handled at Bangui increased from 130,000 tons in 1960 to 220,000 tons in 1967, and this has justified investment in new facilities at that port. Yet in this case, too, some traffic may be diverted if the trans-Cameroon railway is eventually carried through to the CAE.

The second major waterway of the continent is the Niger River, together with its tributary the Benue. Throughout most of the 1950's and early 1960's, traffic remained very constant, so that the importance of these rivers relative to other forms of transport declined steadily. Then the civil war brought it to a halt, and little had been done to re-activate it by 1976. One factor which discourages greater use of these rivers is the marked seasonal variation in their level, and it is hoped that Kainji Dam will assist navigation on the Niger. Locks have been built around the dam, so that a through route from the Niger Republic to the sea now exists, while plans have been made for using the river for the bulky cargoes which might be generated by an iron and steel industry in Nigeria.

The Nile provides a vital transport artery for southern Sudan, but economic development there has been so slight that little traffic is handled. There, too, plans were made some years ago for river control which would have provided an improved waterway, but these have not been implemented, and may perhaps be superseded by a further extension of the railway from Wau to Juba. The fourth great river of Africa, the Zambezi, is little used for transport, but as at Kainji the building of the Cabora Bassa Dam is expected to improve opportunities for navigation. It is notable, however, that very little use is yet made of the 280 km long Lake Kariba, mainly because it does not link places which can provide much traffic. Similarly, navigation is as yet of little significance on Lake Volta.

An almost universal trend in water transport is towards spatial concentration as economies of scale become more significant, and this is clearly demonstrated in East Africa. The steamer services on Lake Kyoga, Lake Mobutu, and parts of the River Nile within Uganda were withdrawn in 1962, their place being taken by a new railway extension and improved roads; and even around the shores of Lake Victoria many small ports have been closed. But at the main ports on that lake facilities have been improved; and its continued importance as a routeway has now been assured by the provision of two train ferries, which can handle traffic between Kenya, Tanzania, and Uganda without the delays and damage previously often caused by trans-shipment.

Inland waterways in tropical Africa therefore present a picture of decline in some places, yet new investment in others. The period of usefulness of some of the poorer waterways for large-scale transport is certainly over, but there are many ways in which water transport still has an important role to play in African economic development. The best of the waterways still provide the cheapest means of moving bulk cargoes, and might assist the exploitation of iron ore in Nigeria or bauxite in northern Ghana. There are areas such as northern Malawi and most of Gambia which are still largely dependent on water transport, and in which economic development must continue to depend upon this until it has reached a level sufficient to justify investment in alternative facilities.

Furthermore, throughout tropical Africa, from the lagoons and creeks behind the West African coast to the Bangweulu swamps in Zambia, many people must still rely on movement by canoe for all their links with others. Indeed, inland waterways provide another clear illustration of the dual economy, and far too little is known about existing patterns and trends in the small-scale or "informal" sector. Perhaps much more should be done to encourage canoe traffic, to accelerate the spread of outboard motors, or to assist the establishment of small enterprises operating motor launches, as a means of meeting some of the real needs of rural dwellers in the riverine areas of Mali, Sudan, or Zaire.

RAILWAYS

Traffic

By the beginning of this century railways had taken over from river transport as the chief means of linking the interior of tropical Africa with the coast, and therefore with the rest of the world. They still account for the greater part of the freight haulage undertaken in the region in terms of ton-kilometres, for although road vehicles may now carry a larger tonnage the distances involved are usually shorter.

Most African railways have witnessed a great increase in traffic since the 1950's as people have become more mobile and an ever greater volume of goods has had to be

TABLE 7.2 TROPICAL AFRICAN RAIL FREIGHT TRAFFIC

	Million ton-kilometres		
	Average 1956–7	Average 1964–5	Average 1972–3
Mauritania	0	3700	6464
Senegal–Mali	350	394	353
Guinea	38	?	250
Sierra Leone	142	205	213
Liberia	130	3100	4500
Ivory Coast–Upper Volta	142	332	514
Ghana	312	353	305
Togo	7	7	6
Benin	36	44	113
Nigeria	2066	1991	1358
Cameroon	103	168	330
Congo	138	1350	1630
Zaire	2483	1574	2702
Angola	1243	1623	5070
Mozambique	1840	2379	3430
Malawi	103	94	257
Rhodesia–Zambia (and Botswana)	6361	8392	7510
Kenya–Tanzania–Uganda	2376	3213	4115
Ethiopia	148	210	243
Sudan	1417	2252	2690

Sources: United Nations, *Statistical Yearbook; Industries et Travaux d'Outre-mer.*

moved. Freight movements are much the more important on most lines, and have been growing faster than passenger travel partly because competition from the roads is less intense in the case of freight. However, as Table 7.2 indicates, the rate of growth has differed greatly from one country to another.

The most outstanding change has occurred where new sources of minerals have been tapped, and especially where the minerals are bulky and the sources lie far inland. Twenty years ago there were no railways in either Liberia or Mauritania; today, more rail haulage takes place in each than in any other country in West Africa, though in each case very little is carried other than iron ore and supplies for the mines.

With these two exceptions the greatest increase in traffic in absolute terms in the early 1960's occurred on the systems already most heavily used in the 1950's, and especially on Rhodesian Railways which served both Rhodesia and Zambia until 1967 when much Zambia traffic was diverted from Rhodesia. Transit traffic to and from these two countries also accounts for much of the expansion on the railways of Mozambique and Angola, an expansion that was interrupted in 1975–6 by the closure of the Benguela Railway by the war in Angola, and the sealing of the border between Mozambique and Rhodesia. In East Africa and in Sudan the volume of freight haulage, already higher than in most parts of tropical Africa in 1956, has almost doubled since then. The main areas of production and consumption of such bulky commodities as cotton and petroleum products lie far inland, and the railways still provide the cheapest means of moving them to and from the coast.

In many West African countries railways have presented a much more static picture, expansion of some types of traffic having been offset by the loss of other types to road transport. In Ghana and Senegal, for instance, where most exports are produced and most imports consumed within a short distance of the coast, little or no more rail haulage takes place now than in the mid-1950's. In Nigeria the total volume of traffic is far greater, and the railways are still vital for moving the bulky groundnut crop from the north; but even there it increased only slowly between 1956 and 1963, and then it began to fall again even before the civil war brought severe disruption. In Sierra Leone, where road competition was keenly felt, the level of traffic on the antiquated line across the country fell so far that it was closed in 1974, although a shorter mineral line remained open for two more years. A sharp contrast is provided by Ivory Coast, where the economic boom of the late 1950's brought a rapid doubling of rail traffic; but even there it grew much more slowly during the 1960's.

Improved Equipment

Where traffic has increased on the systems established early in this century, it has often been necessary to invest large sums in new rolling stock and other improvements. Many lines follow a very circuitous route, and others have steep gradients, largely because costly earthworks could not be undertaken when they were built. These features limit their capacity, and in order to handle more traffic several stretches have been realigned in recent years. Nearly all the lines in tropical Africa are single-track only, and capacity has often been increased by providing more and longer passing loops. In a few places, especially where two lines converge as between Dondo and Beira, a second track has had to be laid. It has also been necessary to re-lay many lines such as all those in East Africa, with heavier track, in order to withstand a greater intensity of traffic. This has also been done in Rhodesia and Zambia, and other improvements in the railways of those countries have included the installation of the world's longest section of Centralized Train Control.

Other recent developments are less directly related to increased traffic, and some even represent efforts to regain lost traffic by lowering costs. One of the most widespread changes is that from wood or coal to oil fuel. In some cases existing locomotives have been adapted to use oil for raising steam, but the oil is also used in many new diesel units. On many systems electrification has been considered, but traffic has still rarely been found sufficient to justify it. An exception is provided by Zaire, where 700 km of the Kinshasa–Dilolo–Lubumbashi railway, which lies far from other sources of power, were electrified between 1952 and 1963. A similar change on the Matadi–Kinshasa line will surely take place when the country's economy fully recovers from its post-independence dislocation, and when the Inga power scheme is implemented.

New Railways

More striking than these changes in traffic patterns and equipment are the new railways that have been opened (Map 7.5 and Table 7.3). Tropical Africa is one of the few parts of the world where railway building is still taking place on a substantial scale. The great period of railway building ended in the 1930's, and for twenty years few new lines were laid: but since the early 1950's there has been renewed activity, and almost every year has witnessed the opening of some new railway (Plate 19).

Several of the new railways have been built to assist in mineral exploitation, and follow the traditional pattern of a simple line leading inland from the coast. The longest of these is that opened in 1963 in Mauritania, running 650 km from Nouadhibou (formerly Port Étienne) to the iron deposits of F'Derik and Tazadit. Several problems hindered its con-

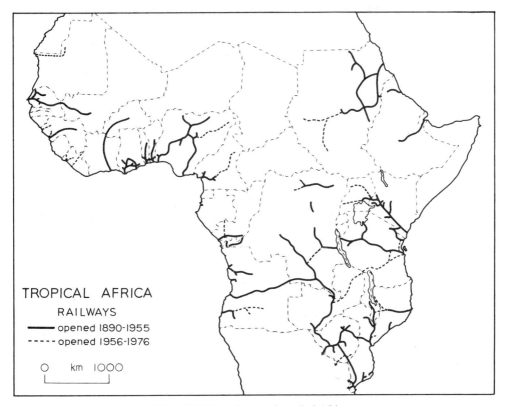

TROPICAL AFRICA
RAILWAYS
—— opened 1890-1955
----- opened 1956-1976

O   km   1000

MAP 7.5. The railways of tropical Africa.

struction, ranging from the physical obstacle of shifting sand dunes, to the political obstacle of Spanish territory which had to be circumvented at great cost. Operating costs are very low, however, for there is a constant stream of iron ore to be shuttled down the whole length of the line, and the modern equipment is specially designed for this purpose. This in turn means that the railway has created relatively few jobs, employing little over 1000 people compared with 15,000 on the railways of Ghana which carry far less traffic.

A similar railway is that which runs from Buchanan to the iron mines of Mount Nimba in Liberia, also opened in 1963 (Map 4.3). This is already one of the most heavily used in tropical Africa, such is the volume of ore to be moved. Although built by the mining company, it is open to public traffic, and the prospects for this developing are greater than in Mauritania. The line could assist in timber exploitation, for example, and it may eventually handle some transit traffic from Guinea, especially since the ore deposits extend across the border. The other Liberian iron ore developments have also involved railway construction (Table 7.3), but these lines are at present for the exclusive use of the mining companies.

The country in which the greatest additions have been made to an existing railway system is Sudan, where the line from Khartoum and Sennar to El Obeid has been extended far to the west and south (Map 7.6). The land traversed by these extensions is remarkably flat, and construction costs were relatively low; but it is not highly productive, and traffic prospects are poor, even though the lack of good roads ensures that such traffic as there is

TABLE 7.3 TROPICAL AFRICAN RAILWAY CONSTRUCTION, 1956–76

		Length (km)	Date of completion
ANGOLA	Sa da Bandeira–Serpa Pinto	501	*c.* 1960
	Dongo–Cassinga	80	1967
CAMEROON	Yaoundé–Belabo	296	1969
	Belabo–Ngaoundéré	327	1974
	Mbanga–Kumba	31	1969
CONGO	Dolisie–Mbinda	283	1962
GABON	Libreville–Booué–Franceville	695	In progress
GHANA	Achiasi–Kotoku	70	1956
GUINEA	Conakry–Fria	143	1958
	Kamsar–Sangarédi	137	1973
LIBERIA	Bomi Hills–Mano River	83	1961
	Buchanan–Mount Nimba	267	1963
	Monrovia–Bong	77	1964
MALAWI	Mpimbe–Mozambique border	99	1970
	Salima–Lilongwe	66	In progress
MAURITANIA	Nouadhibou–Zouérate	650	1963
MOZAMBIQUE	Inhaminga–Marromeu	87	1969
	Nova Freixo–Vila Cabral	260	1969
	Nova Freixo–Malawi border	76	1970
NIGERIA	Kuru–Maiduguri	635	1964
RHODESIA	Mbizi–Chiredzi	90	1965
	Rutenga–Beitbridge	140	1975
SUDAN	Er Rahad–Nyala	700	1959
	Babanusa–Wau	450	1962
TANZANIA	Mnyusi–Ruvu	190	1963
	Kilosa–Kidatu	109	1965
	Dar es Salaam–Zambia border	970	1974
UGANDA	Kampala–Kasese	333	1956
	Jinja–Bukonte	68	1961
	Soroti–Pakwach	343	1964
ZAIRE	Kamina–Kabalo	450	1956
	Aketi–Bumba	182	1974
ZAMBIA	Kapiri Mposhi–Tanzania border	890	1975

Sources: Diverse.

will move by rail. The motive for building these lines was probably as much political as economic in view of the prevailing southern discontent with rule from Khartoum, and if they are to make much economic impact this will require active steps to promote the development which they make possible.

The Nigerian railway system has been enlarged by a 635 km line from Kuru near Jos to Maiduguri in the extreme north-east, which was opened in stages between 1962 and 1964. As in Sudan, the terrain presented few problems and construction costs were relatively low; but north-east Nigeria is better served by roads, and the new railway is not automatically assured of all the traffic in the area. It has reduced the cost of moving groundnuts from the district to the coast, but it has not had much immediate impact on the country through which it passes. Even over a longer period it is unlikely that the railway itself will stimulate development, as was suggested in the reports recommending its construction.

The most immediately successful of the new rail extensions, like the entirely new lines, are those related to mining developments. The working of manganese in southern Gabon required the construction of a branch in Congo from the Pointe Noire–Brazzaville line to Mbinda, which is linked by a cable way to the mine. The mineral traffic on this line is already

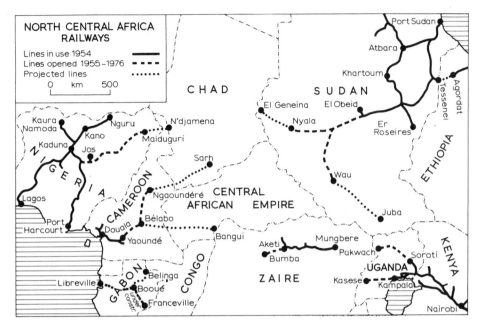

MAP 7.6. Railways in north-central Africa.

very heavy, and it is also handling timber extracted from previously inaccessible parts of Congo. Another heavily used new branch line is that serving the Fria bauxite deposits in Guinea.

The length of railway in Uganda has been much increased by extensions to Kasese in the west and Pakwach in the north. The first made possible copper mining at Kilembe, and the second replaced an out-dated water transport system. Both are handling sufficient traffic to justify their construction, but neither has had any great visible impact on the districts which it serves.

The Portuguese retained a strong faith in railways as agents in economic development through the 1950's and 1960's, and undertook much new construction in both Angola and Mozambique (Map 7.7). In Angola the Moçamedes line was extended from Sa da Bandeira (now Lubango) to Serpa Pinto (now Menongue), and a branch was built to tap the Cassinga iron deposits. On the Benguela Railway a short spur was built to the Cuima iron mines in 1962, and further north a line was begun from Luanda onto the Uige Plateau with the object of assisting agricultural development and no doubt also security. For the same reasons the line leading inland from Nacala in northern Mozambique was extended as far as Vila Cabral. A branch from this has now been built into Malawi, mainly to reduce pressure on the port of Beira by transferring traffic to the under-used port of Nacala. A similar diversion was achieved in 1955, when a long new line was laid from Rhodesia to Maputo.

These new primary lines and extensions account for most recent railway building in tropical Africa. In general they represent a continuation of what has often been termed the "colonial" pattern of links between the interior and coastal ports. There are still few of the lateral lines which produce true rail networks, such as are found in the Maghreb and South Africa. The attainment of independence has certainly brought greater interest in lines designed to aid internal or intra-African movements, but few have yet been built.

151

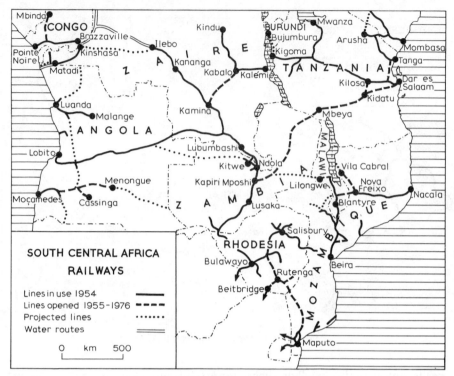

MAP 7.7. Railways in south-central Africa.

Among the lateral links which do exist two were opened as early as 1956. One runs from Kotoku on the eastern Ghana line to Achiasi on an older branch from the western line, thus providing a direct connection between Accra and Takoradi. The building of such a line at that date reflected both Ghana's relative prosperity and the position of Takoradi as its only deep-water port. The traffic handled has not fully justified the investment, especially now that Tema port has been built and road competition for short-distance traffic has become very severe. The other link line is longer, extending 450 km from Kamina in northern Shaba region of Zaire to Kabalo, from which older lines run to Kindu on the navigable Zaire River and to Kalemie on Lake Tanganyika (Map 7.7). This line could greatly assist internal movements although its original primary purpose was to provide a greater range of possible outlets for the minerals of Shaba.

The only important lateral line built since 1956 is that linking the main railway across Tanzania with the northern Tanzania–Kenya–Uganda system. This link, opened in 1963, was designed in part to permit the interchange of rolling stock between the two systems, which have traffic peaks at different seasons, but it was also intended to assist trade between Kenya and Tanzania and inter-district trade within Tanzania. The line is indeed carrying such traffic, though it is not possible to determine whether it has led to an increase in such movements since various other circumstances which affect them have also changed.

Developments of the 1970's

Rail traffic is still increasing in most tropical African countries, and technical improvements are still being made on many lines. Certain new railways are under construction, and many more are planned, representing all stages from further simple routes to the coast to links between different systems. Mineral exploitation continues to justify new primary lines such as that which was opened in 1973 for the haulage of bauxite from the Sangarédi deposit in Guinea. Plans for the first railway within Gabon, originally due to run from Libreville/Owendo to the Belinga iron ore deposit, 565 km inland, have existed for many years, but they cannot be fully implemented until it becomes economically worth while to work this deposit. However, construction of the first 330 km section of the line to Booué began in 1973, since this will permit shipments of at least 1 million tons a year of timber from the interior of the country: and this is now being continued a further 360 km to Franceville in the south-east, serving more timber areas and also the Moanda manganese mines where production could expand far beyond the capacity of the existing outlet through Congo. The whole line is due to be completed in 1980, and will represent an investment of over $500 million, difficult terrain and inflation together having raised construction costs to a level that few other African countries could afford.

Extensions to or branches from existing railways are planned in many countries, sometimes to tap mineral deposits but more often to assist agricultural development. The most important extension undertaken in the early 1970's is in Cameroon, where the Douala–Yaoundé line has been carried 630 km further inland to Ngaoundéré at a cost of $73 million (Map 7.6). This is expected to assist both cash crop and livestock development in northern Cameroon and to permit the exploitation of local bauxite to supply the Edéa aluminium works. It may perhaps also tie the north and south closer together socially and politically. If further funds can be found, the line is to be continued to Sarh (formerly Fort Archambault) in Chad and a branch built to Bangui in the Central African Empire.

The extension of the Cameroon railway into Chad and the CAE is but one of many proposals designed to provide areas in the interior with improved access to the sea. Another plan is for a direct link in Zaire between Kasai Province and Kinshasa, which would enable traffic to and from Shaba to use the *route nationale* without involving trans-shipments to river steamers. An important choice which has to be made in this regard is between an 850 km link from the present K-D-L terminus at Ilebo (formerly Port Francqui) to Kinshasa, and a 1400-km line from Kananga (formerly Luluabourg) passing through Tshikapa and Kikwit, which might cost twice as much but which would not duplicate the existing river route and might assist the development of areas of greater economic potential. There are also firm plans for extending the Kinshasa-Matadi railway as far as Banana, where the scope for new port development is much greater.

The most important of all the recent railway-building projects is certainly the construction of the 1860-km line from Kapiri Mposhi on the old main railway in Zambia to the Tanzanian port of Dar es Salaam (Map 7.7). Many plans for such a line had been made during the colonial period, but there never appeared to be sufficient justification for it until UDI in Rhodesia forced Zambia to seek new routes to the sea. Even then neither the World Bank nor individual Western countries were prepared to support the scheme, and it was China which agreed in 1967 to finance and to build the railway, which was expected to cost about $400 million. Track-laying began in 1970, and with the help of a workforce of 15,000 Chinese and 30,000 local people the line was completed in 1975, well ahead of schedule.

In terms of the political circumstances of 1967 the line was fully justified, and within a few months of opening it was carrying most of Zambia's copper exports since the border with Rhodesia had recently been closed and the alternative route to Lobito was disrupted by conflict in Angola: but as a new political pattern emerges not only in Angola and Mozambique but also in Rhodesia, the need for this further outlet for Zambia may be less evident. If this railway were assured of all Zambia's export and import traffic, it could undoubtedly be profitably operated, but it may have to share this traffic with other railways as well as with the parallel tarred road and oil pipeline. On the other hand, the railway may also assist trade between the two countries, and permit both agricultural and mineral development in southern Tanzania—and perhaps even industrial development based on the coal and iron ore deposits there. Ultimately, therefore, this could prove to be much more than another line linking the interior with the coast, and it could have a substantial impact on the space-economy of both countries.

It was noted above that many governments are interested in improving facilities for intra-African trade, but the prospects for such trade are rarely sufficiently promising to justify the building of new railways specifically for this purpose. Perhaps in time the demand for intra-African movements will increase so much that it will be possible to implement such proposals as those for lines from both Nigeria and Cameroon across Chad to Sudan. These would together provide tropical Africa with an integrated trans-continental network. On the other hand, before that time arrives it may become possible to depend on cheaper road and air transport for most movements of this type.

ROAD TRANSPORT

Traffic

In most tropical African countries road traffic increased extremely rapidly during the 1950's, and in many of them roads first challenged railways as the chief means of transport during this period. Traffic has continued to grow everywhere in the 1960's and 1970's, though generally at a rather slower rate. In contrast to the railways, the roads are particularly important for the movement of people, and the majority of the vehicles using them are private cars although there are some interesting variations in this respect from one country to another (Table 7.4). The total distribution of vehicles within tropical Africa shown on Map 7.8 is therefore greatly influenced by the distribution of high-income groups, especially Europeans. However, the situation is now changing somewhat, for one of the features of the past two decades has been the emergence of a car-owning African elite in each country, and another has been a remarkable proliferation of cars used, legally or otherwise, as taxis.

Many of these taxis and also many buses, especially the "Mammy-wagons" of West Africa, in fact often carry a surprising quantity of goods, even when they are also crammed with passengers. In addition, much short-distance freight haulage now takes place by lorry, while most of the goods carried on the railways make a short journey by lorry to or from a station. Partly in order to avoid the handling which this involves, ever longer journeys with ever bulkier loads are now being undertaken by road vehicles. Although road transport is still generally more expensive than rail, in tropical Africa it is often quicker, and everywhere it is more flexible. Capacity can be built up gradually as demand develops, and goods can be moved in small quantities to or from a large number of points. For these reasons the share of freight movement handled by road is increasing steadily in most parts of the region.

The ratio between vehicles and population differs greatly from one country to another, but this is one respect in which the gap between the richer and poorer countries has recently

TABLE 7.4. TROPICAL AFRICA: MOTOR VEHICLES IN USE (000 vehicles)

	Total 1956	Total 1972	Private cars 1972	Commercial vehicles 1972	Increase 1956–72	
					thousand vehicles	Vehicles per thousand people
Rhodesia	81	195	130	65	114	20
Kenya	57	133	112	21	76	6
Zaire	49	143	74	69	94	4
Nigeria	37	189	120	69	152	3
Zambia	37	123	70	53	86	20
Ghana	28	71	40	31	43	5
Angola	26	149	115	34	123	20
Mozambique	24	111	89	22	87	10
Tanzania	24	73	35	38	49	4
Senegal	24	67	43	24	43	9
Uganda	24	37	27	10	13	1
Cameroon	21	76	39	37	55	9
Ivory Coast	20	147	90	57	127	21
Sudan	20	50	29	21	30	2
Ethiopia	15	54	41	13	39	1
Guinea	8	21	10	11	13	3
Congo	7?	27	17	10	20	17
Malawi	7	18	10	8	11	2
CAE	6	11	7	4	5	2
Mali	6	11	5	6	5	1
Sierra Leone	5	32	21	11	27	10
Somalia	5	16	8	8	11	3
Benin	4	22	14	8	18	6
Chad	4	11	5	6	7	2
Gabon	3	17	10	7	14	27
Togo	3	16	10	6	13	6
Upper Volta	3	16	8	8	13	2
Niger	3	15	7	8	12	3
Liberia	2	22	12	10	20	12
Rwanda	2	8	5	3	6	2
Burundi	2	7	5	2	5	2
Mauritania	1	9	4	5	8	7
Gambia	1	5	3	2	4	8

Source: United Nations, *Statistical Yearbook.*

been somewhat narrowed at least in relative terms. In some poor countries which had very few vehicles in the mid-1950's, such as Niger and Upper Volta, the number in use has more than quadrupled in fifteen years, although the total is still very small (Table 7.4). In some of the more prosperous countries, notably Rhodesia, the rate of growth has been much slower, although the absolute numbers of new vehicles have been far greater.

Not surprisingly, the most impressive increase in vehicle numbers in relation to population has taken place in countries which have enjoyed an economic boom in recent years, notably Ivory Coast and Gabon. A similar increase had taken place in Ghana in the early 1950's, but there subsequent growth, particularly of commercial vehicle traffic, has been remarkably modest. The same is true of Uganda, and perhaps both there and in Ghana more commercial vehicles were in use in the mid-1950's than the demand really warranted. All types of road traffic have also increased relatively slowly in Kenya, where European

155

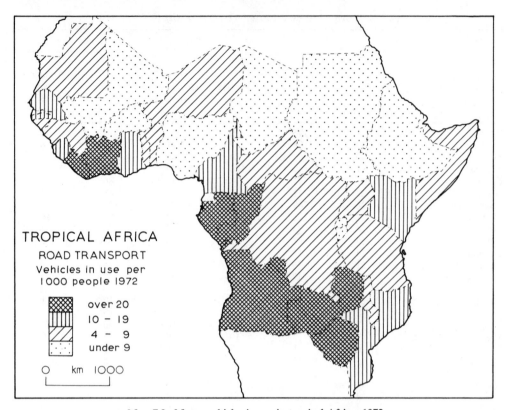

MAP 7.8. Motor vehicles in use in tropical Africa, 1972.

settlement has passed its peak, and such settlement certainly contributed to the more rapid increase in vehicle registrations in Angola and Mozambique during the 1960's, for most of the new Portuguese settlers in the towns owned a car and those in the country generally owned a lorry or van. Among the larger countries, Sudan and Ethiopia are those in which road transport has made least progress in terms of vehicles in use.

It would be interesting to know where most of the vehicles travel within each country, and especially whether traffic is increasing more rapidly in the large towns and their immediate surroundings, or in the more remote rural areas. Unfortunately, very little is known about traffic patterns in most African countries; but most of the counts that are made suggest that it is on the roads that are already most heavily used that the most rapid increase is occurring. Thus while contrasts in traffic density between countries may in some cases have been reduced, within countries they have generally increased. This is certainly the impression gained from driving on almost deserted roads across, say, much of Nigeria, and then finding oneself in the jammed streets of Lagos.

Road Construction

The increasing importance of road transport has necessitated large expenditure on road improvements in most countries (Plate 20). Since the traffic is generally heavily concentrated in the most developed parts of each country, it is there that most improvements have been made: but at the same time many new highways have been built into less developed dis-

156

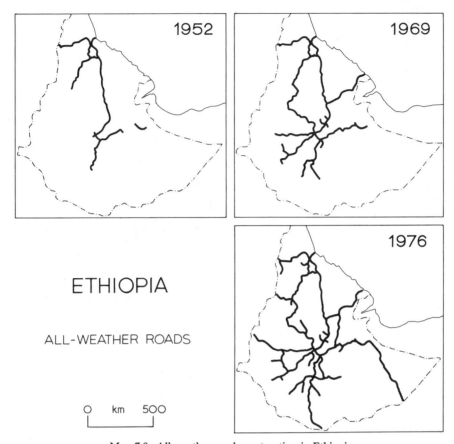

MAP 7.9. All-weather road construction in Ethiopia.

tricts, and many minor roads have been built to serve communities which previously had no road access.

Among the countries in which roads have been given a particularly high priority for development expenditure is Ethiopia, where poor communications are clearly a major obstacle to economic advance, and where the role of railways is very small. The Italians were very active in road building there during their brief occupation, but during the 1940's many of the roads which they had built fell into disrepair. In recent years many have been reconstructed, largely with American funds, and various other new roads have been built (Map 7.9) such as that following the Awash valley from Awash township to Tendaho, and another leading south to the Kenya border.

Much has also been done recently with American funds in Liberia, which, in contrast to Ethiopia, had witnessed very little road construction before 1952. There were only 400 km of public roads in the whole country in that year, but by 1964 the figure had been raised to 2700 km (Map 4.4). Part of the expenditure incurred has in fact sometimes been criticized on the grounds that some roads have been built to a higher standard than the level of traffic warrants. In parts of Nigeria the road network was quite dense even in the early 1950's, but many of the roads were not good enough to withstand the traffic which was developing, and much has since been spent on improvements (Map 7.10). In addition some

157

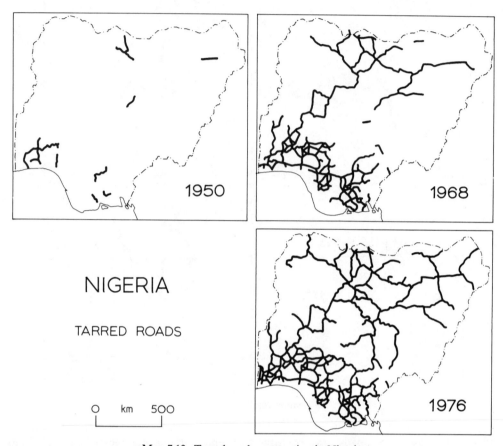

1950

1968

NIGERIA

TARRED ROADS

0   km   500

1976

MAP 7.10. Tarred road construction in Nigeria.

important new roads have been built, such as that linking Lagos and Ibadan with Benin city and the east, which incorporated a $15 million bridge over the Niger River.

New and improved roads were given a high priority by the Portuguese in Angola and Mozambique, partly to assist economic development, but also to assist in security operations. In Mozambique a long new section of road has provided for the first time an all-season link between Maputo and Beira, while Angola now has one of the most extensive networks of tarmac highway in tropical Africa (Map 7.11).

Countries in which less attention has been given to road improvements in the last twenty years include Rhodesia, Ghana, Sudan, and Gabon. In both Rhodesia and Ghana the road network was already exceptionally good in the early 1950's, and has been considered adequate to withstand the subsequent increase in traffic. In fact many roads in Ghana have since fallen into serious disrepair, the best-known development there having been the opening of a multi-lane motorway between Accra and Tema considerably in advance of traffic requirements. In Rhodesia the main change has been the complete tarring of many roads which formerly had just two strips of tar along their length.

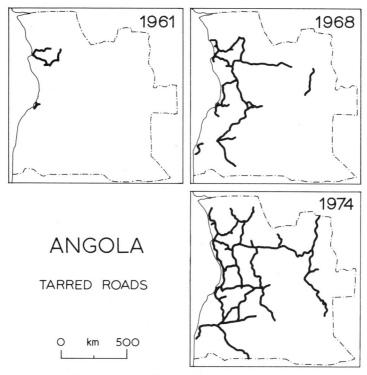

MAP 7.11. Tarred road construction in Angola.

The situation is very different in Sudan and Gabon, both of which were very poorly served with roads in the 1950's and are little better served today (Map 7.12). In Sudan most roads are still only open for part of the year, and the only tarmac road outside the towns is that which has progressed very slowly from Khartoum towards the Gezira. There is probably no other country in which emphasis has been placed so heavily on rail rather than road development, one reason being that whereas the terrain is generally suitable for railways, road-building material is scarce in most districts. Gabon does not even have any railways yet, and is therefore so poorly equipped with surface transport that it is unusually dependent on air transport. However, with the aid of oil revenues, and in an effort to spread the benefits of these more widely, a substantial road-building programme is now planned.

The distribution of road construction within each country reflects both the pattern of economic development and that of other transport facilities. Many of the apparently isolated sections of tarmac road shown on Map 7.12, for example, are feeders to railways. In general, however, the past two decades have witnessed a change in the formerly widespread policy of giving a low priority to roads between centres already linked by rail. It is only during this period, for instance, that the roads from Lagos to northern Nigeria and from Mombasa to the highlands of Kenya have been tarred. While these road improvements clearly could be delayed no longer, there has not always been as much co-ordination between new road and rail developments as there might have been, often because different bodies have been responsible for the planning of each. Thus in Uganda fewer feeder roads were built in the 1950's to the western railway extension than had been intended, and in the 1960's plans were made to reconstruct and tar the Soroti–Gulu road whilst the northern rail

159

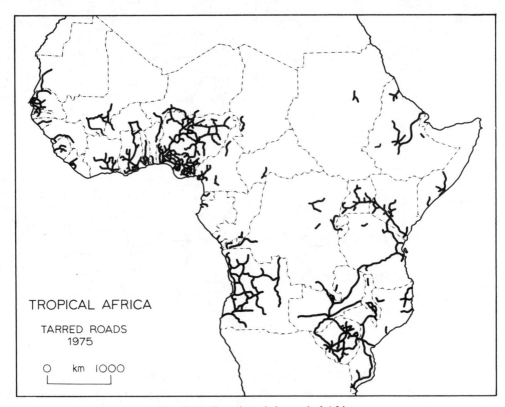

MAP 7.12. Tarred roads in tropical Africa.

extension was being laid parallel to it. Fortunately, priority in road improvement was then switched to the Kampala–Gulu road, which is complementary to the rail network.

One of the ways in which road development can most effectively complement the rail network is in linking one African country with another. In the 1950's there were still few truly international highways, but much has been done to remedy this situation even if not on the scale of the Pan-American highway. In West Africa, for instance, there is now a tarred road from Nigeria across Benin and Togo to Ghana, while in Upper Volta priority is being given to the reconstruction of the roads to the borders of Ghana and Mali rather than that between the country's main towns, which are connected by rail. In Kenya the improvement of the Mombasa–Nairobi road was followed by the tarring of the links with Tanzania and Uganda, and now a new route has been forged across the arid north to Ethiopia. The road between Tanzania and Zambia was inadequate for the heavy traffic which resulted from the diversion of Zambian overseas trade after Rhodesia's UDI. Priority was therefore given in both countries to its improvement, and the whole of the Zambia section was tarred in 1967–9 at a cost of $35 million, while the Tanzania section was completed two years later.

It is extremely difficult to assess the benefits of new road building, but it is a task which must be attempted in many parts of tropical Africa to assist in the formulation of future investment policies. It is clear at least that the local impact is by no means the same everywhere. In Nigeria the opening of new roads has often led to immediate changes in the

PLATE 17. Port development at Mombasa, Kenya. The old wharves along the shore of Mombasa Island have recently been supplemented by additional berths at Kipevu on the mainland, shown here in the foreground.

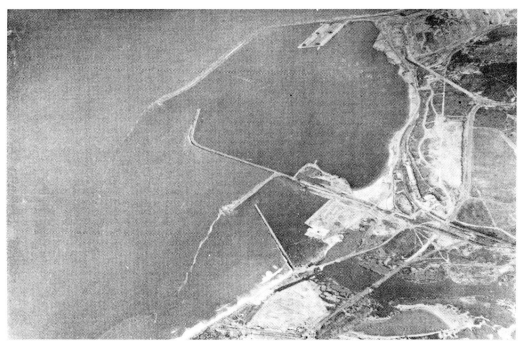

PLATE 18. Port development at Tema, Ghana. In this case the 1950s witnessed the construction of an entirely new artificial harbour, beside which an industrial town is growing.

PLATE 19. Railway construction in Uganda. After descending into the rift valley the western Uganda extension had to traverse the swamps fringing Lake George, involving considerable costs.

PLATE 20. Road construction in Zambia. Another economic problem in both rail and road building projects in many areas (such as between Zambia and Tanzania) is the need to cross vast tracts which offer little traffic, present or potential.

PLATE 21. Ibadan, the largest "traditional" city in tropical Africa. The impact of European administration was here relatively slight, and even today the city is changing only slowly.

PLATE 22. Nairobi, perhaps the epitome of the "colonial" city. The city developed very rapidly as the headquarters of the British administration in Kenya, and is again growing rapidly in the post-independence period. This is involving both the expansion of the business area from the foreground to the right of the picture, and the rising of new blocks in the administrative zone behind.

PLATE 23. The University of Ghana, Legon, is one of a number of institutions which are playing a vital role in African development although they are sometimes critically viewed as "ivory towers".

PLATE 24. Certainly higher education for the elite must be matched by efforts to spread education far more widely among the new generation and even among the old, as here in northern Ghana.

pattern of settlement and trade, whereas in most parts of East Africa this process seems to take place more slowly. The savings in vehicle operating costs resulting from any particular type of road improvement may be similar from place to place, but it is much more difficult to generalize about the effect that these savings will have on development at either end of an improved road.

As with other means of transport the benefits of road building will be greatest where problems of inadequate communications are clearly hindering development. In some countries one of the most urgent problems is now the easing of traffic congestion in the cities, as has lately been partially achieved in Lagos at a cost of $25 million by the opening of a second bridge between the island and the mainland. However, most recent investment has been allocated to the improvement of existing roads between towns. Parts of the West African forest belt, for example, now have a relatively elaborate system of tarred roads, reflecting both climatic conditions which frequently put earth roads out of use, and an unusually high density of traffic. On the other hand, there are many areas, especially in the savanna lands, where even the main roads will be able to withstand any likely traffic in the near future without a tarred surface, but where at present all communications are cut in the rainy season. In many cases only a modest expenditure is required to ensure that the roads do not become impassable under any normal weather conditions. Even this does not exhaust the range of investment possibilities amongst which priorities must be allocated, for in every country there are many communities who have no road access at all. The building of even unpretentious dry-weather roads to serve these people may permit commercial activity where none took place before, and in this way may sometimes produce the greatest developmental impact for a given expenditure.

AIR TRANSPORT

In Africa, as elsewhere, the role of air transport is restricted, for despite all the advances of modern technology it is still expensive. Nevertheless, it has a very important contribution to make to African development. It shares with road transport the advantages of great flexibility and a relatively low ratio of fixed capital costs to operating costs, so that it can be built up from small beginnings in line with demand; and, unlike road transport, it is particularly suited to the long-distance movements between scattered "islands" of development which the requirements of this continent often involve. Furthermore, air transport suffers from less competition in tropical Africa than in areas where surface transport facilities are more highly developed.

For these reasons, air transport is already a well-established feature of the African scene, and is now expanding very rapidly (Table 7.5 and see Table 7.8). Between 1958 and 1967 passenger traffic on the airlines of tropical Africa rose by 12% a year, while cargo traffic rose by 20% a year. In 1967 the totals amounted to 2500 million passenger-km and 100 million ton-km of freight movement. Each represented less than 2% of the world total, but it is notable that the rate of growth was above the world average, so that in this respect at least there is some evidence that tropical Africa may have been catching up with more developed regions. More recently, however, the rates of increase have slowed to 10% annually in each case, comparable to the world average. The air services are very widely distributed, for every state has at least one airport. Most have several, so that air transport meets some needs for internal movement as well as linking the state with other parts of the world.

TABLE 7.5. TRAFFIC OF MAJOR AIRLINES IN TROPICAL AFRICA

	Million passenger-km					Cargo: million ton-km		
	1960	1964	1968	1972	1974	1960	1968	1974
Air Afrique	—	537	646	853	1110	—	55	119
East African Airways	194	357	666	860	1019	3	22	27
Air Zaire	?	117	331	524	655	?	9	34
Ethiopian Airlines	105	213	299	431	455	4	16	17
Nigerian Airways	38	191	149	321	355	1	4	7
Sudan Airways	46	134	152	158	244	1	3	4
Ghana Airways	60	118	132	135	149	0	5	4
Central African Airways	142	129	160	—	—	1	2	—
Zambia Airways	—	—	—	320	326	—	—	20

Sources: Diverse national.

The rapid expansion of traffic has involved substantial investment in new airport facilities as well as the purchase of aircraft for the new or greatly expanded African airlines. The frequency of flights on many established routes has been increased, but new routes have also been opened up, and there is more evidence of a general change in the network than in the case of either railways or roads.

New Airports

Most African countries do not lag so far behind other parts of the world in terms of airport facilities as they do in most other forms of transport infrastructure. Many were provided with international airports in the pre-war and early post-war periods; and much recent investment has been devoted to the improvement of these, partly to satisfy the standards required by international airlines, and partly because an airport more than anything else forms the window through which a new nation is seen by others. Examples include the building of a new 3000 m runway at Accra in 1961, at a cost of $5 million, and the expansion of Bangui airport to international standards in 1965–7 at a cost of $6 million. Other recent developments of this type have taken place at Lungi airport, which serves Freetown, and at Salisbury, which now has one of the longest runways in the world. In addition, improvements have been made at many of the small airfields which are used for domestic services, some of which have recently been provided for the first time with a tarmac runway and landing aids.

However, some completely new airports have been built, such as those opened at both Kinshasa and Nairobi in 1958, in each case to replace one that could no longer meet the demands made on it and could not easily be enlarged. A similar development has taken place at Lusaka, where a new airport costing $16 million, and capable of receiving all aircraft then in service, was opened in 1967. Rwanda had no international airport at the time of independence, so in the late 1960's one was built at Kigali, where only a tiny airstrip had existed previously. The process has continued in the 1970's: thus 1973 witnessed the completion of a new airport at Bamako and the start of one at Douala.

New Airlines

Many of the airlines now operating from African countries have been established in the period since the various states gained independence, though there are several important exceptions such as Ethiopian Airlines and East African Airways. Most of the states of former French West and Equatorial Africa joined in forming Air Afrique in 1961, and more recently most of them have also established their own national airlines to operate their domestic services. Thus Air Senegal was formed in 1963 and Air Bangui in 1966. Regrettably perhaps, some of the inter-territorial airlines inherited from the colonial period have been split up. Thus the West African Airways Corporation, established as a subsidiary of BOAC, gave way in 1958 to Ghana Airways and Nigeria Airways; in 1967 Central African Airways was dissolved and replaced by three national airlines; and in 1976 East African Airways seemed likely to disintegrate.

In some cases the benefit resulting from the creation of national airlines must be sought in terms of either prestige or security rather than economics; but some of the larger African airlines, such as Ethiopian Airlines and Air Zaire, are successful commercial concerns and provide a valuable source of income for the states which own them. Nevertheless, as in many other parts of the world, the proliferation of rival airlines does lead to some duplication of services, and there is a case for some degree of rationalization.

New Routes

A comparison between the route networks of 1956 and 1976 indicates both a general expansion and some significant changes in the overall pattern. The main demand for air transport during the colonial period was for movement between the metropolitan powers in Europe and their African colonies. Even today, the best connections from most African countries are still with the former metropolitan power; but these have increasingly been supplemented by flights to other European capitals, and even to other parts of the world. Substantial changes of this type occurred, for instance, in Ghana in the late 1950's and Ivory Coast in the early 1960's (Table 7.6). On the other hand, poorer countries such as Benin or Malawi cannot offer sufficient traffic to justify such a development. It is also

TABLE 7.6. AIR ROUTES TO EUROPE FROM SELECTED WEST AFRICAN AIRPORTS

| | Weekly flights from | | | | | | | | | |
| | Accra Ghana | | | | Abidjan Ivory Coast | | | Lagos Nigeria | | |
	1956	1962	1970	1976	1962	1970	1976	1962	1970	1976
Austria	—	—	—	—	—	—	—	—	—	1
Belgium	—	—	—	—	—	1	1	—	1	1
Denmark	—	—	—	—	—	—	—	—	—	2
France	—	—	2	1	14	18	14	2	2	3
Germany (E.)	—	—	—	—	—	—	—	—	—	1
Germany (W.)	—	2	2	1	—	—	—	3	2	3
Greece	—	—	—	—	—	—	—	—	—	1
Hungary	—	—	—	1	—	—	—	—	1	—
Italy	6	4	5	5	—	2	2	5	5	5
Netherlands	—	4	2	2	—	2	—	2	2	3
Portugal	2	2	1	—	—	—	—	—	—	—
Spain	—	1	1	—	—	2	1	1	3	1
Switzerland	—	3	2	2	—	2	3	3	3	3
United Kingdom	7	6	6	6	—	—	—	8	10	14
USSR	—	1	—	1	—	—	—	—	1	—
Yugoslavia	—	1	—	—	—	—	—	—	—	—

Source: ABC World Airways Guide.

TABLE 7.7. INTRA–AFRICAN AIR ROUTES FROM SELECTED WEST AFRICAN AIRPORTS

	Weekly flights from								
	Monrovia Liberia			Abidjan Ivory Coast			Lagos Nigeria		
	1962	1970	1976	1962	1970	1976	1962	1970	1976
Angola	—	—	—	—	—	—	—	—	1
Benin	—	1	1	4	5	10	2	3	4
Cameroon	—	2	2	3	5	7	4	4	4
Congo	—	1	—	—	2	4	1	1	3
Eq. Guinea	—	—	—	—	—	—	—	—	1
Ethiopia	1	—	—	—	—	4	1	3	4
Gabon	—	—	2	—	2	7	—	1	3
Gambia	2	2	5	2	2	5	—	2	2
Ghana	8	10	8	9	9	10	12	13	14
Guinea	—	—	—	1	2	—	—	—	—
Ivory Coast	5	11	12	—	—	—	3	7	8
Kenya	—	1	3	—	—	—	1	3	5
Liberia	—	—	—	5	11	12	3	7	7
Mali	—	—	1	3	2	4	—	—	—
Mauritania	—	—	—	—	1	1	—	—	—
Niger	—	—	—	4	3	4	—	—	2
Nigeria	3	7	7	4	7	9	—	—	—
Senegal	9	8	9	9	7	12	2	5	5
Sierra Leone	5	10	12	3	7	9	—	5	3
Sudan	2	—	—	—	—	—	2	2	1
Tanzania	—	—	1	—	—	—	—	—	1
Togo	—	—	1	2	4	8	2	3	5
Uganda	—	1	—	—	—	—	—	3	1
Upper Volta	—	—	—	3	3	3	—	—	—
Zaire	2	1	2	—	—	2	2	3	4

Source: ABC World Airways Guide.

notable that most of the change had taken place by about 1966, since when patterns have been relatively stable. Indeed, in some cases numbers of flights have been cut back, partly through the use of larger aircraft.

Air routes joining one tropical African country with another were very poorly developed at the time of independence, except where they formed parts of inter-continental routes, or where a high degree of economic integration had been achieved. By 1970 East African Airways operated flights from Nairobi to Dar es Salaam forty-five times a week and to Entebbe thirty-seven times a week, but this was not matched anywhere else. Yet the position has generally improved in recent years, especially with the introduction of flights across the continent from east to west (Table 7.7). It is certainly for this type of connection, which at present generally involves the movement of people rather than bulky produce, that air transport is particularly well suited; and there is every prospect of further expansion, especially if closer Pan-African ties bring a greater demand for movements of this type.

Air transport is used for internal movements far less than in most Latin American countries, but some extensions to domestic services have taken place. In many countries, such as Nigeria and Ethiopia, these developed rapidly in the first decade after World War II, and the subsequent period has been one of consolidation. In others, however, such as Gabon and Mauritania, in each of which the population is very thinly spread and poorly served with surface transport, many new domestic routes have been opened up since 1956 (Map 7.13).

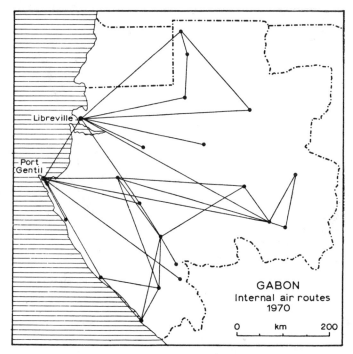

MAP 7.13. Internal air routes in Gabon.

   The new African airlines have developed their international route networks partly at the expense of the well-established European airlines, but partly by increasing the frequency of flights on existing routes and even by establishing new routes. At the same time new routes have been established by other European airlines, especially by those of countries which had no colonial territories in Africa, such as Switzerland, the Netherlands, the Soviet Union, and the Scandinavian countries. One of the major United States airlines also now operates services to tropical Africa, and East Africa's important ties with India are reflected in air routes crossing the Indian Ocean. Thus whereas before independence Dar es Salaam airport was used only by BOAC, Central African Airways, and East African Airways, it now handles the planes of eighteen airlines. Nairobi is now the best connected of all airports in tropical Africa, with twenty-six airlines providing direct links with over forty places outside East Africa, even excluding operators of charter flights.

   There are some exceptions to the general pattern of expansion. In some countries the network of domestic services provided in the early post-war period has proved too costly to operate, and certain routes have had to be abandoned. Nigeria provided an example of this even before the strife of 1967–9 brought further withdrawals of services. In Senegal and Liberia certain services have been cut following major road improvements.

   A further reason for changes in the pattern of routes is the increasing range of modern aircraft. In the past, services between Europe and tropical Africa normally involved a stop in North Africa, but this is no longer necessary. Similarly, the number of flights calling at Kano in northern Nigeria has fallen, as it has become possible for aircraft to fly from Europe to Lagos or Accra without a stop. Political considerations have brought a sharp reduction in the number of flights between tropical and South Africa, and flights to Europe by South

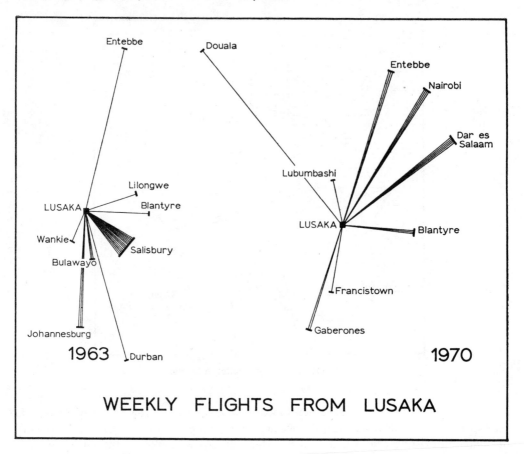

MAP 7.14. The changing pattern of air routes from Lusaka, Zambia, to destinations in other African countries.

African Airways can now stop only in Rhodesia, Gabon, and Ivory Coast. In addition all flights between Zambia and Rhodesia have ceased, but this has been counter-balanced by a great increase in flights between Zambia and East Africa (Map 7.14).

New Traffic

All the new routes that have been established, together with increasing frequencies and larger planes on existing routes, have made possible the great increase in traffic noted above. This growth is best measured by the number of passengers and volume of cargo handled at the main airports of the region (Table 7.8). Where there has been only a small increase in traffic this is generally the result of changing political patterns, as in the case of Brazzaville and Salisbury. In most cases there has been a steady expansion, and in some a phenomenal growth.

The greatest expansion in absolute terms in the late 1950's and early 1960's occurred in countries which already generated substantial air traffic in the mid-1950's, such as Rhodesia, Kenya, and Ghana. In Ghana growth was especially rapid around 1960, and has slowed down in more recent years as a result of unfavourable economic and political conditions. In

TABLE 7.8. AIRPORT TRAFFIC IN TROPICAL AFRICA

Major airports	Thousand passengers embarking and disembarking		Hundred tons of cargo loaded and unloaded	
	1962	1972	1962	1972
Salisbury	354	444	24	32
Nairobi	240	823	52	225
Dakar	144	237	39	68
Kinshasa	131	266	67	185
Lagos	115	290	72	?
Accra	111	209	12	29
Douala	101	234	92	159
Dar es Salaam	93	239	21	46
Abidjan	93	276	29	116
Brazzaville	73	88	?	92
Conakry	56	90	?	13
Luanda	51	141	9	38
Entebbe	49	169	7	43
Libreville	48	164	17	144
Blantyre	45	225	?	18
Maputo	44	186	5	39
N'djamena	43	64	107	115
Addis Ababa	32	198	7	58
Lusaka	?	192	?	49
Khartoum	?	170	?	60

Sources: United Nations, *Air Transport in Africa*; International Civil Aviation Organization, *Digest of Statistics*; National sources.

Kenya, however, it has been accelerating, partly as a result of the rapid development of the tourist industry. The most remarkable traffic growth of all has occurred in Ethiopia, partly because of the new role of Addis Ababa as the headquarters of the OAU and the UN Economic Commission for Africa.

There has also been a rapid expansion of traffic, from small beginnings, in such countries as Gabon, as a result of the impact of new mining enterprises. Between 1960 and 1967 the number of passengers using both Libreville and Port Gentil airports quadrupled. Even countries such as Togo, which have had new development of this type only on a smaller scale, have experienced a rapid increase in air traffic.

In general the rate of growth has been even higher for cargo than for passenger traffic, although the latter is still much the more important almost everywhere. Perhaps the most notable cargo movement, that of meat from Chad to Cameroon and Congo was well established in the 1950's, and has expanded very little: but many other movements such as that of fresh fruit from Nairobi to Europe, have increased at a very rapid rate.

CONCLUSIONS

No fundamental change has taken place in the broad pattern of transport in tropical Africa in recent years, even though many important individual developments have occurred. The most impressive of these are essentially of the type that is often termed "colonial", for they are designed to assist the export overseas of such primary products as the iron ore of Liberia. While some of the new ports, railways, and roads have assisted the spread of commercial activity to new areas, most of the transport investment that has taken place has tended to consolidate well-established patterns. A circular process is at work whereby the colonial transport network has greatly influenced the spatial pattern of economic development, and this in turn determines where most of the demand for improved transport facilities arises.

To some extent the perpetuation of the present pattern may represent the best use of scarce resources, but there is an undoubted need for some improvement of facilities for movement within and between African countries. A little progress has indeed already been made in this direction. The main role of the ports and railways is still the handling of overseas exports and imports, and most new investment in these fields has been undertaken for this purpose; but the transport media which are expanding most rapidly today, roads and airways, are gradually providing improved communications within tropical Africa.

Although transport facilities reflect mainly economic needs, there are many ways in which the political map still has a great influence on the transport map. One recent development which exemplifies this is Mauritania's iron-ore railway, which makes a long detour around former Spanish territory. Sometimes the political pattern may lead to what in economic terms may constitute a duplication of facilities. Certain of the new ports that have been built, and also perhaps the laying of a railway as well as a pipeline and tarred road between Zambia and Tanzania, provide examples of this. It does not, of course, follow that such developments should not take place, for the political circumstances may fully justify them. On the other hand, political barriers to movement should be reduced wherever possible. In general the trend is now towards greater co-ordination between at least some African countries in respect of transport facilities; but this is certainly a field in which there is scope for far more integration in the future, for instance between former British and former French territories in West Africa.

The improvement of communications undoubtedly has a great role to play in the economic development of tropical Africa, although experience in several countries in recent years has shown that investment of this nature will not automatically bring about such development. Railway building, for example, is unlikely to have the same dramatic effects now as it had early in this century, when it often provided the first means of transport other than human porterage, and when in many places there was no entrenched pattern of commercial activities. The improvement of transport facilities is only proving beneficial where their inadequacy previously formed a barrier to development or where it threatened to do so as demands increased. It is usually of particular value where simultaneous investment is made in other fields to take advantage of the opportunities which the new facilities provide.

Undoubtedly there will be a need for further improvements in the near future to handle increasing quantities of exports and imports, to permit closer relations between African states, and to assist the expansion of the internal exchange economy within each of them. New transport facilities may also enable the processes of economic development to permeate more thoroughly to every part of each state, though it can be argued that as far as industry and services are concerned they are likely to assist even greater concentration in the existing foci of activity rather than to lead to greater dispersal. This need for investment in transport will continue to be greater in tropical Africa than in many other parts of the world as long as most people gain their livelihood by producing bulky goods rather than by providing services. As improvements take place there must be close co-ordination between the various transport media to ensure that the new developments are complementary to each other rather than a mere duplication of facilities. There is no single answer for tropical Africa to the question of the relative merits of each means of transport, for the situation differs greatly from place to place. In many cases it is necessary to invest in two or more simultaneously if each is to yield the greatest possible benefit.

There is little doubt that some new ports will have to be built in the near future, though there are strong arguments for acknowledging the universal trend towards port concentration and allocating most investment to the improvement of the busiest existing ports. The age of railway building may be over in many countries, but not necessarily in tropical Africa as a whole. A railway still often provides the most economical method of moving large quantities of bulky produce between fixed points, and new lines may be essential to certain development projects especially in the field of mineral exploitation. However, as in the case of ports, it can be argued that the largest share of investment should be used for the improvement of existing facilities, particularly since railway operation benefits considerably from economies of scale.

The situation is perhaps different in the case of road development. As traffic increases many of the present main roads will have to be improved, notably those linking neighbouring territories not connected by railways. However, there is a case for giving greater emphasis to the extension of the road network to reach as large a proportion of the population as possible. In many places there is an urgent need for new low-cost local roads to reduce the great burden of headloading, and perhaps for a subsidized supply of bicycles. For local movements there is no real alternative to road transport, whereas for long distance movements not only rail but also air transport provide alternatives.

While improved railways may continue to handle most of the bulky freight traffic especially on routes between the interior and the coast, air transport is becoming increasingly important particularly for passenger movement. The recent rapid development of air transport is likely to continue, in certain cases for internal movements within states, more extensively to link tropical Africa with other continents, but perhaps especially to connect the various isolated islands of economic development within the region.

The pattern of transport development in the future will, of course, be much affected by new technological advances. For instance, an increasing range of commodities are now being moved by pipeline. It is possible that soon even iron ore or bauxite may be transported most economically in this way, especially if a pipeline extends out to an offshore terminal and therefore takes the place of both railway and port facilities. If technical advances could greatly lower the cost of air transport, this could be of enormous value to tropical Africa, enabling many parts of the region to bypass other stages of transport improvement. In such a situation as this, transport might again provide a key to revolutionary economic changes, as it did seventy years ago.

SELECTED READING

The most useful general discussions of transport in Africa are:
    W. A. HANCE, *African Economic Development* (New York, 1967), ch. 5;
    A. M. KAMARCK, *The Economics of African Development* (New York, 1971), ch. 8;
    G. H. T. KIMBLE, *Tropical Africa* (New York, 1960), ch. 11.
Several important recent transport developments are discussed in:
    G. ARNOLD and R. WEISS, *Strategic Highways of Africa* (London, 1977).
Detailed studies of African ports are provided in:
    B. S. HOYLE and D. HILLING (ed.), *Seaports and Development in Tropical Africa* (London, 1970);

B. S. Hoyle, *The Seaports of East Africa* (Nairobi, 1967);

R. J. Peterec, *Dakar and West African Economic Development* (New York, 1967).

Navigation on two African rivers is the subject of:

B. J. Turton, River transport in the less developed countries, in B. S. Hoyle (ed.), *Spatial Aspects of Development* (London, 1974), pp. 323–44.

Examples of new railway construction are discussed in:

K. M. Barbour, Survey of the Bornu railway extension, *Nigerian Geographical Journal* **10**, 11–28 (1967);

J. B. Murairi, Incidences économiques de la jonction des chemins de fer BCK et CFMK, *Cahiers Economiques et Sociaux* **8**, 515–76 (1970);

A. M. O'Connor, *Railways and Development in Uganda* (Nairobi, 1965).

The fullest discussion of road transport for an African country is:

R. Hofmeier, *Transport and Economic Development in Tanzania* (Munich, 1973).

A useful study of air transport is:

S. Reichman, *Air Transport in West Africa* (Paris, 1965).

Studies covering various modes at the national scale include:

A. Huybrechts, *Transports et Structures de Développement au Congo* (Paris, 1970) (on Zaire);

R. N. van chi Bonnardel, four papers on Senegal in *Bulletin de l'IFAN* 32–33 (1970–1).

A valuable attempt to construct and test a general model of transport development, but with special reference to Africa, is:

E. J. Taaffe *et al.*, Transport expansion in under developed countries, *Geographical Review* **53**, 503–29 (1963).

This paper and applications of the model to East Africa and Liberia are reproduced in:

B. S. Hoyle (ed.), *Transport and Development* (London, 1973).

8

URBANIZATION

ONE change that is commonly associated with economic development is the growth of towns and cities, and such urban growth is undoubtedly one of the most widespread processes taking place in tropical Africa today. The towns have been expanding rapidly throughout most of this century, and the total number of urban dwellers in the region is now roughly doubling every ten or twelve years. This is a more rapid rate of increase than in any other large region of the world, and is in some ways a very disturbing phenomenon. Even the largest cities in tropical Africa, Lagos and Kinshasa, are small in comparison with Calcutta or São Paulo, having about 2 million inhabitants each, and it is doubtful if the region can yet be considered "over urbanized". But many problems arise from the rapidity of the urban growth, especially since the population is generally increasing much faster than employment opportunities. The growth has taken place from such a low base that the proportion of the whole population that lives in towns is still small; yet these towns play a role in the life of most African countries quite out of proportion to the size of their population. They act as focal points in the political, social, and economic affairs of each country, and even people who have never visited a town are profoundly affected by decisions made there and by transactions undertaken there.

Some of the activities already discussed, notably manufacturing, normally take place in the towns; but so also do many others, sometimes labelled together as "services", which have not been considered individually. The most important of these services are wholesale and retail trade, which must develop as subsistence production gives way to production for sale, and administration, which always seems to occupy a rapidly increasing number of people as economies and societies become more complex. Others are education and medical facilities, which form important parts of the development programmes of all African states, and which are often concentrated in the urban areas. There are a few towns which depend largely on some productive activity such as mining or manufacturing, but the chief function of the great majority is the provision of services for the people of the surrounding area.

In some parts of tropical Africa substantial towns have been in existence for many centuries. In West Africa, for example, there was during the medieval period a series of towns on the southern margin of the Sahara, of which Timbuktu was perhaps the most renowned. A little to the south, Kano has a history extending back well over 700 years. in the forest belt even further south, town development did not begin so early, but Kumasi In Ghana, Abomey in Benin, and many of the Yoruba towns of south-west Nigeria were well established before the Europeans penetrated inland (Plate 21). In many other areas, however, there is no indigenous urban tradition, and all towns have been established since the arrival of the Europeans (Plate 22). In Zambia and Rhodesia, for instance, none of the present towns were founded before 1890.

In tropical Africa as a whole, the majority of towns and cities are of colonial origin, and while some of these were founded several centuries ago, especially around the coast, most of their growth has occurred during this century. Furthermore, most of the indigenous towns which have grown rapidly have done so to a large extent as a result of colonial influence. Even where administration was not in the hands of any European power, as in Ethiopia, contact with Europe has made a large contribution to the urban development that has taken place. The distribution, and the character, of the towns and cities therefore constitutes an important part of the colonial legacy inherited by the new states of tropical Africa. The continuing urban development in these states may follow closely the pattern that has been set during the first half of this century: or it may take new forms and produce a very different distribution pattern within the next few decades.

THE DISTRIBUTION OF TOWNS IN THE MID-1950's

The distribution of towns shown on Map 8.1 includes all those that had a population of over 50,000 by the mid-1950's. There was a fairly even spread of urban development over much of tropical Africa; but several large tracts were devoid of towns of this size, notably

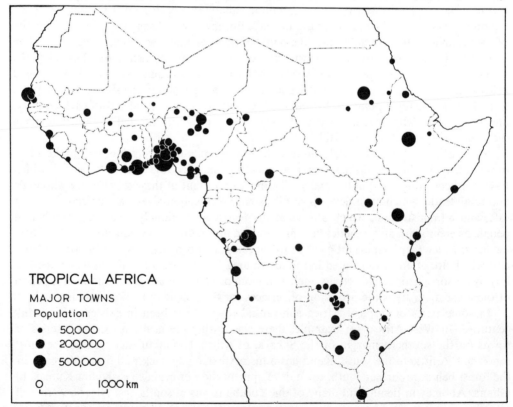

MAP 8.1. The population of the 100 largest towns of tropical Africa.

the Sahara, parts of the equatorial rainforest zone, and much of the savanna belt of south-central Africa. By contrast, the map shows certain marked concentrations, notably in south-west Nigeria where many large towns lie within 50 km of each other. The rest of Nigeria was also by then more urbanized than most parts of tropical Africa, and in the whole country the 1952–3 census recorded nineteen towns of over 50,000, their combined population exceeding 2 million. A second cluster had developed on the Copperbelt of Zambia and Zaire, where there were seven towns with over 50,000 inhabitants by 1955. This stood out in sharp contrast to all the surrounding areas, where towns were few and small.

Since many of the towns arose primarily as central places serving the needs of the people in the surrounding country, one of the basic factors affecting their distribution was the general density of population in each area. Thus the largest zones with no towns occurred in desert and semi-desert areas where a harsh environment supported very few people. However, the proportion of the total population living in towns differed greatly from one

TABLE 8.1. URBAN POPULATION OF TROPICAL AFRICAN COUNTRIES, 1955–70

	Population in towns with over 20,000 in 1955 (000)	Proportion of total population (%)	Population in towns with over 20,000 in 1970 (000)		Proportion of total population (%)	
			1955	1970	1955	1970
Angola	260	6	310	720	7	13
Benin	80	5	100	290	6	11
Burundi	40	2	40	80	2	3
Cameroon	180	4	280	770	7	13
CAE	80	7	170	380	14	23
Chad	50	2	90	260	4	7
Congo	120	17	150	350	20	29
Ethiopia	700	4	780	1,470	5	6
Gabon	0	0	30	150	4	16
Gambia	20	7	20	40	7	9
Ghana	600	10	680	1,730	12	20
Guinea	70	3	90	300	4	8
Ivory Coast	170	6	230	860	8	20
Kenya	360	5	400	890	5	8
Liberia	40	4	60	180	6	12
Malawi	60	2	80	200	3	5
Mali	90	3	130	320	4	6
Mauritania	0	0	10	30	1	3
Mozambique	180	3	220	520	4	6
Niger	20	1	50	170	2	4
Nigeria	3,300	8	4,500	9,500	11	15
Rhodesia	480	15	510	880	16	17
Rwanda	0	0	10	30	0	1
Senegal	450	16	500	1,060	18	27
Sierra Leone	80	4	100	240	5	9
Somalia	150	8	180	440	9	16
Sudan	520	5	580	1,200	6	8
Tanzania	250	3	340	760	4	6
Togo	50	4	60	180	5	9
Uganda	120	2	150	440	3	5
Upper Volta	80	2	90	230	2	4
Zaire	1,150	8	1,500	3,600	11	17
Zambia	410	14	440	1,120	15	27
TROPICAL AFRICA	9,200	6	12,800	29,500	8	12

Sources: Diverse.

173

country to another (Table 8.1), and a second factor affecting the urban pattern was the level of economic development achieved in each area. Thus the large size of Accra and Kumasi, and of Salisbury and Bulawayo, reflected the relative prosperity of Ghana and Rhodesia. Conversely, towns were small and few in such poor countries as Malawi and Niger. Contrasts in both population density and income levels were often as great within as between countries, and the distribution of urban development within, say, Cameroon or Sudan, could be largely explained in terms of these.

Since the economy of most tropical African countries was even more heavily dependent on agriculture in the 1950's than today, differences in agricultural productivity, especially in terms of export crops, were of particular significance for the pattern of urban development. For example, income from cocoa contributed greatly to the high level of urbanization in Ghana, and to the concentration of it in the south of that country. It should be noted, however, that it assisted the growth of Accra, outside the cocoa belt, as well as Kumasi within it. In contrast to some other parts of the world the impact of mining on town growth was slight. In Ghana and Tanzania, where mining was important, and even in Liberia and Sierra Leone, where it dominated the commercial economy by the mid-1950's, the main towns lay far from the mineral workings. The only major exception was the Copperbelt area.

Some countries which were neither very densely populated nor particularly prosperous were nevertheless relatively highly urbanized. In some of these cases cultural factors were of greater importance. The large size of Addis Ababa was certainly related in part to the pattern of highly centralized authority in Ethiopia, while from Sudan to Mali, but especially in northern Nigeria, there seemed to be some association between Islam and a tradition of town life. The outstanding concentration of large towns in south-west Nigeria cannot be explained entirely in terms of dense population and relative prosperity. It seems to have resulted in part from a preference for urban living amongst the Yoruba, even when they depended mainly on farming for their livelihood. Conversely, in Uganda, where the towns housed an exceptionally small proportion of the population, there was a marked preference for rural living; and the daily flow of people from their farms to places of employment in the towns in that country contrasted with the flow in the opposite direction around the towns of south-west Nigeria.

Since most tropical African towns developed as a result of contact between indigenous and alien groups, and in the 1950's were still sustained in large measure by the colonial relationship, their distribution reflected the spatial pattern of this contact. In particular, there was a concentration of the towns along the coasts, notably along the West African coast from Dakar to Douala and in countries such as Mozambique which depended heavily on transit traffic from inland states. Many inland centres also developed as transport foci, and while some, such as Timbuktu, declined long ago with a changed orientation of trade, others such as Kano expanded partly as a result of their location on new routeways. Modern rail and road routes contributed greatly to the growth of Salisbury and Bulawayo in Rhodesia, while other towns such as Kinshasa (then Leopoldville), Kisangani (then Stanleyville), and Bangui arose at strategic points on inland water routes.

The political map also had significant effects on the pattern of urban development, a tract of country being more likely to have a large town within it if it formed a political entity than if it formed part of a larger unit. Thus the great size of Kinshasa reflected the size of the area which it administered, and Kisangani and Lubumbashi would probably have grown more if they had been capitals of small states rather than merely provincial headquarters. The large population of both Dakar and Brazzaville certainly depended on the extent of the area which each administered under the French; and, conversely, the political structure partly explained the small size of towns in the other countries which lay within French West Africa and French Equatorial Africa.

THE RECENT AND CURRENT GROWTH OF THE TOWNS

In almost every part of tropical Africa the towns are at present rapidly expanding both in population and in physical extent. Furthermore, the proportion of the total population of each country living in towns is rising year by year. Over tropical Africa as a whole the rate of urban growth has probably been fairly steady throughout the past twenty years, and does not yet show any sign of decreasing. In some individual countries it was especially rapid in the late 1950's, and appeared to be related mainly to the process of economic development. In others it has been even more impressive in the 1960's, and sometimes seems to have been stimulated, to at least a comparable extent, by increasing political consciousness since independence. Unfortunately this can result in the population of the towns rising faster than economic opportunity, and the resulting urban unemployment is becoming a serious problem in many African countries.

The statistical data available on this increase in urban population are very limited, for there are few countries in which two reliable censuses have been taken. Even where reliable figures exist, they often do not faithfully reflect the urban population, but rather that occupying certain administrative areas. However, it appears that the number of people living in towns of over 20,000 more than trebled between 1955 and 1970, from 9 million to 29 million. The proportion of the total population of tropical Africa living in towns of this size rose during this period from about 6% to about 12%. It can be argued that these figures in part reflect general population growth rather than urbanization, especially since a modest growth through natural increase alone could bring some centres into the over-20,000 category for the first time. But even if the same towns are included at each date (Table 8.1), the rate of growth is far higher than the rate for the whole population of tropical Africa.

Certainly much of the growth in urban population must be attributed to natural increase, for in contrast to some other parts of the world this appears to be at least as rapid in African towns as in the rural areas. A large proportion of urban dwellers are in the 15–45 age range, and this contributes to a high birth rate, although this is off-set in some places by a heavy preponderance of males. Medical facilities are generally much better than in the countryside, especially perhaps for mothers and infants, and this lowers the death rate.

The areas where men greatly outnumber women in the urban population are those where a great deal of migration from the countryside to the towns takes place. Census figures suggest that less than one-third of the inhabitants of many towns were born there. Since much of this migration is temporary, it need not necessarily contribute to town growth, but in many countries it is in fact making a great contribution at present. Those coming temporarily for employment are tending to stay longer, and more than in the past bring wives and children with them. At the same time there is an increasing amount of permanent movement from homes in the countryside to a new life in the town. It is also likely that there is much movement between towns, and that migration often involves a first step from a rural area to a small town and a second from the small town to a city.

The growth in population has, of course, involved a rapid expansion of the physical components of the towns, including both residential areas and the zones in which their

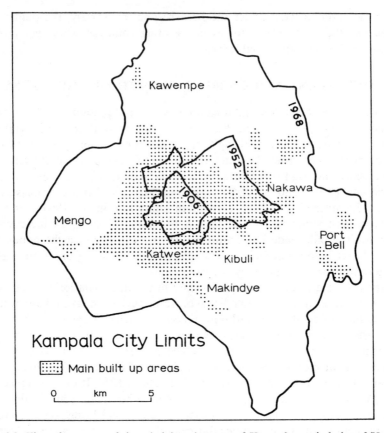

MAP 8.2. The enlargement of the administrative area of Kampala, capital city of Uganda. Minor boundary changes may have occurred at other dates.

administrative, commercial, and industrial functions take place. The building and construction industry has in fact been one of the most active sectors of the economy in many tropical African countries in recent years, and has been extremely important in terms of employment. The physical growth of the towns has included both a greater intensity of development in the older urban area, and the extension of the margins of the built-up area across land which was formerly rural in character. This has sometimes been matched by an enlargement of the administrative area of the town (Map 8.2), but elsewhere most of the sprawling new development lies outside municipal boundaries. It is this situation which renders exact measurement of population growth particularly difficult.

THE DISTRIBUTION OF URBAN EXPANSION

The remarkable increase in urbanization which has taken place over the past two decades has almost invariably taken the form of expansion of existing towns rather than establishment of new urban centres. Tema in Ghana and Nouakchott in Mauritania are rare exceptions. Inevitably, however, the rate of expansion has differed from one country to another, and also from one town to another within each country. A general impression of

TABLE 8.2. THE POPULATION GROWTH OF MAJOR TROPICAL AFRICAN CITIES, 1955–75

	Population (000)				
	c. 1955	*c.* 1960	*c.* 1965	*c.* 1970	*c.* 1975
Ibadan	500	560	620	700	800
Addis Ababa	430	490	580	850	1100
Lagos	360	600	1000	1500	2000
Kinshasa	**349**	500	800	**1323**	2000
Accra	**290**	**388**	530	**739**	1000
Khartoum	**246**	350	500	700	900
Dakar	**231**	**375**	460	600	800
Salisbury	220	270	320	**386**	560
Nairobi	200	270	380	**509**	720
Luanda	180	**225**	300	**475**	—
Kano	180	230	300	400	—
Bulawayo	170	200	220	**246**	340
Lubumbashi	**143**	200	250	**318**	—
Kumasi	140	**218**	270	**345**	—
Maputo	130	**179**	250	**378**	—
Mombasa	130	170	210	**247**	340
Abidjan	**128**	220	340	550	900
Dar es Salaam	120	170	240	340	500
Kampala	110	160	240	330	—
Douala	110	150	200	280	—
Lusaka	70	100	150	**238**	430
Kananga	50	100	200	**429**	—

Sources: The data are taken mainly from national sources, and have been estimated by extrapolation where figures are available only for other years.

Notes: The data are for the whole agglomeration rather than for the municipal area. Census figures are in bold type.

the distribution of this urban growth is provided by Table 8.1. Some of the more reliable data which exist for various individual cities are presented in Table 8.2.

Most of the features of the distribution of towns in the mid-1950's which were discussed above, are still quite apparent today, for in absolute terms most urban development has taken place in the areas which were already most highly urbanized at the time. The results of the 1973 Nigeria census, which might have been fairly accurate for the towns, have not been released, but comparison between the census of 1952–3 and that of 1963 suggests that the pre-eminence of Nigeria in the total urban pattern of tropical Africa has at least been maintained. The number of towns there with more than 50,000 inhabitants appears to have increased over that period from nineteen, with a total population of 2 million, to over fifty, with a total population of 7 million. The results of the 1963 census are disputed, however, and there is little doubt that the population of some centres was overstated. Furthermore, while there is no doubt that the urban population of Nigeria has expanded extremely rapidly, it is notable that the census figures show an almost equally rapid growth rate for some rural areas. In the highly urbanized former Western Region there is no evidence of much change in the proportion of the whole population who live in towns. Likewise in another country where cultural factors seem to have encouraged a relatively high degree of urbanization, Ethiopia, the number of urban dwellers has not increased greatly as a proportion of the total population (Table 8.1).

It can be argued that these countries already had a larger urban population in the 1950's than the economy could easily support, and that the scope for further urbanization was therefore limited. Conversely, there was particularly great scope in countries such as

177

Uganda and Tanzania, where cultural factors had not encouraged a high level of urbanization. There resistance to living in towns is now diminishing, and the rate of urban growth is especially high, even though the absolute numbers involved are still small. These are two of the countries in which only a small proportion of each town's population was born there, and in which migration has accounted for a large part of the urban growth. Throughout East Africa more of the men migrating to the towns for work are now settling there with their wives, and this is leading to accelerated population growth as these young couples produce their families.

The distribution of urban population in tropical Africa still largely reflects population densities and levels of income, neither of which have changed fundamentally in recent years. Among the countries in which a high level of urbanization depends essentially on a relatively dense and prosperous agricultural population, Ghana has maintained its lead, with an increase of urban population at a rate comparable to that for the whole of tropical Africa. The rate has been much higher, however, in neighbouring Ivory Coast, reflecting its booming economy, and the emergence of that country as one of the more highly urbanized of African countries represents a major change in the total urban pattern. The expansion of Abidjan is very striking not only from population estimates, but also on the ground.

The Copperbelt is still outstanding as the only cluster of towns based upon a mineral deposit. In the Zambia and Zaire sections together there are now eight towns with over 50,000 inhabitants, which together house well over a million people compared with 550,000 in 1955. Elsewhere such large new mining developments as those in Liberia and Gabon have had some impact on the pattern of urban population; but although this has been rising rapidly in these countries, most of the growth has occurred in the capital cities, and there are still no large towns around the mines. Similarly, no urban development has taken place at the site of such major power projects as Kariba and Akosombo.

Despite the break of political ties with Europe the extent of concentration of towns along the coasts is as great as ever. In 1955 there were nineteen towns of 100,000 in tropical Africa excluding Nigeria, of which eight were on the coast. In 1970 the equivalent figures were forty-three and eighteen. The significance of a coastal location partly reflects the continuing importance of sea-borne trade in the economies of most African countries; but in the case of many coastal capitals such as Conakry or Freetown only a small proportion of the growth now depends directly on their port functions.

The main effect of political independence has been to increase the significance of the political map for the distribution of urban development, and especially to stimulate the rapid growth of the national capitals. It is notable that one of the countries in which the rate of urban expansion has been relatively slow is Ethiopia, where the 1960's were not marked either by especially rapid economic development or by the transition from colonial rule to independence. The rapid growth of the towns in countries such as Guinea and Tanzania, and especially of capital cities, has certainly been encouraged by independence and by the growing political consciousness mentioned above. People from all parts of those countries are drawn to Conakry and Dar es Salaam much more strongly now that these are identified as "their" capital cities, and now that people are more aware of their attractions (Map 8.3).

Although in each case the absolute figures are still extremely low, the rate of urban growth has been especially rapid in Rwanda and Mauritania, each of which was administered from a capital outside its boundaries during the colonial period. The rapid increase

178

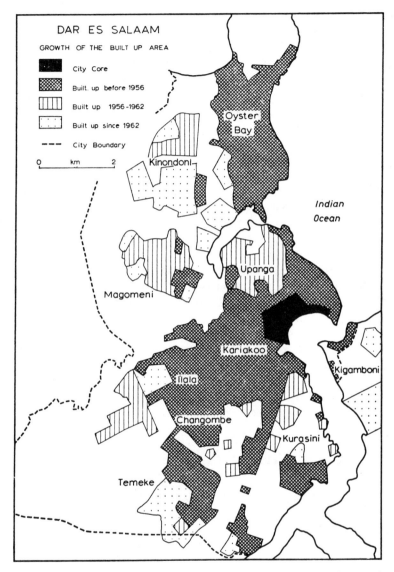

MAP 8.3. The growth of the built-up area of Dar es Salaam, capital of Tanzania.

of population in the towns, and especially the capitals, of most of the former members of the French federations in Equatorial and West Africa reflects in part the decentralization of administration from Brazzaville and Dakar. So also does the relatively slow growth since 1960 of Brazzaville, which has lost a large part of its *raison d'être* now that it administers only a country of less than a million people. In this context the continued rapid growth of Dakar is rather an anomaly. Changing political patterns also help to explain the relatively slow growth of the towns of Rhodesia in the 1960's, as the administration in Salisbury and to a lesser extent the industries both there and in Bulawayo have ceased to serve Zambia and Malawi as well as Rhodesia.

179

One general consequence of the achievement of independent status by so many countries during the past decade, and the consequent growth of national capitals, has therefore been a rather wider spread of urban development at an international level than might otherwise have been the case. Urban growth has not been concentrated into a few giant centres to the same extent as in some parts of the world. While the greatest absolute increase in population has taken place in the largest cities, the rate of growth of these has not in general been any higher than that of those smaller centres which serve as national capitals.

THE DISTRIBUTION OF GROWTH WITHIN COUNTRIES

A rather different issue is the relative rate of growth of the largest cities and the smaller towns within each country. While it is probably not possible to reach any firm conclusion on this for the whole of tropical Africa, a survey of the situation in a number of countries may give some indication of a general trend.

In West Africa the country in which population growth is best documented is Ghana, where censuses were taken in 1948, 1960, and 1970. During the first period the total population of the country rose by 63%, but the ninety-eight towns which had over 5000 inhabitants in 1960 increased in population by 116%, from 0.72 million to 1.55 million. The rate of growth was even higher in the largest cities, taken alone, for both the second city, Kumasi, and the capital, Accra, increased in population by 166%. The 1970 census results show that this trend continues (Table 8.3), and in the 1960's Accra was even forging ahead of Kumasi. The most rapid expansion of all is that of Tema, which has developed from a small fishing village into a major port and industrial centre. However, in many respects, Tema can be considered as a detached part of the Accra urban complex, for they are only 30 km apart, and may well coalesce into a single conurbation in the future.

TABLE 8.3. TOWN POPULATION GROWTH IN GHANA

Urban agglomeration	Population (000)		% increase 1960–70
	1960 census	1970 census	
Accra–Tema	415	739	78
Kumasi	218	345	59
Sekondi–Takoradi	123	161	31
Tamale	58	99	71
Cape Coast	57	71	25
Koforidua	54	70	30

Source: Censuses of 1960 and 1970.

In Nigeria the results of the 1963 census give some indication of change since the 1952–3 census, even though the figures must be treated with caution. Some of the large Yoruba towns expanded only slowly, including the largest of all, Ibadan; but others more than doubled in population, and Ilorin, the most northerly of these towns, appears to have quadrupled. Growth was very rapid in most of the larger towns of the east and north, especially Kaduna, the former northern regional capital. A trend towards capital city dominance became apparent for the first time, as the federal capital, Lagos, overtook

Ibadan as the largest urban centre in the country during this period. The city population rose by about 150%, a rate comparable to that in many other towns, but it also spilled over into Mushin and other adjacent municipalities, so that the population of the whole agglomeration rose from 323,000 to over a million.

Ivory Coast, Liberia, Sierra Leone, Guinea, Togo, and Mali are all examples of countries with a single dominant city which is growing very rapidly, and various small centres which show no signs of rivalling it. The recent burst of development in Ivory Coast was mentioned above, and population surveys taken for medical purposes in 1955 and 1963 suggest that it has not been confined to Abidjan. While the population of the capital rose from 128,000 to 285,000 between these years, that of the next seven towns together rose by a similar proportion, from 88,000 to 195,000. Nevertheless, in absolute terms it was in Abidjan that most of the urban development was concentrated. Such evidence as is available indicates that the less dramatic expansion in the other countries followed a similar pattern.

In eastern Africa the pattern of urban development differs greatly from one country to another. In Ethiopia the relatively slow growth noted above seems to apply equally to the small towns such as Harar, Dessie, and Jimma, and to the capital city, Addis Ababa. In Sudan growth has been fairly slow in most small towns, population increasing 50% to 80% between 1956 and 1973 in Wad Medani, El Obeid, and Atbara; but Khartoum, the capital, and Port Sudan have expanded considerably. Within greater Khartoum, which has trebled in population over this period, the growth has been very evenly divided between the three component units—the city proper, Khartoum North, and Omdurman.

In Kenya urban development began much more recently, except at the coast, and is now taking place at a more rapid rate throughout the country. The rate of growth between the census dates of 1948 and 1962 was remarkably similar in most of the towns, large and small. The population of Nairobi, the capital, rose from 119,000 to 267,000, and that of the next six towns together rose from 130,000 to 286,000. However, since independence Nairobi has forged ahead, and the 1969 census recorded a population of 478,000 (admittedly for an enlarged municipal area) compared with 371,000 for the next six towns. This trend is confirmed by data on construction. In 1964–7 new buildings worth $26 million were erected for private ownership in Nairobi, while the equivalent figure for Mombasa was $4 million, for Thika (developing as an industrial outlier of Nairobi) $1 million, and for the next four towns together only a further $1 million. Since 1967 Nairobi has enjoyed an even greater building boom: during 1967–9 the city council approved plans for new private buildings worth $78 million and government buildings worth $17 million, and in 1970 seven large blocks were rising in the city centre, including one of twenty-seven storeys.

In Tanzania all the towns grew considerably between the 1948 and 1957 censuses, but the growth was faster in the capital, Dar es Salaam, than anywhere else. In general this trend was confirmed by the 1967 census (Table 8.4), the population of the capital rising between 1957 and 1967 from 129,000 to 273,000, while that of the next ten mainland towns together rose from 166,000 to 288,000. The main exception is provided by Arusha, which has expanded as a secondary industrial centre, and as the new headquarters of the East African Economic Community.

In south-central Africa the dominance of the capital city is clear only in Angola and Mozambique, where this situation has certainly been maintained by the recent pattern of urban development. In Angola, for instance, Luanda was six times larger than the second town in 1960 and eight times larger in 1970, while it accounted for just half the value of new buildings in all towns completed in 1963–6. In Malawi the situation is unusual in two

181

TABLE 8.4. TOWN POPULATION GROWTH IN TANZANIA

	Population (000)			% increase 1957–67
	1948 census	1957 census	1967 census	
Dar es Salaam	69	129	273	112
Zanzibar	47	63	81	28
Tanga	22	38	61	60
Mwanza	11	20	35	75
Arusha	5	10	32	225
Moshi	8	14	27	96
Morogoro	8	15	25	74
Dodoma	9	13	24	76
Iringa	6	10	22	116
Kigoma–Ujiji	?	16	21	31
Tabora	13	15	21	36
Mtwara-Mikindani	?	15	20	33
All towns of over 20,000	138	250	641	—
Total urban population	269	427	773	81
Total Tanzania population	7,627	8,951	12,231	37

Source: Tanzania, *Recorded Population Changes, 1948–1967.*

respects. Firstly, Blantyre is clearly the dominant urban centre, even though the colonial administrative capital was Zomba, 70 km away. Secondly, government policy now aims to spread development from the south to the centre of the country by shifting the administration to Lilongwe. A costly building programme has begun there, and it is expected to develop into a major urban centre during the next decade.

In Zambia, too, the Government is anxious to spread development to the smaller centres, though not by such drastic measures; but it is the largest towns that are expanding most rapidly at present (Table 8.5). The situation is particularly interesting since there is great rivalry between the capital, Lusaka, and the Copperbelt towns, and also between the various towns which together make up the Copperbelt. In the years since independence Lusaka has been growing fastest of all, although it is not yet clear whether this is only a

TABLE 8.5. TOWN GROWTH IN ZAMBIA

	Population (000)			Value of building plans passed (k.m.)	
	1956 estimate	1963 estimate	1969 census	1962–5	1968–71
Lusaka	71	114	238	25.6	55.8
Kitwe	70	115	179	7.4	20.6
Ndola	69	89	151	9.2	23.2
Mufulira	56	75	101	2.0	1.3
Luanshya	52	72	90	1.6	3.0
Chingola	—	56	93	2.6	3.7
Chililabombwe	—	30	40	—	—
Kalulushi	—	17	24	—	—
Kabwe	30	47	67	2.2	11.4
Livingstone	29	34	43	2.2	4.3

Sources: Zambia, *Statistical Yearbook*, and *Economic Survey.*

TABLE 8.6. TOWN GROWTH IN RHODESIA

	Population (000)				Value of building plans passed ($Rh.m.)	
	1956 estimate	1961–2 census	1969 census	1976 estimate	1964–8	1969–73
Salisbury	226	311	386	570	71	248
Bulawayo	170	211	246	340	23	80
Umtali	34	43	46	62	3	19
Gwelo	31	38	46	64	4	19
Wankie	23	22	21	28	—	—
Que Que	17	26	33	48	3	16
Gatooma	?	15	21	33	3	4

Source: Rhodesia, *Monthly Digest of Statistics.*

temporary phase associated with the nation-building process. On the Copperbelt, Kitwe has emerged as the dominant centre, and in addition to expanding its mining and industrial activity, it is challenging Ndola's former supremacy as the commercial focus of the area.

In Rhodesia also the pattern is unusual in that not one but two towns dominate all others, Bulawayo having shown remarkable resilience despite the location of the administration at Salisbury. However, a comparison between official estimates for 1956, the 1969 census and further official estimates for 1976 suggest that growth in population has recently been much more rapid in Salisbury than in either Bulawayo or the next four towns together (Table 8.6). Between 1964 and 1973 Salisbury accounted for 65% and Bulawayo for 20% of the value of building plans approved in all the urban centres of Rhodesia, indicating that the pre-eminence of the capital city is probably being increased further as these plans are implemented.

It is clear that in many tropical African countries there is a dearth of medium-sized towns, the most common situation being that of one dominant city and only very small regional centres. This has sometimes been attributed to the former colonial status of these countries, and there is no doubt some truth in this. It was easier for alien administration and trade to be channelled through a single centre than through many. But there is also much evidence to suggest that over tropical Africa as a whole the attainment of independence has contributed to an even greater concentration of activity in the national capitals than during the colonial period, even though many governments are opposed in principle to such a trend. There is, for instance, no counterpart in most of the smaller towns to the parliamentary buildings, government offices, and embassies that have appeared in the capital cities. District administration generally continues to operate in much the same way as it did before independence.

There are countries such as Zambia in which urban development is divided between a number of large centres, all of which are growing rapidly, but even in these the capital is increasing its dominance. There are others, such as Cameroon and Benin, in which development is divided between an administrative capital and a commercial capital. However, the general pattern is one in which there is a single dominant city in each country: and although this is not always experiencing the most rapid growth of all, it is usually expanding faster than most of the smaller towns. Undoubtedly in every case the greatest growth in absolute terms is taking place there.

In so far as the growth of the capital cities results from new functions acquired on independence, it may be to some extent a temporary phenomenon. Yet where the capital is also the largest urban centre, many other factors favour particular rapid growth there, even after the immediate effects of independence has passed. Manufacturing provides a case in point, for as it expands it shows a marked tendency to locate in the existing major urban centres. There is no sign of new industrial towns arising, comparable to those which grew on the coalfields of Europe in the eighteenth and nineteenth centuries. Most of the industries depend on the expanding domestic market, and are market- rather than power-orientated in their location. The main power stations are often in the capital cities, but even where this is not the case power is generally transmitted to them for consumption there. This tendency is strengthened by the fact that new industries are often based on import substitution, and are appropriately located in the centres from which the imported products were formerly distributed.

The general trend seems to be towards an increasing concentration in the field of social services also, as new universities and new hospitals with specialized facilities are established in the capital cities. In many countries investment in educational and medical facilities has expanded more rapidly both in the capital and in the rural areas than in the smaller towns.

A trend towards concentration of urban development would not be surprising in the light of the experience of other continents. As towns grew over the centuries in Europe they formed a widely dispersed pattern; but where most urban development came later, as in Latin America and Australia, in an age of much improved communications and increasing economies of scale in commerce, industry and even services such as medicine, the pattern is one of a few large towns, sharply differentiated from the numerous small local centres. While there is no certainty that Latin American experience will be repeated in Africa, it seems quite likely.

CHANGES IN THE CHARACTER OF THE TOWNS

In some ways the character of urban development in Africa is changing more rapidly than its distribution, especially in the centres that were of colonial origin. One important example is provided by the employment structure, and especially the role of what has some-times been termed the "informal sector". Until the 1950's there was a sharp contrast be-tween old cities such as Kano and Kumasi where large numbers of people were self-employ-ed, especially in petty trade, and colonial cities such as Nairobi and Dar es Salaam where most of the labour force were wage-earners employed by government or large-scale private enterprise. As these forms of employment have failed to expand at the same rate as the urban population, and as opportunities for small-scale indigenous enterprise have opened up, a large "informal sector" has emerged in such cities. The term is open to question, since it covers a wide range of activities—legal and illegal—and many of these are closely dependent on the large-scale sector, but this component of the urban economy, to which the influential ILO report on Kenya drew particular attention, is now often much more impor-tant than official policies and plans might suggest.

With regard to the physical form of the towns, the contrasts between indigenous centres such as Ibadan, European-created centres such as Salisbury, and also hybrid or inter-mediate centres such as Khartoum and Lagos, are almost as great now as in the 1950's, as most have expanded around the framework already established. With respect to the towns of colonial origin in particular, each tends to have fairly distinct zones corresponding to its major functions (Map 8.4), and this pattern is more often being consolidated than

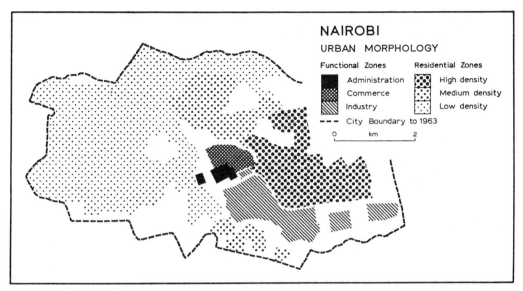

MAP 8.4. The physical structure of Nairobi, capital city of Kenya. Although the map is inevitably somewhat generalized, marked contrasts between zones are clearly apparent on the ground. The extent of the municipal area has now been greatly increased, but most of the present built-up areas lie within the 1963 boundary.

altered. Nevertheless, various changes in the form of the towns have commonly occurred during the past twenty years.

The attainment of independence has been marked in several countries by the erection of new parliamentary buildings, and sometimes of new tall blocks for government departments, nationalized corporations, and political party headquarters. The administrative zone has therefore often been completely transformed in appearance within a few years (Plate 22). Another development directly related to the attainment of independence has been the establishment of diplomatic missions by foreign countries. In some of the smallest countries these are still few in number, but in such countries as Nigeria, Ghana, and Zaire there are forty to fifty, all located in the national capital.

The greatest amount of development of administrative functions and buildings has taken place in cities such as Abidjan, Bamako and Lusaka, which have become true national capitals only since independence. Much has occurred also in Addis Ababa, since it houses both the UN Economic Commission for Africa and the OAU. The least has taken place in the cities of Salisbury, Bujumbura, Dakar, and Brazzaville, which administered larger areas in the past than they do today, and where the expansion of national government activity has merely filled the vacuum left by the termination of federal administration.

While the relative importance of commerce has often declined somewhat, especially in the capital cities, some expansion in this function in absolute terms has taken place everywhere. In many cities it is only during the past twenty years that the first tall office blocks have been erected, and the first large department stores have been opened. Thus in Ibadan it is only during this period that the skyline of iron roofs has been broken by the multi-storey Co-operative building and Cocoa House. Among the largest commercial buildings to be opened in many of the capitals are new hotels, designed to accommodate the increased flow of visiting politicians, diplomats, and businessmen as well as tourists. During 1967 for in-

185

stance, hotels each involving capital expenditure of over $3 million were under construction in Nairobi, Dar es Salaam, Kampala, Lusaka, and Abidjan.

The commercial development most closely related to political change is perhaps the nationalization or partial nationalization of concerns such as the copper mines of Zambia and Zaire. This has involved the establishment of new headquarters within the country concerned, though often in the national capital rather than within the mining area. Another change is the establishment of national offices by large concerns which formerly conducted business in several countries from one regional headquarters. This has been very clearly apparent in East Africa, where the oil companies, for example, decentralized their operations from Nairobi to Dar es Salaam and Kampala soon after independence.

The growth in population of nearly all the towns of tropical Africa has involved a great expansion in the extent of their residental areas, as well as an increase in the density of settlement in some of the older ones, sometimes to a level of very serious overcrowding. Some changes in the character of the residential areas have also taken place in many towns. During the colonial period they tended to be divided along racial lines, in the early years by law but later generally only by custom and income. This pattern has not immediately disappeared as the African nations have gained independence, especially since the alien groups still fall almost entirely within the highest income groups, but it has become more blurred as increasing numbers of Africans have been able to move into such high-class residential areas as Oyster Bay in Dar es Salaam and Ikoyi in Lagos.

Another important development has been the building of housing estates for lower-paid workers on a much larger scale than in the past. They were a familiar feature of towns in Rhodesia and Zambia many years ago, but in many West African towns there were none before the late 1950's, most people living in privately built houses often paying a high rent for one or two rooms. Yet however rapid this development in such cities as Nairobi, Lagos, and Abidjan, it has nowhere kept pace with the rising population, and has often consisted of housing that is far too costly for those in greatest need; and a striking feature of most African towns today is an extensive peripheral zone of crudely built shacks, sometimes disparagingly termed a "septic fringe". In several cities such areas, consisting partly of illegal squatter settlements and partly of settlements established with the approval of the traditional authorities often just outside the city boundaries, now house over half the urban population: and "informal sector" house-building constitutes a major economic activity.

This is not an entirely new phenomenon, but it is one which has increased immensely within the post-independence period; and although it has not yet reached the same proportions as in many parts of Latin America, it presents the present generation of African town planners with some of their most difficult problems. It is by no means obvious what the official reaction to these spontaneous settlements should be. Some observers consider that they provide an appropriate transition for newcomers to the city between rural and urban life, although it should be noted that they are often not occupied primarily by new arrivals, most of whom lodge with kinsmen before establishing their own home. Many of these settlements are certainly unsatisfactory in their present form, especially with regard to sanitation, but they do represent people providing what governments have been manifestly unable to provide—housing for large numbers at a cost that the majority can afford. Thus rather than being prohibited, as in Nairobi until recently and in Salisbury still, or even largely ignored, as in Abidjan where attention has been concentrated on high standard residential areas for a minority, they might be encouraged especially in planned locations where at least basic services such as water supplies and sewerage have been made available.

The well-established site and service schemes of Lusaka perhaps offer one promising approach, although the cities of tropical Africa are sufficiently diverse that a single formula is unlikely to be appropriate for all of them.

CONCLUSIONS

The cities and towns of tropical Africa are growing rapidly, although the rate and the nature of urbanization varies considerably from place to place. In general this growth is likely to continue in the years ahead. In certain countries it is perhaps taking place at too great a pace, and outrunning the expansion of urban functions, thus creating a serious problem of unemployment. For this reason in some countries in which large numbers of people have been moving to the towns governments are attempting to resist the tide and even to encourage a movement back to the land wherever possible. The attractions of town life are so strong, however, that in every country not only the total number of people but also the proportion of the whole population living in an urban environment continues to rise year by year.

This process of urban expansion is intimately related to the whole course of social, political and economic development, for it is the towns which are the spearheads of most forms of change. Modernization in tropical Africa can be seen as a process that is gradually diffused from urban nuclei into the countryside. It is to the towns that the farmers send their cash crops; it is from them that their radio programmes are received; and it is in them that their future is discussed by the politicians. Conversely, any form of development within each country is reflected in some way in the towns. For each new agricultural research centre that is established, for each new mine that is opened up, even for every new school that is built, more administrators are employed there and new opportunities for trade are created there.

Despite the rapid rate of growth, the pattern of urban development seems to be changing remarkably little. Certain alterations in the spatial structure within each city and town can be seen in many countries, as, for instance, in the blurring of the former sharp distinctions in the residential areas occupied by different races, and the establishment of large areas of spontaneous low-income settlement. And there is some evidence that the contrasts between cities of European origin and those which owe much to African initiative are becoming less clear. For instance whereas in the towns of Zambia males greatly out numbered females until the early 1960's, as they still do in Salisbury and Bulawayo, a rapid change from circular migration of men to long-term migration of whole families had even by 1969 produced a sex ratio as balanced as that in most West African cities. In most ways however, urban development in independent Africa is taking place upon the framework established by the colonial powers rather than striking out in new directions.

Similarly, in so far as it is possible to discern a general trend in the distribution of urban growth, it is for the existing pattern to be ever more deeply entrenched, as the greatest amount of development takes place in the centres which are already dominant. The attainment of independence by a large number of small states has contributed to some dispersal of city growth, as each state has sought to be independent of all others in terms of urban functions. Within each country, however, evidence of dispersal is very rare: much more often there are signs that the dominance of the largest city, usually the political and commercial capital, is increasing. Indeed, one possible implication of increasing economic, and especially political, integration amongst African states, is that the trend towards dispersal

187

on an international scale might be reversed, so that urban growth throughout tropical Africa as a whole might become highly concentrated within a very few centres.

This tendency towards concentration is of course not confined to Africa. In many regions in which urban development dates mainly from the recent period of good communications and ever-increasing economies of scale in commerce, industry and even social services and administration, the pattern is one of a small number of large cities. This is not generally welcomed by governments, since it creates severe problems both in the overgrown cities and in the undeveloped areas far from them. It can be overcome to some extent by official action, although generally only at some cost, particularly in terms of individual freedom of action. Whether government policy in each country is to accept the present and emerging patterns, or to attempt to modify them, the distribution, as well as the nature, of current urban growth should be understood. Since there is much that is not yet known about this, there is scope for much more investigation in the field of African urbanization not only by sociologists but also by geographers.

SELECTED READING

On the pattern of urban development in tropical Africa up to the late 1950's, see:
  R. W. STEEL, The towns of tropical Africa, in K. M. BARBOUR and R. W. PROTHERO (eds.), *Essays on African Population* (London, 1961), pp. 249–78.
More recent extensive reviews are:
  W. A. HANCE, *Population, Migration and Urbanization in Africa* (New York, 1970), ch. 4;
  P. VENNETIER, Le développement urbain en Afrique tropicale, *Cahiers d'Outre Mer* 85, 5–62 (1969);
  P. VENNETIER, *Les Villes d'Afrique Tropicale* (Paris, 1976).
From the immense sociological literature one might pick out:
  P. C. W. GUTKIND, Tradition, migration, urbanization, modernity and unemployment in Africa, *Canadian Journal of African Studies* 3, 343–66 (1969);
  W. J. and J. L. HANNA, *Urban Dynamics in Black Africa* (Chicago, 1971).
Many useful papers may be found in:
  CENTRE NATIONAL DE LA RECHERCHE SCIENTIFIQUE, *La Croissance Urbaine en Afrique Noire* (Bordeaux, 1972);
  S. EL SHAKHS and R. OBUDHO (eds.), *Urbanization, National Development and Regional Planning in Africa* (New York, 1974);
  H. MINER (ed.), *The City in Modern Africa* (London, 1967);
  D. J. PARKIN (ed.), *Town and Country in Central and Eastern Africa* (London, 1975).
There are useful papers on West Africa by M. L. McNULTY and on East Africa by E. W. SOJA and C. E. WEAVER in B. J. L. BERRY (ed.), *Urbanization and Counterurbanization* (Beverly Hills, 1976).
An outstanding analysis of urbanization in one country is:
  A. L. MABOGUNJE, *Urbanization in Nigeria* (London, 1968).
Individual city studies focused on recent change include:
  A. SECK, *Dakar: Metropole Ouest-Africaine* (Dakar, 1970);
  E. P. SKINNER, *African Urban Life: The Transformation of Ouagadougou* (Princeton, 1974).
Studies concerned with urban employment problems include:
  ILO, *Employment, Incomes and Equality: Kenya* (Geneva, 1972);
  ILO, *Abidjan: Urban Development and Employment* (Geneva, 1976).
Housing for the urban population is the subject of:
  J. HUTTON (ed.), *Urban Challenge in East Africa* (Nairobi, 1972);
  M. PEIL, African squatter settlements, *Urban Studies* 13, 155–66 (1976).
The process of rural–urban migration is examined in:
  J. C. CALDWELL, *African Rural–Urban Migration* (Canberra, 1969);
  R. DENIEL, *De la Savane à la Ville* (Paris, 1968);
  H. HEISLER, *Urbanization and the Government of Migration* (London, 1974);
  J. GUGLER, Migrating to urban centres of unemployment in tropical Africa, in A. H. RICHMOND and D. KUBAT (eds.), *Internal Migration* (Beverly Hills, 1976),
the first three being case studies of Ghana, Ivory Coast, and Zambia respectively.

9

EXTERNAL ECONOMIC RELATIONS

POLITICAL independence has not brought economic independence to the countries of tropical Africa. Indeed, all are still heavily dependent in many ways on other parts of the world. Most are firmly locked into the peripheral part of a spatial economic system that is centred on North America and Europe. There is much-heated debate on how far continuing relationships with the Western industrialized countries either help or hinder the development process, and no agreement is likely to be reached since they help some forms of development but hinder others. There is naturally resentment at forms of neo-colonialism that limit the freedom of action in the development field for African governments, and some ties have been severed with beneficial results: yet recent experience does not suggest that any African country would be helped in its economic aspirations by a policy of extreme isolation. Political independence has provided the opportunity to choose whether and where to build up new relationships, but even any sudden re-orientation has generally involved some economic disruption or sacrifice.

The nature and extent of the changes that have taken place differ greatly from one country to another. Some have broken away from the former metropolitan power in every possible way, while others have retained very close links. Some have established much closer ties both with other parts of the economically developed world, and with other tropical African countries, than they had during the colonial period: in other states little change of this nature has occurred.

Some of the relationships are primarily political, and these still include constitutional ties as well as military treaties and the exchange of diplomatic missions. Others are essentially economic, and it is these which are of most direct concern for the pattern of African development. The most important form of relationship, and that on which most information is available, is trade. Its importance has been highlighted by the severe impact that rising import prices, especially for oil, have had on most African economies in the 1970's, along with the increased differentiation between the exporters of oil (and to a lesser extent some other commodities such as phosphates) and their less-fortunate neighbours. The gradual rise in the total value of tropical Africa's external trade from $US6000 million in 1956 to $18,000 million in 1972 largely reflected an increasing volume, but the further rise to $25,000 million in 1974 was due largely to higher prices.

Private investment from other parts of the world remains important to most tropical African countries, although the sources have been changing substantially; and a distinctive feature of the 1960's was an increased, though still pitifully small, flow of financial and technical aid to these as to other less-developed countries, both from the more prosperous countries and from organizations such as the World Bank. It is notable that the flow of such aid then diminished slightly in real terms in the early 1970's, partly because the value of much aid in its present form is increasingly being questioned.

Other relationships which directly affect African economic development range from the international migration of labour and the transmission of skills and technology, to currency arrangements, and groupings of commodity producers such as OPEC. A full discussion of these would require a book to itself, and so the geographical pattern of only a limited range of relationships is considered here.

THE COLONIAL POWERS

Most of the new states of tropical Africa still have much closer ties with the former colonial power than with any other country. While the political links have weakened greatly they have rarely disappeared completely, and the economic connections which arose from these are in many cases still as strong as ever. All former British territories except Sudan have remained within the Commonwealth, and all those administered by France, except Guinea, at first remained in a French community and then became associate members of the European Economic Community under the Yaoundé Convention in 1964. Zaire and Somalia have retained ties with Belgium and Italy respectively, and they too became associate members of the EEC. Angola, Mozambique, and Guinea-Bissau were, of course, still administered by Portugal throughout the 1960's.

The continuing economic ties with the former colonial powers are clearly illustrated by the pattern of external trade (Tables 9.1 and 9.2). The geographical patterns of private

TABLE 9.1. EXTERNAL TRADE OF TROPICAL AFRICA

| | Values in $US million | | | | | |
| | Exports | | | Imports | | |
	Average 1956–7	Average 1966–7	Average 1974–5	Average 1956–7	Average 1966–7	Average 1974–5
TOTAL TRADE	3100	4900	12100	3300	5100	14000
Western Europe	2220	3310	6100	2070	2940	6500
United States	340	550	1400	280	520	1340
Japan	40	230	660	160	270	740
Eastern Europe	10	80	130	30	90	190
USSR	10	50	220	0	60	150
China	10	30	220	20	80	330
Middle East	40	90	240	110	160	880
North Africa	40	40	150	30	50	130
South Africa	70	170	(300)	200	290	(500)
TROPICAL AFRICA	?	220	1020	?	250	1130

Sources for Tables 9.1, 9.2, 9.4–9.8, and 9.10: United Nations, *Yearbook of International Trade Statistics*; International Monetary Fund, *Direction of Trade*.

Notes: Tropical African exports do not equal other countries' imports from tropical Africa noted in later tables (and above) because of freight and other charges. No data exist for trade in 1956–7 within such units as French West Africa or the Federation of Rhodesia and Nyasaland (or for the direction of trade of Rhodesia in 1974–5).

TABLE 9.2. TRADE PATTERN OF SELECTED AFRICAN COUNTRIES

	% with former metropole			% with other western Europe		
	1956	1967	1975	1956	1967	1975
Sudan	31	16	11	24	32	31
Ghana	41	29	15	18	27	33
Nigeria	54	29	18	24	41	38
Ex-French West Africa	66	43	36	12	20	29
Zaire	47	30	26	28	31	40
Angola and Mozambique	31	34	14	39	30	28

investment and official aid are in many respects very similar (Table 9.3). Thus of the $1500 million or so provided annually to tropical Africa as official aid between 1965 and 1972, just half came directly from West European countries compared with $200 million from the USA, $200 million from the Soviet bloc and China, and $300 million from multilateral agencies (these including the EEC).

TABLE 9.3. AID TO SELECTED AFRICAN COUNTRIES FROM OECD COUNTRIES
AND MULTILATERAL AGENCIES
Net flow of official development assistance in $US million

Recipient	1969–71 Average			1974–5 average
	Bilateral flows	Leading donors as %	Total flows	Total flows
Ghana	62	US 46; UK 25	72	80
Kenya	48	UK 48; US 14	74	121
Nigeria	103	US 44; UK 21	143	95
Tanzania	54	US 22; UK 12	70	219
Cameroon	32	France 54; US 14	55	84
Ivory Coast	44	France 70; Germany 12	62	90
Niger	29	France 69; Canada 18	39	114
Senegal	35	France 68; Germany 12	55	115
Burundi	11	Belgium 79; France 10	17	39
Rwanda	14	Belgium 66; Germany 7	19	63
Zaire	62	Belgium 70; US 17	86	189
Somalia	13	Italy 45; US 33	23	51
Angola	15	Portugal 99	15	2
Mozambique	39	Portugal 98	39	6
Ethiopia	58	US 48; Sweden 22	76	121
Liberia	11	US 87; Germany 11	15	16

Source: OECD, *Development Co-operation 1973* and *1976*.
Note: No equivalent data for aid from USSR and China are available, but figures for aid commitments are given in Table 9.9.

France is still the leading trading partner of most of its former colonies (Table 9.4), and although its share has fallen everywhere it accounts even today for almost half the external trade of several of them, such as Senegal, Niger, and the Central African Empire. With the exception of Guinea, and for a short period Mali, these countries have not radically altered their orientation, and therefore wherever total trade has expanded rapidly, as in Ivory Coast, trade with France has also increased. In addition, France continues to provide the largest share of aid to most of its former colonies through the Fonds d'Aide et de Co-opération (Table 9.3). Many of the poorer states, such as Upper Volta and Benin, depend on French

TABLE 9.4. THE SHARE OF FRANCE IN THE TRADE OF
FORMER FRENCH WEST AFRICAN COUNTRIES

	Exports % to France		Imports % from France	
	1961	1975	1961	1975
Benin	73	24	59	30
Guinea	18	8	12	29
Ivory Coast	52	27	70	39
Mali	18	22	68	33
Mauritania	32	21	82	57
Niger	78	67	77	42
Senegal	76	51	66	43
Togo	58	40	42	32
Upper Volta	11	24	61	43

grants to balance their annual budgets as well as to pay for such developments as new hospitals or roads. Amongst the prosperous nations of the world France has an outstanding record, for it is the only country whose overseas aid programme during the 1960's consistently represented more than 1% of national income. Government grants and loans to tropical African countries then amounted to about $300 million a year. Thirdly, most private investment in Francophone Africa is still undertaken by French companies. It is these, for example, which have played a key role in the rapid economic development that has taken place in Ivory Coast. Firms such as Société Commerciale pour l'Ouest Africain (SCOA) and Compagnie Française d'Afrique Occidentale (CFAO) still dominate the commercial life of this and several other countries. Indeed, it is often argued that the economic boom in Ivory Coast has brought more benefit to France than to the people of that country.

The situation in Guinea provides a sharp contrast, for when that country opted for complete independence in 1958 France responded by cutting off connections to the greatest possible extent. All aid ceased immediately, trade decreased sharply, and no new investment took place other than in the FRIA bauxite development which was too far advanced to be called off. Relations with the former colonial power also became strained in Mali after 1960, and although France remained a major trading partner and source of aid there, its importance in relation to other countries declined greatly for a while.

Even in the years before independence, Britain did not dominate the external trade of most of its colonies to the same extent as France, especially those in East Africa where no imperial preference operated. Its share has since dropped further, particularly in Ghana and Nigeria (Table 9.2), yet even today Britain is still the leading trading partner of most of the Commonwealth countries. Similarly, Britain is still the chief source of aid for some of these countries, although since the volume of such aid has not matched that provided by France for its former colonies other sources have also been keenly sought. The flow of private capital from Britain also continues on a substantial scale, as exemplified by the investments of Brooke Bond tea in Kenya, British Petroleum in Nigeria and Lonrho in many African, countries. As in the case of France, this is matched by a flow of profits in the opposite direction.

Despite the abrupt withdrawal of the Belgians from Zaire in 1960, connections with Belgium are still strong, and the share of that country in the external trade of Zaire remains remarkably high. For several years after independence the copper industry remained firmly in Belgian hands, and although it was eventually nationalized, both money and men from

Belgium are still very much involved in it. Belgium also remains the chief source of imports and of aid for both Burundi and Rwanda (Table 9.3). Similarly, the Italian interest in Somalia is still considerable, even though that country has turned to some extent towards the eastern bloc and Italy is no longer its chief trading partner. The Italians also developed interests in Eritrea during their brief occupation, and even elsewhere in Ethiopia, and Italy is still the chief supplier of Ethiopia's imports and the third market for its exports. It remains to be seen how far independent Angola and Mozambique will retain economic ties with Portugal.

A wide range of factors combine to encourage the maintenance of the close economic relationships inherited from the colonial period. They include currencies based on the pound and the franc, legal systems based on those of the respective colonial powers, and the well-established position of British, French, Belgian, and Italian firms in all forms of economic activity including banking and wholesale trade. In France and Italy tariff preferences and subsidized guaranteed markets for African produce remained for some years after independence, although these have now gradually been eliminated. A more lasting consideration is language, which affects all types of relationship from business to educational assistance.

OTHER WESTERN EUROPEAN COUNTRIES

In several tropical African countries economic relationships with western Europe as a whole are as strong as ever, for the shift away from the former colonial power has been largely to its European neighbours (Table 9.2). This has meant that new links have been forged by Britain, France, Belgium, and Italy, while an even more significant change has been increased contact between West Germany and tropical Africa (Table 9.5).

One important factor in this development has been the establishment of the EEC. Not only did Zaire, Rwanda, Burundi, Somalia, and all the former French territories except Guinea, become associate members of this community in the early 1960's, but also, partly as a result of Britain's entry, all the Commonwealth countries in Africa, and also Guinea,

TABLE 9.5. WEST GERMAN TRADE WITH TROPICAL AFRICA

	Values in $US million					
	Exports			Imports		
	1958	Average 1967–8	Average 1974–5	1958	Average 1967–8	Average 1974–5
TROPICAL AFRICA	190	380	1620	310	620	2290
Of which:						
Angola	11	35	57	10	20	68
Gabon	?	4	26	?	18	103
Ghana	12	26	96	50	30	62
Ivory Coast	?	28	57	?	61	184
Kenya	?	28	75	?	20	65
Liberia	19	14	172	16	72	59
Nigeria	33	64	498	45	71	1032
Zaire	24	25	143	39	41	92
Zambia	?	16	73	?	82	238

Note: No figures are available for the 1958 trade with individual countries within customs unions.

Guinea-Bissau, Ethiopia, and Liberia became associates under the Lomé Convention in 1975. The associate members have revised their trade tariffs to give equal preference to all the European members; and they benefit from a common aid fund to which all the European members contribute and which had already amounted to $1300 million over the period 1958–69. West Germany and Netherlands have in this way been able to increase their share of the trade of such countries as Ivory Coast and Gabon, and have also begun to provide them with aid, although their share is still small compared with that of France.

Association with the EEC is a result as well as a cause of trade diversion for such countries as Nigeria, where the share of EEC countries in total imports had risen from 18% to 27%, and in exports from 22% to 33% between 1956 and 1966. EEC and especially West German trade with countries such as Liberia and Angola also expanded in the 1960's, sometimes as a result of investment by firms from that country, and sometimes following indirectly from aid agreements. Netherlands and Italy also extended their African interests beyond the original associations of the EEC, the Italian interests including the construction of the Kariba, Volta, and Kainji dams, and involvement in several other activities such as road and air transport in Zambia and oil refining in Tanzania.

THE UNITED STATES

Whereas Latin America lay very largely within the economic and political sphere of influence of the United States even before World War II, and South-east Asia came within it in the immediate post-war years, American influence in tropical Africa was still extremely slight in the mid-1950's. Even today, most of the countries of the region have much weaker connections with the United States than with western Europe; and that country has fewer relationships with tropical Africa than with any other part of the non-communist world. Yet there has been a substantial increase in trade, aid, and political interaction in recent years. Most African countries sent one of their first ambassadors to Washington, have received some American aid, and conduct an increasing volume of trade with that country. The United States is less interested than western Europe in trade with Africa for its own sake, though there are a few commodities of which supplies from Africa are becoming

TABLE 9.6. UNITED STATES TRADE WITH TROPICAL AFRICA

	Values in $US million					
	Exports			Imports		
	Average 1956–7	Average 1967–8	Average 1974–5	Average 1956–7	Average 1967–8	Average 1974–5
TROPICAL AFRICA	220	480	1490	360	630	5190
Of which:						
Angola	16	38	58	38	70	434
Ethiopia	8	35	52	22	48	61
Gabon	?	4	46	?	13	195
Ghana	10	49	89	46	67	148
Ivory Coast	?	13	64	?	63	137
Liberia	16	43	80	36	52	111
Nigeria	16	60	411	34	40	3552
Uganda	0	3	12	17	48	70
Zaire	60	50	167	110	41	73

increasingly significant; but it is even more concerned that the region should lean towards the West rather than the East in terms of the division of the world into great power blocks.

American exports to tropical Africa increased in value only from $215 million in 1956 to $350 million in 1964, but they had reached $850 million by 1972. Imports for these years were respectively $370 million, $570 million, and $950 million. This trade expansion was remarkably evenly distributed over the region, but was particularly marked in Liberia, Ethiopia, Ghana, and Nigeria (Table 9.6). The Liberian state was, of course, established by American Negro settlers, and it has always been closely tied to the United States as exemplified by its use of American currency. Ethiopia does not have such close connections, but nor does it have a legacy of a colonial relationship with western Europe. Ghana and Nigeria are the two countries which have shown most interest in importing from the United States goods formerly imported from Europe, partly because independence there brought abolition of imperial preference. In many other Commonwealth countries there never was such preference, while the former French territories continued to give preference to goods from France together with its EEC partners.

As Table 9.6 also shows, the pattern of American trade with tropical Africa has been completely transformed by the rise in oil prices. Not only did the value of US imports increase sixfold between 1972 and 1974, but the share of Nigeria in the total rose to 70%, while the other main oil producers, Angola and Gabon, became the second and third sources of US imports. By 1975 oil revenues had also permitted Nigeria to take a share of American exports three times larger than any other country.

American private investment in tropical Africa has also increased greatly, from a cumulative total of about $250 million in 1956 to $600 million by the mid-1960's and almost $2000 million by 1972. Such investment was always much less evenly spread than trade, Liberia alone accounting for about $70 million in 1956 and $200 million ten years later. Its distribution has somewhat widened, for the American investment in the Ghana aluminium smelting industry has been followed more recently by participation in the Boké bauxite development in Guinea and several new industries in Zaire, while the chief sphere of activity has become the oil industry of both Nigeria and Angola.

In both trade and investment American interests are still greater in South Africa than in most parts of tropical Africa, and apart from oil exports the form of economic relationship of most significance for this region is now certainly government aid. Between 1961 and 1965 American direct aid to tropical Africa amounted to $1750 million, though for the next five-year periods it fell to little over $1000 million, while the United States also contributes substantially to multilateral aid. In this respect also Liberia, Ethiopia, Ghana, and Nigeria have been particularly prominent; and some aid is now being given to Guinea, which is loosening its post-independence ties with the eastern bloc without turning back to France. But the largest amount of assistance of all has gone to Zaire, which has desperately needed aid to repair its economy, and which is potentially one of the most influential countries of the region.

JAPAN

A remarkable development of recent years has been a great increase in contacts with Japan, which has been looking to tropical Africa both as a source of raw materials such as metal ores and as a market for its rapidly expanding manufacturing industries. Exports from this region to Japan rose from $30 million in 1956 to $220 million in 1966 and $600

TABLE 9.7. JAPANESE TRADE WITH TROPICAL AFRICA

	Values in $US million					
	Exports			Imports		
	Average 1956–7	Average 1967–8	Average 1974–5	Average 1956–7	Average 1967–8	Average 1974–5
TROPICAL AFRICA	130	250	1140	30	350	1280
Of which:						
Angola	0	10	28	0	15	106
Ghana	25	18	41	0	27	74
Kenya	8	20	88	5	7	27
Mozambique	1	19	31	0	18	74
Nigeria	49	26	435	0	16	364
Sudan	6	21	75	6	20	22
Zaire	4	13	53	1	12	85
Zambia	1	29	80	1	153	232

million in 1972. Imports from Japan rose from $120 million in 1956 to $530 million in 1972 (Table 9.7). The next three years brought a further sharp increase in the value of trade with Japan, but in contrast to trade with the United States imports increased faster than exports since Japan obtains little of its oil from Africa.

Japan does import enough oil from Nigeria to make that country its leading source of imports from tropical Africa in 1974 and 1975, but previously the main development had been in copper shipments from Zambia, for which Japan became a major customer in the 1960's. It is certainly oil revenues which have made Nigeria the chief African purchaser of Japanese goods, accounting for 40% of the tropical African total in 1975. Apart from this, the trade is very widely distributed, Japan being an important supplier for most countries but nowhere absolutely dominant. Even in the 1950's Japan was second to the colonial power in several countries, including both Nigeria and Ghana. Since then it has come to occupy second or third position in many more.

Relationships with Japan have not been confined to trade, for Japanese firms are now investing in many types of industry in tropical African countries from ocean fishing in Ghana to textile manufacture in Kenya. The most important example in the 1960's was investment in the expansion of the Zambian copper industry, which has been followed by even larger investments in this field in Zaire. Japanese firms are also interested in African sources of iron ore, and followed up their recent investment in Swaziland by substantial contributions to the expansion of iron mining in Angola and investigations in Mozambique.

THE SOVIET BLOC

Soviet economic ties with tropical Africa are still very poorly developed in comparison with those of western Europe, or even the United States and Japan. Nevertheless, relationships with the Soviet bloc were so slight during the colonial period that the rate of growth of all forms of contact has been quite striking. The attainment of independence by the countries of tropical Africa, and the desire of many to take up a non-aligned position in relation to the Western and Eastern powers, has coincided with a move on the part of the USSR to increase contacts with all parts of the world.

The value of trade between the USSR and tropical Africa rose from under $20 million in 1956 to $100 million in 1965 and $400 million in 1975 (Table 9.8). The trade is much more

TABLE 9.8. SOVIET TRADE WITH TROPICAL AFRICA

	Values in $US million					
	Exports			Imports		
	Average 1959–60	Average 1969–70	Average 1974–5	Average 1959–60	Average 1969–70	Average 1974–5
TROPICAL AFRICA	20	70	150	40	110	230
Of which:						
Cameroon	0	1	2	0	8	38
Ghana	5	12	24	20	25	45
Guinea	5	13	25	2	3	12
Mali	0	5	9	0	1	1
Nigeria	0	7	26	5	24	108
Somalia	0	3	22	0	0	3
Sudan	5	18	18	5	28	5

localized than that of western Europe, the United States, and Japan, for many African countries still have virtually no trade with the USSR, and the four states of Ghana, Guinea, Nigeria, and Sudan account for a large proportion of the total. In Guinea the reorientation of trade after independence was so great that the USSR became the leading trading partner for a few years, but it has now lost that position. On the other hand, the expansion of trade in some other countries, including Nigeria, began some years after independence, and the Soviet Union's share in their trade is still very small.

The first flow of financial aid from the USSR occurred only in 1959, yet by 1971 commitments for aid had reached $700 million (Table 9.9). The geographical distribution of this aid is similar to that of trade, except that Ethiopia has also been a major beneficiary, notably

TABLE 9.9. EASTERN BLOC AID COMMITMENTS TO TROPICAL AFRICA ($US m.)

	Values in $US million			
	Cumulative Total to 1971			Additions 1972–4
	E. Europe	USSR	China	All
TROPICAL AFRICA	345	690	990	950
Of which:				
Congo	—	9	25	44
Ethiopia	17	102	84	3
Ghana	102	89	42	65
Guinea	25	165	66	112
Kenya	—	44	18	—
Mali	23	56	50	10
Nigeria	42	7	—	56
Somalia	6	66	132	1
Sudan	123	64	80	85
Tanzania	6	20	256	74
Uganda	—	16	15	—
Zambia	—	6	218	161

Sources: OECD, *Flow of Resources to Developing Countries 1973*; United Nations, *Statistical Yearbook 1975*.

in the form of the Assab oil refinery. Contacts of other types, such as educational scholarships, show a very similar pattern. Despite this growth, the volume of both trade and aid was still smaller for the whole of tropical Africa during the 1960's than for Egypt alone (where Soviet aid financed the great Aswan Dam), and there is a great potential for further relations with the USSR. In particular, it offers a huge potential market for some products of tropical agriculture, such as cocoa and coffee, for the present Soviet consumption of these is extremely low.

There is also much scope for increased trade with the other countries of eastern Europe, although this is already rather better developed than trade with the USSR, especially in the case of Poland and Czechoslovakia. These two countries together import more from and export more to tropical Africa than does the USSR. Tropical Africa's relationships with these countries have developed alongside those with the USSR, and are in most respects very similar. In addition to trade, some technical assistance has been received and diplomatic missions have been established. The geographical distribution of such contacts closely parallels that of Soviet contacts (Table 9.9), but there are exceptions such as the particularly close ties between East Germany and Zanzibar.

CHINA

The extent of Chinese involvement in tropical Africa is often exaggerated in western circles, for at least in terms of economic relationships it is no greater than that of the USSR. The distribution of Chinese influence in the 1960's was also very similar to that of Soviet influence, perhaps surprisingly so in view of the political differences which have arisen between those two countries in recent years. The first contacts of any significance were those made with Guinea in 1959 and with Ghana and Mali in 1961. There was some perceptible change after the rift with the Soviet Union, however, and attention was then directed to eastern Africa. Diplomatic relations were established with such countries as Somalia and Tanzania in 1961–2 and small-scale aid agreements quickly followed. Some trade then began to develop with these countries, and with Sudan and Uganda also. By the early 1970's the links with Guinea, Mali, and Somalia had weakened, and the main ties were with Tanzania and Zambia.

Communist China is now recognized by and has embassies in more than half the states of tropical Africa, although almost half, including most of the French-speaking countries, still recognize Taiwan instead. Much Chinese literature reaches Africa, and broadcasts from Pekin beamed to tropical Africa increased from $3\frac{1}{2}$ hours a week in 1956 to 86 hours in 1963. The value of trade has increased from less that $5 million in 1956 to $120 million in 1967 and $360 million in 1972, and aid has expanded with the establishment of large textile mills in several countries and particularly with the financing of the new Tanzania–Zambia railway in 1970, this being by far the largest Chinese commitment in the region (Table 9.9). China sees a distinct role for itself in tropical Africa, especially since, unlike the USSR, it can claim to be on the side of the coloured peoples of the world in any conflict with the white peoples. Yet up to the present it has not succeeded in carving out any distinct sphere of influence, and it still has very much weaker connections in tropical Africa than has western Europe or even the United States. It is clearly not easy for China to establish contacts, for the African countries are in general interested only when there is some economic advantage to be gained thereby. Furthermore China is itself such a poor country that it can neither afford to give much aid nor offer a large market for most African exports, although this situation may change substantially as development proceeds there.

THE MIDDLE EAST

Middle Eastern countries such as Iran and Saudi Arabia have long been important trading partners of many African countries, but only as suppliers of oil. This trade has increased in volume even though Nigeria has displaced these suppliers in some countries, while it has risen enormously in value as a result of the oil price rise of the 1970's. Thus the share of Iran and Saudi Arabia in the total imports of Kenya rose from 7% in 1971 to 23% in 1975.

While oil revenues are permitting many Middle Eastern countries to increase their imports substantially, very few of these imports are obtained from tropical Africa. However, oil money is beginning to flow from the Arab members of OPEC in the form of private investment and official aid. Kuwait was quoted as a source of finance for several new enterprises set up by international consortia in 1975 and 1976, for example. Total commitments of official financial assistance on concessionary terms made to tropical Africa by OPEC countries amounted to over $200 million in 1974 and over $350 million in 1975. One of the most distinctive features of this aid is provided by its geographical distribution. The dominant commitments were to the countries with the greatest cultural affinity with the Arab states, for Sudan accounted for 25%, Somalia for 25%, and Mauritania for 18%.

SOUTH AFRICA

One of the most striking changes in the external relationships of several tropical African countries since independence has been a severing of connections with the Republic of South Africa. During the 1950's that country was an important source of manufactured goods for East Africa and Zaire as well as the former Federation of Rhodesia and Nyasaland and the Portuguese territories. It also provided a useful market for tropical produce such as coffee and cocoa, although its main import from the countries to the north was migrant labour. In many other fields also, relationships were close during the colonial period, and the Republic could be considered the leading member of a southern African community, setting an example at least in economic development which other members might follow. However, the country has set an example in social organization which is abhorrent to most other countries in the world, and especially to those of tropical Africa: and it is because of this that one country after another has broken its ties with South Africa as soon as the attainment of independence has given it the opportunity to do so. The most important economic consequence has been the cessation of all trade on the part of such countries as Kenya and Tanzania. Another striking change has been the re-routing of airways services mentioned in Chapter 7.

Although this change affected the relationships of most tropical African countries with South Africa in the 1960's, it did not extend to the countries which had the closest relationships. Portugal put into practice in Angola and Mozambique different social policies from those operating in South Africa, but it showed no interest in joining any boycott of the state which could do most to help it to maintain its rule in those territories. Even when independence was finally attained, Mozambique could not break all its ties, the Cabora Bassa power project and the dependence of Maputo port on South African traffic providing clear illustrations. In Rhodesia strong disapproval of South Africa was often expressed in the past, and there was a notable wish to avoid subservience to this powerful neighbour, but since UDI the Rhodesian regime has seen closer contacts with South Africa as essential to its survival. Even Zambia and Malawi retain most of their links with South Africa, in each case as a matter of economic necessity. The two countries differ in that the government of Malawi under Dr. Banda declares that South Africa's social policies are irrelevant in this context, and is actively encouraging closer ties, whereas the Government of Zambia is seeking ways of reducing the dependence on South Africa which it inherited from the colonial period. This dependence is particularly great in the case of supplies for the mining industry, which developed to a large extent as an offshoot of the South African mining industry and is still partly financed and managed from that country; and ironically it has temporarily increased in other respects also as a result of diversion of trade with Rhodesia since UDI. The most important of Malawi's links with South Africa is still migration for employment, but examples of the new ties are the financing and construction by South African concerns of many buildings in the new capital at Lilongwe and the new rail link eastwards towards Nacala.

RELATIONSHIPS WITHIN TROPICAL AFRICA

One of the most remarkable features of African external relationships during the 1950's was the small extent of contact between many neighbouring territories, and especially between countries in different parts of the continent. Important changes in this situation are now beginning to take place, for the attainment of independence has in many cases been followed by the establishment of closer ties between tropical African states. Pan-Africanism has become a movement of some significance, and much energy has been devoted to the attainment of greater unity in both political and economic spheres.

The clearest expression of the new political relationships amongst African countries was provided by the establishment of the Organization of African Unity in 1963, with its headquarters in Addis Ababa. This has the support of all the independent states of tropical Africa, and has assumed a role of considerable importance in the political affairs of the region. Naturally it has not brought complete unity on all matters, but it has played a valuable part in resolving certain conflicts between African nations, and in tackling such problems as that of refugees. The equivalent body concerned with economic matters is the United Nations Economic Commission for Africa (UNECA), which also has its headquarters in Addis Ababa, and which has assisted the exchange of information between countries. It has also undertaken numerous studies of the possibilities of economic integration and co-operation in Africa, although with few practical consequences as yet. Another organization of increasing importance in the field of economic affairs is the African Development Bank, established in 1964 and supported by the majority of African countries.

As early as 1961 most of the former French territories were loosely associated in the Union Africain et Malgache, but the establishment of the OAU led to the dissolution of this body in 1963. Contacts between most French-speaking countries remained close, however, and two years later on the initiative of President Houphouet-Boigny of Ivory Coast, a new Organization Commune Africaine et Malgache was formed. Although this body has no executive powers it provides a useful forum for discussions and a potential pressure group in relations with other parts of the world: but it has been weakened by the departure of Cameroon, Chad, Congo, and Zaire in 1972–3, due in part to its additional role as a vehicle for the maintenance of French influence.

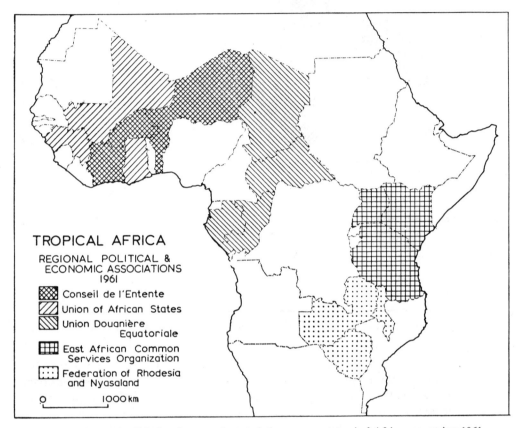

MAP 9.1. Formal political and economic associations amongst tropical African countries: 1961.

Multinational institutions have been established not only at the continental but also at the regional level, although not always with lasting success (Maps 9.1 and 9.2). Indeed, except on a local scale as in the case of Somalia, Cameroon, and Tanzania, most attempts at regional integration made from a political basis have failed. One such attempt dating from the colonial period was the Federation of Rhodesia and Nyasaland: others of the post-independence period were the Mali Federation and the Ghana–Guinea union. On the other hand, efforts to achieve regional integration from an economic basis have been rewarded with some success. In East Africa the customs union between Kenya, Tanzania, and Uganda survived along with most of the common services which they inherited from British rule, and after some periods of strain a new East African Community was established in 1967. Interest in co-operation over a wider area of eastern Africa then increased, and applications to join the new community were made by Burundi, Ethiopia, Somalia, and Zambia: but by the mid-1970's conflicts among the three members made collapse seem more likely than enlargement.

201

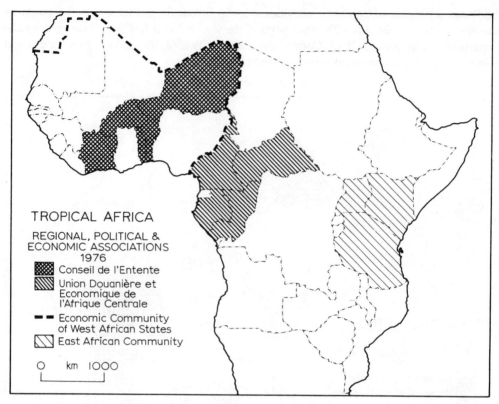

MAP 9.2. Formal political and economic associations amongst tropical African countries: 1976.

The four successor states of French Equatorial Africa (CAE, Chad, Congo, and Gabon) also retained their customs union, and were joined in 1961 by Cameroon. In 1966 the bonds were strengthened by the transformation of the customs union into the Union Douanière et Economique de l'Afrique Centrale, which allowed for joint preparation of economic plans and policies and a solidarity fund to assist the poorest members, Chad and the Central African Empire. In 1968, however, Chad, and for a short period CAE also, joined with Zaire in a new "union", and although this has been very ineffective it has weakened the original grouping. Unlike the East African Community states, the UDEAC states, along with Chad, still share a central bank (still based in Paris up to 1976, but now moved to Yaoundé). Ultimately, it might be very advantageous if a single equatorial African grouping could be created, but the former French states fear the likely dominance of Zaire within such a community.

In West Africa the economic bonds between states had still not been effectively institutionalized by the early 1970's, although many proposals for economic association between various groups of states had been made. Agreements for a customs union amongst the former French territories exist, but they have never been fully implemented. The most important tie so far has been the Conseil de l'Entente, which was formed by Ivory Coast, Upper Volta, Niger, and Benin in 1960 and joined by Togo in 1966. The main effect of this grouping has been to increase the influence of Ivory Coast over its poorer neighbours in return for some financial subsidy through a solidarity fund. Integration over a wider area

202

has been hindered both by different colonial backgrounds and by the disparate sizes of individual countries. However, 1975 witnessed the signing of the ECOWAS treaty by 14 West African countries, and this may provide the basis for closer economic integration throughout the region if its objectives can be fulfilled.

The opportunities for the supply of government aid or private investment funds from one tropical African country to another are very limited, so economic relationships take the form mainly of trade. Much trade between neighbouring countries is unrecorded, but probably the greater part is now officially declared. The general picture is one of expansion, though not at a rate notably faster than that of foreign commerce as a whole. There have been a few instances of rapid growth during certain periods, notably amongst several of the states of former French West Africa and within the East African and Equatorial customs unions in the 1960's, and in respect of oil shipments from Nigeria and Gabon more recently (Table 9.10). However, these are offset by the falling off of the most important intra-African trade flow of the 1950's, that between Rhodesia and Zambia, consequent upon the break-up of the federation and especially Rhodesia's UDI.

One of the factors which had hindered greater intra-African trade is the inadequacy of the transport links between many neighbouring countries. The improvement of these has been a matter of great concern to many tropical African countries, and to UNECA and the African Development Bank. Some of the improvements that have been made were noted in Chapter 7, along with some of those still in the planning stage. The network which can be altered with least difficulty is that of air routes, and it is this which has witnessed the greatest change over the past decade. This change also reflects the fact that the increasing contacts between African states have as yet taken the form mainly of the movement of government officials and diplomats rather than of goods.

A more fundamental limitation to the opportunities for intra-African trade is that so many countries have similar economies. Most have little to offer to their neighbours,

TABLE 9.10. THE LEADING RECORDED INTERNATIONAL TRADE FLOWS WITHIN TROPICAL AFRICA, 1964–74

	Values in $US million		
	1964	1969	1974
Rhodesia–Zambia	86	28	8
Rhodesia–Malawi	16	13	22
Kenya–Tanzania	37	36	54
Kenya–Uganda	35	44	77
Kenya–Zambia	1	12	31
Tanzania–Kenya	11	11	27
Tanzania–Zambia	1	16	30
Uganda–Kenya	20	22	11
Gabon–Cameroon	1	7	20
Gabon–Senegal	0	5	15
Cameroon–Gabon	1	5	16
Nigeria–Ghana	11	5	57
Nigeria–Ivory Coast	1	1	50
Nigeria–Senegal	0	0	29
Nigeria–Sierra Leone	1	2	17
Ivory Coast–Senegal	4	9	22
Ivory Coast–Upper Volta	3	6	27
Ivory Coast–Mali	2	2	32
Senegal–Ivory Coast	6	7	22
Senegal–Mauritania	1	1	19

for the commodities of which they produce a surplus are rarely in great demand elsewhere in the region. This situation is likely to change only slowly, as new forms of economic activity develop, and especially as industrialization proceeds. Unfortunately, the problem then arises that it is the more industrialized countries that stand to gain most from the trade, leading to ever greater disparities in development. It is already clear, for example, that Kenya or Ivory Coast can sell more to their poorer neighbours, such as Somalia or Upper Volta, than they wish to purchase from them. This problem of the unequal distribution of benefits perhaps provides the most serious obstacle to closer economic integration in tropical Africa today.

CONCLUSIONS

No attempt can be made here to establish the extent to which the development of tropical Africa is constrained by its condition of dependence on other parts of the world. It is clear,

TABLE 9.11. TROPICAL AFRICA: DEPENDENCE ON EXTERNAL TRADE

	$ million imports 1974	$ imports *per capita* 1974	$ imports per $ thousand of GNP 1974
Gambia	47	90	520
Liberia	288	170	500
Somalia	129	42	440
Sierra Leone	220	81	410
Kenya	1026	79	390
Benin	146	49	390
Mauritania	144	110	380
Zambia	910	192	370
Gabon	382	670	340
Congo	206	160	340
Tanzania	813	55	340
Ivory Coast	969	150	330
Senegal	498	105	310
Zaire	1051	43	300
Mali	130	23	290
Malawi	188	38	280
Upper Volta	145	25	270
Cameroon	437	62	250
Togo	120	55	220
Ghana	822	86	200
Chad	87	22	200
Sudan	642	42	190
Rwanda	58	14	190
Niger	97	22	180
Rhodesia	550	90	170
CAE	60	34	160
Mozambique	467	52	150
Angola	614	97	140
Nigeria	2772	42	130
Guinea	85	16	130
Burundi	43	12	130
Uganda	213	19	100
Ethiopia	273	10	100

Sources: UN, *Yearbook of International Trade Statistics*; IMF, *International Financial Statistics; World Bank Atlas.*

however, that there are great geographical variations in the intensity of this dependence. An indication of the role of exports in the economy of certain African countries was given in Chapter 1, while variations in the relationships of imports to national income across the whole region are shown in Table 9.11. A different aspect of dependence is illustrated in Table 9.12, which shows striking contrasts in the amount of aid that has been flowing to particular countries from the West and from multilateral agencies. It is unfortunate that data for flows from the eastern bloc cannot be incorporated, for such flows reflect dependence to an equal degree, but they have not been large enough to affect the total picture drastically. Even the total aid and trade patterns taken together would not of course tell the whole story. For instance, while on these criteria Rhodesia shows a higher degree of self-reliance than any other tropical African country, it has clearly been highly dependent on South Africa in many ways ever since UDI. Nevertheless, it is evident that the extent of dependence on either trade or aid is far greater in some countries, both poor and relatively

TABLE 9.12. TROPICAL AFRICA: DEPENDENCE ON OFFICIAL AID
FROM OECD COUNTRIES AND MULTILATERAL AGENCIES
Net flow of official development assistance, 1972–4 average

	$ million	$ per capita	$ per $ thousand of GNP
Mali	70	13.1	155
Niger	81	18.9	150
Rwanda	38	9.5	122
Upper Volta	60	10.5	115
Chad	46	11.8	112
Somalia	30	10.0	103
Burundi	28	7.9	85
CAE	29	16.8	78
Benin	27	9.1	73
Gambia	6	12.8	70
Mauritania	26	21.1	68
Malawi	35	7.4	53
Togo	28	13.3	51
Congo	19	22.5	48
Senegal	75	16.3	47
Tanzania	103	7.1	44
Zaire	147	6.2	42
Kenya	94	7.6	36
Cameroon	62	9.0	35
Ethiopia	74	2.8	28
Gabon	29	55.1	28
Guinea	18	3.5	28
Ivory Coast	63	10.0	22
Liberia	12	7.3	21
Sierra Leone	11	4.1	20
Zambia	41	8.8	17
Sudan	45	3.0	13
Ghana	44	4.8	11
Mozambique	18	2.1	11
Uganda	18	1.7	7
Angola	26	4.5	6
Nigeria	77	1.2	4
Rhodesia	0	0.0	0

Sources: OECD, *Development Co-operation Review; World Bank Atlas.*

prosperous, such as Somalia, Mauritania, and Liberia, than in others, including Nigeria, Sudan, Ethiopia, and Mozambique, as well as Rhodesia, where the role of the internal exchange economy is greater.

In the 1950's the external relationships of nearly all tropical African countries were clearly dominated by their ties to one or another of the European colonial powers. Today the situation is much less clear; but there have certainly been two changes of particular geographical interest. One has been the increasing diversity in the spatial pattern of such relationships for most individual countries, and the other has been the emergence of sharp contrasts between one African country and another in the orientation of external connections.

In some of the former French territories the attainment of political independence has brought little change in economic relations apart from some spread of contacts from France to the EEC as a whole. The significance of this for economic development is hard to assess, for while Ivory Coast has clearly gained great material benefits from its continued ties to France, these have not helped Upper Volta to make much economic progress. All these countries remain firmly linked to the Western powers, as also does Liberia, but the majority of African countries have taken up a "non-aligned" position in terms of the East–West division, and have established at least token connections with the communist countries. Yet most still have far closer relations with western Europe and even the United States, including in most cases membership of the Commonwealth or associate membership of the EEC. A few countries which retain such institutional ties have nevertheless developed economic and cultural contacts of some significance with the eastern European countries, the USSR and China: notable examples are Somalia, Tanzania, Mali, and more recently Angola and Mozambique. Sudan and Ethiopia also have important links with the communist world as well as the West. The country which took the most active steps to change its orientation after independence was Guinea, but relationships with the Soviet bloc and China have not invariably proved a success there, and by the 1970's Guinea was looking increasingly to the West again.

One matter on which most African states are agreed is that a desirable future change is to increase the extent of relationships within tropical Africa. Yet in this respect there are even greater differences between one country and another in recent trends and in the present situation. For some, connections with other African countries are of major importance; for others, they are of very little practical significance. Probably there are also differences between them in the potential value of establishing closer links within tropical Africa in the future, but in general there is a pressing need for greater integration within tropical Africa, as has been forcefully argued by Green and Seidman, and indicated, though less emphatically, by Robson and others. The more prosperous parts of the world may be persuaded to do more to assist African development, by easing trade restrictions and by improving not only the volume but also the terms of aid. More assistance may also come from those Middle Eastern countries to which oil is now bringing great wealth. Ultimately, the current discussions about a New International Economic Order may— indeed must—be followed by actions. Meanwhile all African countries must take every opportunity to help themselves, both individually as exemplified by Tanzania's policies of greater self-reliance, and collectively by greater co-operation among themselves.

SELECTED READING

Among the many books on African external relations are:
A. A. MAZRUI, *Africa's International Relations* (London, 1977);
W. A. NIELSEN, *The Great Powers and Africa* (London, 1969);
I. W. ZARTMAN, *International Relations in the New Africa* (New York, 1966).

On the continuing ties with Europe, see:
S. AMIN, *Neo-colonialism in West Africa* (London, 1973);
J. BOURRINET, *La Co-opération Economique Eurafricaine* (Paris, 1976);
E. M. CORBETT, *The French Presence in Black Africa* (Washington, 1972);
I. W. ZARTMAN, Europe and Africa: decolonization or dependency? *Foreign Affairs* **54**, 325–43 (1976).

Full details of the patterns of Western aid to Africa are given in:
OECD, *Geographical Distribution of Financial Flows to Developing Countries* (Paris, annual).

A useful case study of such aid is:
K. MORTON, *Aid and Dependence: British Aid to Malawi* (London, 1975).

Interesting papers on foreign private investment may be found in:
C. G. WIDSTRAND (ed.), *Multinational Firms in Africa* (Uppsala, 1975).

Books on the growing links with the Soviet bloc and China include:
B. D. LARKIN, *China and Africa 1949–1970* (Berkeley, 1971);
C. STEVENS, *The Soviet Union and Black Africa* (London, 1976);
B. R. STOKKE, *Soviet and East European Trade and Aid in Africa* (New York, 1967);
W. WEINSTEIN (ed.), *Chinese and Soviet Aid to Africa* (New York, 1975).

On the new dependence on the Middle East see:
E. C. CHIBWE, *Arab Dollars for Africa* (London, 1976).

A full discussion of relationships with South Africa is:
S. C. NOLUTSHUNGU, *South Africa in Africa* (Manchester, 1975).

The literature on relationships among African countries is very extensive, and includes:
P. DIAGNE, *Pour l'Unité Ouest-Africaine* (Paris, 1972);
R. H. GREEN and A. SEIDMAN, *Unity or Poverty?* (London, 1968);
A. HAZLEWOOD (ed.), *African Integration and Disintegration* (London, 1967);
A. HAZLEWOOD, *Economic Integration: The East African Experience* (London, 1975);
B. W. T. MUTHARIKA, *Towards Multinational Economic Co-operation in Africa* (New York, 1971);
P. NDEGWA, *The Common Market and Development in East Africa* (Nairobi, 1968);
P. ROBSON, *Economic Integration in Africa* (London, 1968);
B. VINAY, *L'Afrique Commerce avec l'Afrique* (Paris, 1968).

10

CONCLUSIONS

THERE certainly has been an improvement in material standards of living for some people in most parts of tropical Africa over the past two decades. Many forms of economic development have taken place, from improved methods of cultivation on small farms to the construction of giant power stations, and in aggregate the resulting growth of income has outpaced the steady growth of population. Yet in many ways the period has brought disappointment, for the rate of development has been much slower than many people, and many governments, hoped. It has often been pointed out that the total annual national income of tropical Africa is still smaller than the annual *increase* of income in many years in the United States. The economy of most African countries has certainly expanded no faster than that of most other parts of the world, so that no progress has been made towards narrowing the gap between these countries and the rich nations. Indeed, in absolute terms the gap has widened substantially.

Furthermore, it has been increasingly recognized that development has been distributed within African countries, both socially and spatially, in such a way that it has caused increasing *disparities* of income and welfare. In many countries the most affluent 10% of the population are now much better off than they were twenty years ago, but for the poorest 10%, and perhaps many more, conditions have not improved at all. In so far as the development process has brought greater awareness of this situation among the underprivileged, it has also led to increased *dissatisfaction* with their condition. This may be welcome to those who hope for revolution, but it is not something that is desired by most governments. There are also many ways in which development in Africa has brought increased *dependence* on other parts of the world. The countries with the best record on many of the conventional measures of development, Gabon and Ivory Coast, have clearly had to accept such dependence at least temporarily as the price for their relative prosperity. For all these reasons there has been much rethinking of development policy in recent years, in Africa as elsewhere. Yet no African country has rejected development in some form as a major national goal, and whatever other changes may also be sought all regard accelerated economic growth as a vital component of such development.

It is becoming increasingly clear that in terms of world resources and ecological equilibrium there are "limits to growth", even if there is much dispute on what the limits might be. The discussion often centres on population growth, which is undoubtedly a vitally important issue, but it applies equally to economic growth and thus to development prospects. If it is doubtful that the world could support even its present population at the levels of consumption (and pollution) now prevailing in North America or even western Europe, much less its undoubtedly greatly enlarged future population, then it is quite unrealistic to regard economic development in such regions as tropical Africa as progress towards such consumption levels. The extent of the material development which can be realistically envisaged depends among other things on the future paths of the present developed countries: and it also depends on the nature of the development which is pursued. Undoubtedly, however, the present levels of economic development in tropical Africa, and the present disparities on a world scale, are quite unacceptable to the people of the region.

Thus however strong the arguments for curbing economic growth may be for the world as a whole, and however far African countries may turn away from the present industrialized countries as the model for their own future, there is clearly an urgent need for the rate of economic development in tropical Africa to be accelerated. Every country in the region is striving to achieve this, and the more prosperous countries elsewhere which are providing aid wish to see this happen, provided of course that it does not involve any substantial sacrifice on their part. There is also general agreement, at least in principle, that this development should be spread among a larger proportion of the population rather than benefiting only a few. There is much less agreement on how these aims can best be attained, and every country faces great problems of priorities in the allocation of its resources.

Attempts must therefore be made to evaluate the relative benefits of investment in different forms of economic activity, such as agriculture, mining, and manufacturing. An

TABLE 10.1. INCREASE IN PER CAPITA GNP IN SELECTED AFRICAN COUNTRIES, 1958–73

	Per capita GNP $US		$ absolute increase	% increase
	1958	1973	1958–73	1958–73
Rhodesia	180	430	250	140
Senegal	160	280	120	80
Ghana	140	300	160	110
Ivory Coast	120	380	260	220
Zambia	110	430	320	290
Liberia	100	310	210	210
Cameroon	90	230	140	160
Togo	70	180	110	160
Kenya	70	180	110	160
Nigeria	60	210	150	250
Benin	60	110	50	80
Mauritania	50	200	150	300
Tanzania	50	130	80	160
Chad	50	80	30	60
Malawi	40	110	70	180
Ethiopia	40	90	50	130
Burundi	40	80	40	100
Upper Volta	40	70	30	80

Sources: United Nations, *Yearbook of National Accounts Statistics; World Bank Atlas*; national sources.

Notes: The data available for the remaining countries are even less reliable than these. The figures are for the Gross National Product at current prices, and therefore part of the increase represents inflation rather than increased activity. This problem is even more serious when estimates for 1974 or 1975 are used, as in Map 10.2.

209

even more difficult task is to compare these with the benefits which should result in the long term from improved communications and even perhaps more efficient administration. In terms of the welfare of the people, all these have to be set against better educational and medical facilities. Furthermore, within each of these fields, priorities must be allocated between numerous small-scale and fewer large-scale developments. Often, but not always, this implies a decision between labour-intensive and capital-intensive projects, and this distinction is especially significant since employment opportunities have increased in many countries disturbingly slowly.

In each case there are some general principles that provide guidance, but even these normally depend upon certain basic assumptions about present and future world economic relationships. Discussion of appropriate national and international development *strategies* would therefore require a consideration of the future international economic order that is quite beyond the scope of this book. However, we might note that whatever the broad strategies might be, many specific decisions must be influenced by the particular circumstances of each area concerned. Generalizations are often made about all the less-developed countries, or the so-called "Third World": very few of these are really valid even for all the countries of tropical Africa. The experience of Latin America or India will generally be relevant to the African situation, but it will rarely provide the complete answer. Similarly, a policy on the priority given to industrial development which is right for one African country may not be right for another. In respect of planning decisions, many aspects of the geography of tropical Africa are therefore of great relevance; but an aspect of economic plan-

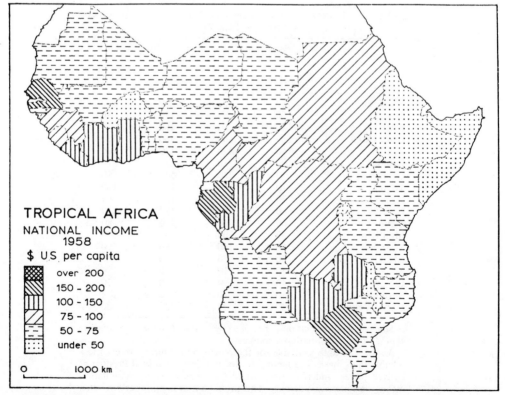

MAP 10.1. National income *per capita* in tropical Africa, 1958.

210

ning to which geography can be applied even more explicitly is the priority accorded to each *area*, whether on an international or a national scale.

The development that has taken place in recent years has been very unevenly distributed, so that income has increased much more rapidly in some countries than in others, and also faster in some districts than in others within each country. Data on the variations within each country are very scarce, and even those which can be gathered on the differences between countries are subject to a wide margin of error. As noted earlier, precise measurements of national income or gross national product are impossible for economies which include a large subsistence element, and the techniques of estimation adopted differ from year to year as well as from one country to another. Nevertheless Table 10.1 and Maps 10.1 and 10.2 give some indication of the spatial pattern of the growth in *per capita* income in recent years (although since the figures refer to incomes at current prices, part of the increase, especially since 1970, reflects inflation rather than a real improvement in living standards). Attempts have been made to calculate growth rates at constant prices, and these form the basis of Map 10.3.

Table 10.1 and the maps indicate that the greatest increase in income in absolute terms has taken place in countries that were already among the most prosperous in the mid-1950's. In Ivory Coast, Gabon, and Zambia, income per head rose by over $200 between 1958 and 1970, and by over $400 between 1958 and 1975, whereas in some of the poorer countries of the region, such as Mali, Upper Volta, and Rwanda, it rose by less than $30 up to 1970 and

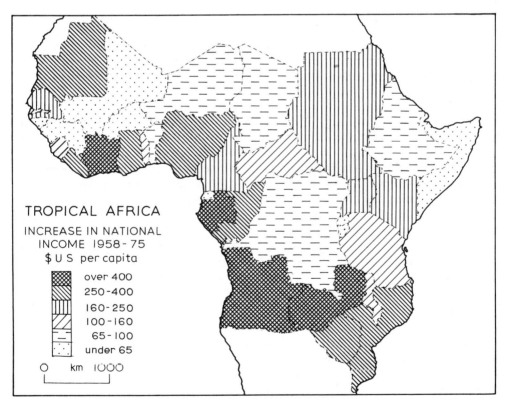

MAP 10.2. Absolute increase in national income *per capita* in tropical Africa at current prices, 1958–75.

211

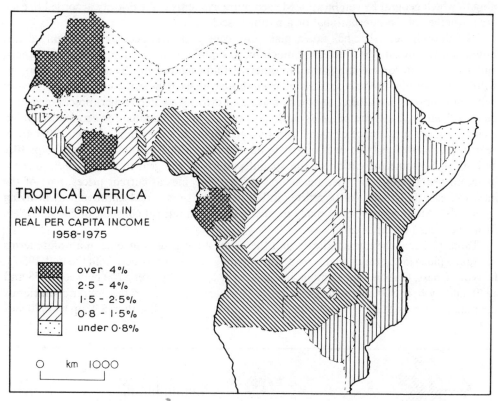

MAP 10.3. Annual growth in real *per capita* income in tropical Africa, 1958–75.

by only about $50 even up to 1975. While Table 10.1 suggests no clear relationship between level of income and rate of growth, when estimates for all countries are considered there is some evidence that the disparity in income between most of the richer and the poorer nations is widening even in relative terms, as the annual *rate* of growth has been higher among many of the more favoured. On the basis of an unusually prosperous agriculture first Ghana and then Ivory Coast roughly doubled their income per head within a decade, and on the basis of mineral exploitation both Gabon and Zambia achieved an even faster growth rate. Most tropical African countries, which started from substantially lower figures, were able to raise these during the 1960's by only 30–50%. Not surprisingly, the poorest countries are generally also those with fewest data on national accounts, but there is no doubt that in some of these, such as Somalia, Mali, and Upper Volta, the level of real income per head has risen very little, if at all, over the past two decades.

There are, of course, exceptions to this general trend. The relatively prosperous Rhodesia, Senegal, and Congo all experienced economic setbacks through the break-up of federations which they dominated; and in each of these countries *per capita* national income in 1970 was only a little higher than in the late 1950's, although it has since risen substantially in Rhodesia and Congo. Conversely, Mauritania has experienced new mineral development on a scale sufficient to raise it from one of the poorest countries of tropical Africa to one with an income level above the average for the region. However, the

212

significance of national income figures (Map. 10.3) may well be questioned in such a country where a large part reflects the operations of one or a few foreign firms.

Since 1970 national income data have been influenced more than ever by both inflation and changes in exchange rates, but a few further trends of this period might be noted. Gabon, Ivory Coast, and Zambia continued to forge ahead in the early 1970's, although Zambia then suffered a severe setback in 1975–6 as copper prices fell. Meanwhile the already very poor Mali, Upper Volta, Niger, and Chad suffered further impoverishment as a result of several years of drought, as did Ethiopia and Somalia also. Among the poorest countries only Malawi experienced a marked improvement in income in the early 1970's. One of the most important recent changes in the patterns across the continent is the result of the sharply increased oil revenues since 1974, which have raised *per capita* income in Nigeria from a level rather below the tropical African average to one comparable with Ghana, and have placed Gabon in a quite exceptional position within the region (whatever figure is adopted for its population).

TABLE 10.2. INCREASE IN COMMERCIAL ENERGY CONSUMPTION IN TROPICAL AFRICA

	Kilograms coal equivalent per capita			% Increase
	1961	1974	Increase	Increase
Rhodesia	575	805	230	40
Zambia	428	557	129	30
Gabon	158	1070	912	580
Congo	139	216	77	55
Kenya	139	177	38	27
Mozambique	120	141	21	18
Senegal	114	184	70	61
Guinea	97	94	—	—
Ghana	94	184	90	96
Ivory Coast	89	370	281	315
Zaire	85	76	—	—
Liberia	72	432	360	500
Angola	72	191	119	165
Sierra Leone	66	123	57	86
Cameroon	58	86	28	48
Sudan	52	125	73	140
Nigeria	39	94	55	141
Tanzania	36	74	38	105
CAE	35	57	22	63
Malawi	34	56	22	65
Gambia	33	73	40	120
Togo	31	70	39	125
Benin	30	42	12	40
Uganda	28	51	23	82
Mauritania	23	112	89	387
Somalia	20	40	20	100
Mali	15	24	9	60
Burundi	11	13	2	20
Rwanda	11	13	2	20
Upper Volta	10	14	4	40
Niger	9	31	22	250
Chad	9	17	8	90
Ethiopia	8	31	23	290

Source: United Nations, *World Energy Supplies.*

The spatial pattern of growth in energy consumption tends to confirm the general trend indicated by national income figures (Table 10.2). During the late 1950's commercial energy consumption per head of population was fifty times higher in Rhodesia and Zambia, and ten times higher in Ghana and Ivory Coast, than in Upper Volta, Chad, or Ethiopia. Even in relative terms the gap is just as wide today in most cases, while in absolute terms it is much wider. The greatest rise in energy consumption has generally occurred where mineral exploitation has expanded, notably in Gabon, Liberia, and Mauritania, but there has also been rapid growth in Ivory Coast. In Ghana the increase was remarkably slight until 1966, but the use of Volta power for aluminium smelting has now brought a sharp rise there too. Even in Rhodesia, Congo, and Senegal, much more energy is now being consumed per head of the population than in the 1950's. Meanwhile, most of the poorest countries of the region still await the type of development which will raise their commercial energy consumption above its present minute level.

Since so many African countries are heavily dependent upon overseas trade, another useful indicator of the spatial pattern of economic advance is provided by figures for exports (Table 10.3). These naturally reflect, in part, world commodity prices rather than changes within Africa, and they give an exaggerated impression of development in certain countries since some of the earnings are remitted overseas again as company profits. Even so, they help to build up the total picture, and they lend support to the view that a large proportion of the increased income of tropical Africa during the 1960's accrued to the nations which were already in a relatively strong position in the previous decade.

To some extent, export figures may even understate the widening gap since there is no doubt that it is in the more prosperous countries that most has been done to expand the internal exchange economy by industrial development. In some very poor countries industry has grown from such a slight base that the index of manufacturing has risen astronomically, yet these states account for only a very small share of the new industrial capacity of the region.

The areas of relatively intense economic activity in tropical Africa are often likened to islands in a sea of poverty. Even on the basis of data for whole nations, it is possible to see

TABLE 10.3. INCREASE IN EXPORTS FROM SELECTED AFRICAN COUNTRIES

	\$US *per capita*				
	Average 1956–7	Average 1961–2	Average 1966–7	Average 1971–2	Average 1974–5
Zambia	100	110	170	160	230
Liberia	60	65	120	140	240
Ghana	41	41	33	42	75
Zaire	40	25	24	30	45
Senegal	37	34	35	38	88
Ivory Coast	35	42	60	85	180
Benin	8	6	6	14	18
Chad	8	6	9	12	16
Niger	7	6	9	10	16
Ethiopia	3	4	5	6	9
Upper Volta	2	2	3	3	6
Mauritania	2	2	65	90	140

Sources: Diverse.

Note: These are the countries with the highest or lowest figures in 1956–7 with the exception of Gabon, Rhodesia, Mali, Somalia, Burundi, and Rwanda, for which complete figures are not available.

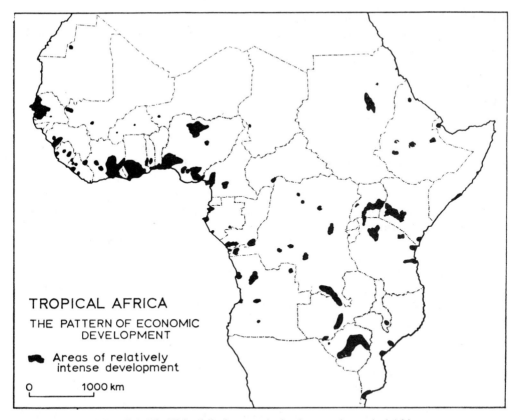

TROPICAL AFRICA

THE PATTERN OF ECONOMIC
DEVELOPMENT

Areas of relatively
intense development

0   1000 km

MAP 10.4. The "islands" of economic development in tropical Africa.

that recent development has followed a similar pattern. The islands of economic development are in fact generally smaller than national units (Map 10.4), so that differences in the
intensity of economic activity and in prosperity, are just as great within each country as
between one and another. Thus just as tropical Africa may be considered part of the periphery in terms of world economic relationships that focus on the North America–Europe
core area, so also a core and a periphery in the sense expounded by Friedmann may be
identified within most African countries. To a large extent it is the development process
which has brought about this differentiation within countries, and which now maintains it
through the dominance/dependence relationships that have been set up between the relatively
prosperous and the particularly poor areas. The spatial pattern of such relationships is a
relatively simple one in countries such as Ivory Coast and Uganda, where the core comprises
the capital city and the most highly developed rural area which surrounds it, but it is much
more complex in countries such as Nigeria, Tanzania, and Zaire, where there are subsidiary
centres of economic power well separated from the capital city. Liberia and Rhodesia are
two countries in which a clear-cut core and periphery dichotomy in non-spatial terms is
reflected in a more intricate pattern on the ground, the core comprising only parts of the
European-occupied half of the national territory in Rhodesia, and consisting of a scattered
set of small enclaves in Liberia.

    As on an international scale, the disparities within countries are not only being maintain-
ed but are often increasing. Through the processes of cumulative causation described by

215

Myrdal, one form of development assists another in the more favoured areas, while the very lack of development hinders economic advance elsewhere. In various respects the processes causing wide regional disparities are operating more strongly in Africa now than in the more developed areas in earlier periods. In Europe development took place more slowly, allowing more time for its diffusion over space; in the United States it took place simultaneously with the settlement of the country by a highly mobile population; in the Soviet Union its spread has been assisted by the strong powers of the government. In tropical Africa the rate of development in certain localities is too rapid, mobility is insufficient, and government powers are too weak to prevent the emergence and the accentuation of these regional disparities, which combine with ethnic differentiation to create for most African countries huge problems of national integration.

In Ghana and Ivory Coast, where all commercial activities are heavily concentrated in the south, most new forms of activity have been established in the same area. In each country, for instance, the south offers every advantage for industrial development, especially in terms of markets: and the Volta and Kossou power projects serve to confirm this situation. Efforts to improve standards of living in the north of each country have achieved very little, and the prospects for the future are not much better. In Sudan it is the north which is the most prosperous area and the south which is particularly poor; and the few major growth points in the economy, notably the extension of irrigation schemes and the growth of manufacturing, are all located in the north.

In Zambia there is an extremely sharp contrast between the zone near the main railway from the Copperbelt to Livingstone and the remainder of the country, and here, too, development over the past two decades have tended to increase the contrast. Zambia is one of the very few countries where a genuine attempt has been made to work out the regional implications of the national development plans, but while the planners have declared their wish to spread economic growth more widely they have been unable to find means of doing much to achieve this. Their efforts may lead to some economic growth in the poorer areas, but it was acknowledged in the 1966–70 plan that the largest share of the new national income was likely to accrue to the areas that were already the most prosperous (Table 10.4). The problem in Malawi is similar, even if the amount of development that might be spread is far more limited, and an attempt there to discourage excessive concentration in the south is taking the form of the establishment of a new capital city in the centre of the country. The wish to spread development to particularly poor areas was also one factor in the more recent decisions to move the capital of Tanzania to Dodoma, and that of Nigeria to a new site near Abuja (Map 1.10).

The sharpest regional contrasts of all are perhaps found in those countries where new mining developments have occurred. As noted in Chapter 4, these have brought great changes to certain very limited areas of Gabon, Liberia, and Mauritania, but have left the way of life and standard of living of people in most other parts of each country almost unchanged. Thus even in these rather rare cases where the spatial distribution of income within countries has been greatly changed, the effect has usually been to create new concentrations of relative prosperity rather than any real dispersal.

One factor that is generally considered largely responsible for the failure of African countries to achieve a higher rate of economic development during the past two decades is their great dependence on world markets for primary products and the general falling trend in prices for these products, at least in terms of purchasing power for increasingly expensive imports. In most development plans there has therefore been a heavy emphasis on reducing

TABLE 10.4. REGIONAL IMBALANCE IN ECONOMIC DEVELOPMENT IN
TWO AFRICAN STATES

Ivory Coast

Region	Income (milliard francs CFA)		Income per head (000 francs CFA)	
	1965	1970 forecast	1965	1970 forecast
North	15	18	19	21
Centre	41	46	36	37
South (excluding Abidjan)	85	104	49	52
Abidjan	63	127	205	255
Total	204	296	51	64

Source: Republique de Cote d'Ivoire, *Loi Plan de Développement,*
1967–70.

Zambia

Province	Income (£m.)		Income per head (£)	
	1964	1970 forecast	1964	1970 forecast
Western	5	11	12	25
Luapula	4	10	12	24
Northern	7	19	12	29
Northwestern	3	9	13	35
Eastern	7	17	14	30
Southern	18	32	37	56
Central	37	85	71	132
Copperbelt	153	259	264	322
Total	234	442	66	101

Source: Republic of Zambia, *First National Development Plan,*
1966–70.
Note: There are still no data for the actual income distribution in
1970 in either country.

this dependence by increasing the extent of internal exchange, and especially of industrialization.

While this is a wise policy for most countries if pursued in moderation, it is unlikely to reduce in any way regional disparities of income either between or within countries. The experience of the past two decades indicates that it is export-orientated activities that are most likely to create new islands of prosperity, or to extend existing islands over larger areas. The most obvious examples are provided by new forms of mineral exploitation, although it has been noted that the impact of these developments has generally been very limited in extent. An expansion of export crop production has in some areas affected more people, even if less dramatically, as in Ghana, central Kenya, and northern Tanzania.

Where substantial progress has been achieved in expanding the internal exchange economy, this has almost invariably taken place in areas that are already relatively prosperous. Only where incomes are high are markets large enough to permit industrial development, while it is in these areas in which industrialization and other forms of urban growth are occurring that a substantial local demand for agricultural produce exists. It is therefore the relatively prosperous Rhodesia, Zambia, Ghana, and now also Ivory Coast, which have been able to expand their internal exchange economies, and especially their manufacturing industries. The opportunities for this in Somalia, Chad, or Rwanda, have been very slight. Similarly, within such countries as Ghana and Zambia it is in the most prosperous areas that most of the new activities directed to the internal market are located.

Another important aspect of government policy in most African countries today is the effort being made to increase economic integration amongst them. This undoubtedly has an important contribution to make to the development of the region as a whole, particularly by giving new forms of enterprise free access to markets larger than national units can provide. There are instances where it might also improve slightly the economic prospects of poor districts, if this poverty results in part from their location on the periphery of individual states. Thus the extension of the East African Community to include Zambia might assist the development of both southern Tanzania and north-eastern Zambia, especially as it would coincide with the provision of new transport facilities across these areas. On an international scale, however, the effects of increased economic integration may well be to accentuate the differences in income levels which already exist. The East African Community has survived only with difficulty the strains imposed by the tendency for development to be concentrated in Kenya, the most economically advanced of the three member states; and the differences in prosperity there are much smaller than in some other parts of tropical Africa where economic integration is proposed. Thus it is likely that an effective common market in West Africa would assist further development, especially of manufacturing, in Ghana and Ivory Coast; but it is less clear how it could help Upper Volta, Niger, or Benin to expand and diversify their economies.

On a national scale, every African government, and on an international scale both the administrators of economic unions, and the donors of aid from overseas, are faced with a dilemma in relation to the distribution of development effort. If it is concentrated in the areas of greatest potential impact, this is likely to increase regional disparities in income: if it is concentrated in the areas of greatest need, this is likely to yield less than the maximum possible return. There is no obvious answer to this dilemma, and an examination of the development plans of African countries formulated in the 1960's shows that this problem has generally, perhaps understandably, been shelved. Some plans state that everything possible will be done to achieve a more even distribution of income, but they have many more development proposals for the prosperous areas than for the poor districts. Other plans discuss all matters at a national level only, but state that more attention will be given to the regional aspects of economic growth in subsequent plans. The donors of aid have found it no easier to decide upon the allocation of their funds between countries, although some efforts have been made in the 1970's to direct more grants and interest-free loans to the poorest countries.

These problems of spatial decision-making have been accentuated by the fact that some aspects of development have spread much more rapidly than others. Just as it has proved easier to expand education than to expand employment in tropical Africa as a whole, so also it has been possible to extend the former more widely than the latter both among and within countries. At the same time unplanned aspects of development or modernization, such as changed consumer tastes, are spreading more rapidly than spontaneous changes in productive activity. The inevitable result is extreme frustration, especially among the younger people, in the areas where opportunities fall far short of aspirations.

218

Perhaps, even apart from considerations of social equity for its own sake, a reduction of regional economic disparities is so vital for the future security of each state, and of the continent, that this will have to be given much greater priority in planning development, especially if the focus is on the development of people rather than the development of natural resources or national aggrandisement. However, it can be argued that the present distribution of population in tropical Africa reflects past rather than present circumstances, and that the strong tradition of population mobility characteristic of most parts of tropical Africa favours a policy of developing the areas of greatest potential and expecting people to satisfy their economic aspirations by moving to these areas. There may be certain areas which are at present poor but which do have great potential, although this potential can generally be realized only by a programme of integrated development involving many aspects of the economic and social infrastructure as well as several forms of productive activity. Every effort must be made first to locate and then to develop such areas. But generally a choice must be made between areas where the economic prospects are brightest and those where the needs are greatest. This decision faces the African leaders who can do so much more now than they could twenty years ago to shape the destinies of their own peoples, and also those in other parts of the world who still exert much influence and can do much to assist in the task of development. Essentially, perhaps, the choice is a political one, though it need not be doctrinaire and may appropriately differ from one country to another depending on the particular circumstances of each. Undoubtedly it should be made in the light of an understanding of the distribution of resources and of existing development, or in other words the economic geography, of tropical Africa and its component nations.

SELECTED READING

Discussions of development planning in Africa include:
U. Damachi *et al.*, *Development Paths in Africa and China* (London, 1976);
M. Gaud, *Les Premiéres Expériences de Planification en Afrique Noire* (Paris, 1967);
A. Seidman, *Planning for Development in Sub-Saharan Africa* (New York, 1974).

Summaries of recent plans may be found in:
UN, *Statistical and Economic Information Bulletin for Africa* 1 (1972) and 4 (1973).

For case studies from a geographical viewpoint, see:
K. M. Barbour (ed.), *Planning for Nigeria* (Ibadan, 1972);
B. W. Hodder and A. M. O'Connor (eds.), *Development Planning in the Third World* (London, in Press).

Among African plan documents, that which gives most attention to spatial patterns is:
TANZANIA, Second Five-Year Plan for Economic and Social Development 1969–1974 (Dar es Salaam, 1969), especially Vol. III.

Increasing interest in this aspect throughout East Africa is also indicated in:
M. Safier (ed.), *The Role of Urban and Regional Planning in National Development for East Africa* (Kampala, 1970).

Much useful material on Africa, as well as a wider context, is provided in:
A. G. Gilbert (ed.), *Development Planning and Spatial Structure* (London, 1976).

Attention is focused upon Nigeria in:
M. I. Logan, The spatial system and planning strategies in developing countries, *Geographical Review* **62**, 229–44 (1972).

Regional contrasts in development or modernization within individual countries are examined in different ways in:
H. I. Ajaegbu, *Urban and Rural Development in Nigeria* (London, 1976);
P. R. Gould, Tanzania 1920–63: the spatial impress of the modernization process, *World Politics* **22**, 149–70 (1970);
J. B. Riddell, *The Spatial Dynamics of Modernization in Sierra Leone* (Evanston, 1970);
E. W. Soja, *The Geography of Modernization in Kenya* (Syracuse, 1968).

An extremely useful continent-wide review of such contrasts is:

J. BUGNICOURT, *Disparités Régionales et Aménagement du Territoire en Afrique* (Paris, 1971).

The conclusion that there are strong forces tending to increase regional disparities in tropical Africa fits in with the propositions put forward in:

A. O. HIRSCHMAN, *The Strategy of Economic Development* (New Haven, 1958);

G. MYRDAL, *Economic Theory and Underdeveloped Regions* (London, 1957).

One of the most perceptive studies of contemporary development processes as they affect different groups, which draws largely upon African examples is:

C. ELLIOTT, *Patterns of Poverty in the Third World* (New York, 1975).

The most useful theoretical framework for further analysis of the spatial dimension of African development is perhaps provided in:

J. FRIEDMANN, *Urbanization, Planning and National Development* (Beverly Hills, 1973).

INDEX

The main references are given in bold type. Where a reference is to a table, map, or bibliographic note only, this is indicated by a letter (t, m, *or* b).

Aba   93, 109, 110m
Abidjan   69, 100, 108t, 111, 118, 130, 135, 139, 141–2, 143m, 163t, 164t, 167t, 177t, 181, 186, 188b
Abuja   216
Accra   110, 162, 163t, 167t, 174, 177t, 180
Addis Ababa   113, 167, 174, 177t, 181, 185
Afam   128, 129m
Afforestation   71, 73, 75
Agriculture   17, 18t, 20, **22–66**, 174, 212, 217, Plates 1–8
Aid   94, 189–90, **191–9, 205**, 207b, 218
Air Afrique   162t, 163
Air transport   138, **161–7**, 169, 170b, 203
Ajaokuta   110
Akjoujt   83
Akosombo   126–8, 178, *see also* Volta
Aluminium   86, **103**, 126–7, 131, 195
Angola   3, 4t, 6, 12, 13, 18t, 31–2, 36, 42–4, 46t, 54, 58–9, 68, 72t, 73, 78, 84, 85, 88, 89t, 104t, 107t, 108, 115–16, 117t, 121t, 132, 139t, 147, 150t, 151, 155t, 156, 158, 159m, 173t, 181, 191t, 193t, 194, 195, 196, 199, 204t, 205t, 206, 213t
Arab funds   61, 86, 199, 207b
Arlit   91
Arusha   114m, 181, 182t
Asbestos   90
Asians   7, 33, 61
Asmara   113

Assaab   108t, 113, 144
Atbara   113, 181
   river   32, 35m, 36
Awash river   123m, 132, 157
Ayamé   130

Baluba   83
Bamako   162, 185
Bananas   28, 37, 55, Plate 4
Bancroft   82
Bandama river   123m, 130
Bangolo   86
Bangui   112, 145, 153, 162, 174
Bauxite   77m, **86–7**, 95, 96, 97b, 103, 127m, 144, 192
Beer   *see* Brewing
Beira   92, 140, 151, 158
Beitbridge   150t, 152m
Belabo   150t, 151m
Belgium   10–11m, 30, 83, 191t, **192–3**
Belinga   86, 144, 151m, 153
Benin   4t, 29, 47, 50–1, 64, 69, 101, 107t, 111–12, 121t, 135, 139t, 142, 147t, 155t, 160, 163, 171, 173t, 183, 191, 192t, 202, 204t, 205t, 209t, 213t, 214t
Benue river   145
Berbera   140
Bia river   130
Biafra   14
Bicycles   138, 169
Blantyre   115, 167t, 182
Boké   86, 144, 195

Bomi hills 84, 85m
Bong mountains 84, 85m
Bonny 79, 80, 143
Booué 151m, 153
Bouali 112
Boundaries 12, 14
Brass 79, 80m
Brazzaville 112, 166, 167t, 174, 179,
    185
Brewing 107, 109, 111, 112, 115, 116
Britain *see* United Kingdom
Buchanan 85m, 92, 95, 102–3, 142
Buganda 14
Bui 127m, 128
Bujumbura 185
Bulawayo 115, 177t, 179, 183, 187
Burundi 1, 3, 4t, 9, 12, 44, 107t, 118,
    155t, 173t, 191t, 193, 201, 204t,
    205t, 209t, 213t
Bwana Mkubwa 82

Cabinda 73, 78
Cabora Bassa 116, 123, 124m, **133**,
    136b, 146, 200
Cambambe 123, 132
Cameroon 4, 8t, 12, 18t, 22t, 30, 34, 44,
    45, 46, 48, 49, 50t, 51, 57t, 58, 59t,
    72t, 73, 103, 104, 106, 107, 108,
    112–13, 118, 121t, 130–1, 139t, 147t,
    150t, 153, 155t, 173t, 183, 191t, 197t,
    202, 203t, 204t, 205t, 209t, 213t
Canning 28, 69, 102
Canoes 68, 70, 146
Capital 33, 93, 100, 122, 124, 134, *see*
    also Investment
Cashew nuts 51, 102
Cassava 37, 38
Cassinga 85, 150t, 151, 152m
Cattle 25, **28**, 38, 53, 62
Cement 104t, **105**, 106m, 109, 111, 112,
    113, 116, Plate 12
Central African Empire 3, 4t, 13, 25,
    30, 38, 46t, 48, 49, 88, 91, 107t, 112,
    121t, 145, 153, 155t, 173t, 191, 202,
    204t, 205t, 213t
Chad 4t, 8, 9, 22t, 25, 28, 46t, 48, 49,

62, 64, 68t, 69, 104t, 107t, 112, 118,
    121t, 153, 155t, 167, 173t, 202, 204t,
    205t, 209t, 213, 214t
Chambishi 82
Chibuluma 82
Chililabombwe 82m, 182t
China 111, 153, 190t, 191, 197t, **198–9**,
    206, 207b
Chingola 82m, 182t
Chiredzi 36, 60, 150t
Chrome 90
Cigarettes 52, 101, 103, 104t, 111, 113
Clothing 104, 109, 110
Coal **80–1**, 93, 97b, 128
Cobalt 78t, 83
Cocoa 17, 27, 29, 39, 42m, **44–5**, 102,
    174, 198
Coffee 17t, 28, **39–44**, 54, 102, 198,
    Plate 4
Colonial legacy 8, 14, 18, 34, 59, 151,
    167–8, 172, 174, 184, 187, 190, 193,
    200
Conakry 167t, 178
Congo 4, 59t, 61, 72t, 73, 78t, 79, 91,
    104t, 105, 106, 107t, 108, 112, 121t,
    139, 145, 147t, 150–1, 155t, 173t,
    197t, 202, 204t, 205t, 212, 213t
    river *see* Zaire river
Conseil de l'Entente 202
Co-operatives 33, 62
Copper 17, 77m, 78t, **81–3**, 89, 91, 93,
    98b, 102, 186, 192–3, 196, 213
Copperbelt 6, 81–3, 94, 115, 173, 178,
    182–3, Plate 11
Core-periphery 215
Corruption 7
Côte d'Ivoire *see* Ivory Coast
Cotonou 142, 144
Cotton 17t, 27, 33, 34–5, 39t, 43m,
    45–8, 53, 100, 102, 104
Crafts 99–100, 119b
Credit 29, 33
Cuanza river 36, 123m, 132
Cuima 85, 151
Customs unions 113, 117, 201, 202, 203,
    see also Economic integration
Czechoslovakia 198

Dahomey *see* Benin (re-named 1975)
Dairying 28, 30, 53
Dakar 101, 108t, 111, 140, 167t, 170b,
    174, 177t, 179, 185, 188b
Dams 32, 35, 70, **120–37**, 146, 194,
    Plates 13, 14
Dar es Salaam 92, 108t, 114, 140, 165,
    167t, 177t, 178, 179m, 181, 182t,
    184, 186
Débélé 86
Dependency 18, 189, 204–6, 208
Dessie 181
Development plans 19, 22, 28, 94, 99,
    216, 218
Diamonds 77m, 78t, **88**, 91, 95, 98b
Dire Dawa 113
Djibouti 4t, 12, 144
Dodoma 182t, 216
Douala 113, 162, 167t, 177t
Drought 1, 22, 28, 48, 62, 69, 213
Dualism 13, 17–18, 96, 146

East African Airways 162t, 163, 164
East African Community 113–14, 181,
    201, 202m, 207b, 218
Economic integration 100, 117, 118–19,
    168, **201–3**, 206, 207b, 218
ECOWAS 202m, 203
Edéa 103, 123, 130–1
Education **7–9**, 34, 184, 198, 218,
    Plates 23, 24
Electricity 92, 103, 106, **120–37**, 148,
    Plates 13, 14
Employment 6, 7, 17, 65, 95, 99, 104,
    109m, 116, 117t, 149, 184, 188b,
    210
Energy consumption 20, 213t, 214
Entebbe 167t
Equatorial Guinea 4t, 12, 44t, 73
Ethiopia 3, 4t, 7, 8, 9, 12, 14, 17t, 18t,
    22t, 25, 28, 29, **44**, 46, 51, 59t, 61, 63,
    64, 72t, 104, 107, 108t, **113**, 117t, 118,
    121t, 132, 134, 139t, 147t, 155t, 156,
    157, 162t, 164, 167, 172, 173t, 177,
    178, 181, 191t, 193, 194, 195, 197,
    201, 204t, 205t, 206, 209t, 213, 214t

European Economic Community 51,
    63–4, 134, 144, 190, 191, **193–4**
Europeans **6–7**, 22, 31, 52–4, 56, 58, 62,
    101, 107, 154, 171–2
Exports 16, 17, 39t, 55, 72, 78t, 89, 90,
    91, 117, **190–8**, 214

Family planning 3
Famine 38, 63
F'Derik 86
Ferkessédougou 61
Fertilizers 24, **26–7**, 29, 53, 55, 70, 89,
    105–6, 111, 116
Fincha 132
Fishing **67–70**, 75b, 196
Flour milling **107**, 109, 112, 116
Food 20, 22, 37–9, 62, 64, 70
Forcados 79, 80m
Forestry **71–5**
France 7, 10–11m, 12, 30, 34, 36, 40,
    49, 63, 69, 72, 79, 86, 131, 163t, 190,
    191–2, 193, 200–1, 207b
Franceville 150t, 151m, 153
Freetown 108t, 140, 162, 178
Fria 86, 94, 95, 97b, 150t
Fuel, wood 71

Gabon 1, 3, 4, 9, 17t, 20, 24, 64, 72t,
    73, 74, 75, **78–9**, 86, 87, 89t, **90**, 91,
    96, 97, 104t, 107t, 108, 112, 116, 117,
    121t, 139, 144, 150t, **153**, 155, 159,
    164, 165m, 167, 173t, 178, 193t,
    194t, 195, 202, 203, 204t, 205t, 211,
    213
Gambia 4t, 12, 48t, 49, 66b, 102, 118,
    121t, 146, 155t, 173t, 204t, 205t, 213t
Gas 80, 93, 110, 128, 130
Gatooma 115, 183t
Germany 85, 163t, 191t, 193, 194
Gezira 26, **34–5**, 46, 49, 66b
Ghana 3, 4, 8, 9, 12, 17t, 18t, 20, 26,
    27, 29, 36, 37, 42m, 44t, **45**, 52, 54,
    58, 61, 62, 64, 66b, 68t, **69**, 72, 74,
    75b, 87, 88, 90, 103, 104, 105, 107,
    108, **110**, 117t, 118, 119b, 121t,

126–8, 135, 136, 139, **141**, 145, 147, 150t, 152, 155, 158, 162t, 163, 166, 173t, 174, 178, **180**, 188b, 191t, 193t, 194t, 196, 197, 198, 203t, 204t, 205t, 209t, 213t, 214t, 216, Plates 3, 14, 18, 23, 24
Gitaru   131
Goats   28
Gold   77m, 78t, **87**
Groundnuts   26, 27, 39t, **48–9**, 101–2, 109
Guinea   4t, 8, 12, 13, 50, 54, 64, 70, 84, **86**, 91, 95, 97b, 103, 108, 111, 121t, 134, 139t, 144, 147t, 149, 150t, 153, 155t, 173t, 178, 181, 192, 193, 195, 197, 198, 204t, 205t, 206, 213t
Guinea-Bissau   4t, 12, 118, 190, 194
Guneid   35, 49, 61
Gwelo   115, 183t

Harar   181
Haute-Volta   *see* Upper Volta
Holle   91
Housing   186–7, 188b
Hydro electricity   *see* Electricity

Ibadan   177t, 180, 185, Plate 21
Ibo   14
Ilebo   152m, 153
Imports   37, 39, 107–8, **190–9**, 204t
Import substitution   103, 184
Independence   6, 10–11m, 12, 18, 178, 183, 184, 185, 189, 192, 200
Industry   18, 20, 22, 92–3, **99–119**, 125, 128, 136, 184, 204, 217, 218, Plates 11, 12
Informal sector   100, 146, 184, 186
Inga   123, **133–4**, 135
Insecticides   26–7, 51
Intermediate technology   100
Investment   79, 80, 82, 84, 85, 86, 112, 126, 129, 133, 134, 153, 189, 192–9, 207b
Iran   199
Iron   17t, 77m, 78t, **83–6**, 90, 93, 95, 97b, 102, 148–9, 196

Irrigation   **34–6**, 55, 60, 61, 66b, 133, 136
Italy   10m, 12, 134, 157, 163t, 191t, 193, 194
Itezhitezhi   126
Ivory Coast   4t, 5, 6, 7, 8t, 9, 13, 17t, 18t, 20, 22t, 26, 27, 29, 33, 34, 39, **40–1**, 42m, 44t, **45**, 46, 48, 50t, 51, 52, 57t, 58, 61, **63–4**, 65, 66b, 69, **72**, 73–4, 75, 86, 102, 104, 105, 106, 107t, 108, **111**, 116, 117t, 118, 121t, **130**, 135, 139, **141–2**, 147t, 148, 155, 163, 173t, 178, 181, 188b, 191, 192, 193t, 194t, 202, 203t, 204, 205t, 209t, 211, 213, 214t, 215, 216, 217t

Japan   69, 83, 86, 190t, **195–6**
Jebba   129m, 130
Jimma   181
Jinja   114, 131

Kabalo   150t, 152
Kabwe   83, 182t
Kaduna   109, 110m, 180
   river   129m, 130
Kafue   118
   river   36, 60, 70, 123, 124m, 125, 126
Kainji   32, 70, 123, 128, **129–30**, 136b, 145, 194, Plates 15, 16
Kamburu   131
Kamina   150t, 152
Kampala   114, 176m, 177t, 186
Kamsar   144, 150t
Kananga   153, 177t
Kano   109, 110m, 165, 171, 174, 177t, 184
Kapiri Mposhi   150t, 152m, 153
Kariba   32, 70, **123–6**, 136b, 146, 178, 194, Plate 14
Kasese   150t, 151
Katanga   *see* Shaba
Kaunda, K.   13
Kedia d'Idjil   85
Kenana   35m, 36, 61

Khartoum 113, 119b, 132, 167t, 177t, 181, 184

Khashm el Girba 35m, 36, 61

Kidatu 123m, 132, 150t, 152m

Kigali 162

Kikuyu 26, 30, 38, 41, 56

Kilembe 91

Kindaruma 131

Kinshasa 101, 112, 118, 135, 145, 153, 162, 167t, 171, 174, 177t

Kisangani 112, 174

Kismayu 140

Kitwe 93, 182t, 183

Koka 123m, 132

Konkouré 103

Kossou 123m, 130

Kpémé 89, 143

Kpong 128

Kumasi 171, 174, 177t, 180, 184

Kuwait 61, 199

Lagos 109, 110m, 118, 128, 140, 161, 163t, 164t, 167t, 171, 177t, 180–1, 184, 186

Land tenure 29–30

Lead 83

Le Marinel 123, 132

Liberia 1, 3, 4t, 12, 13, 17t, 18, 20, 24, 55, **57**, 64, 70, **84**, 85m, 89t, 90, 91, 92, 93, 94, 95, 97, 98b, 102–3, 104t, 107, 108t, 121t, 132, 139t, 144, 147, 149, 150t, 155t, 157, 165, 170b, 173t, 178, 181, 191t, 193t, 194, 195, 204t, 205t, 206, 209t, 213t, 214t, 215

Libreville 144, 153, 167

Lilongwe 150t, 182, 200

Livestock 25, **28–9**, 38, 61–2, 66b

Lomé 135, 142, 143m, 144

Lomé Convention 102, 194

Lourenço Marques *see* Maputo

Luanda 108t, 167t, 177t, 181

Luanshya 82m, 93, 182t

Lubumbashi 177t

Lusaka 94, 115, 162, 166m, 177t, 182–3, 185, 187

Maiduguri 150, 151m

Maize 27, 38, 53

Malawi 4t, 6, 8, 12, 22t, 30, 38, 48t, 51–2, 56, 59t, 60, 74, 96, 104, 105, 107t, 115, 116, 118, 121t, 132, 146, 147t, 150t, 151, 155t, 163, 173t, 181–2, 200, 203t, 204t, 205t, 207b, 209t, 213, 216

Mali 4t, 8, 12, 22t, 25, 28, 34, 36, 38, 46t, 47, 48t, 61, 62, 104, 105, 111, 121t, 146, 147t, 155t, 173t, 181, 192, 197t, 198, 203t, 204t, 205t, 206, 211, 212, 213

Maluku 112

Manaqil 34–5, 46

Manganese 77m, 78t, **87**, 96, 150

Mano river 84, 85m

Manufacturing 18t, 20, 92–3, **99–119**, 184, 214, 218, Plate 12

Maputo 92, 108t, 140, 151, 158, 167t, 177t, 200

Markets, domestic 22, 37, 46, 59, 70, 74, 93, 97, 100, 103–8 *passim*, 109, 112, 115, 117, 118, 134, 184, 217

Markets, overseas 16, 40, 45, 46, 56, 59, 74, 86, 100, 102, 191–9 *passim*, 216

Matadi 112, 140

Mauritania 1, 4t, 17t, 24, 28, 70, 81t, 83, 84, **85–6**, 89t, 90, 91, 92, 96, 97, 108, 112, 121t, 139, 147, 148–9, 150t, 155t, 164, 173t, 178, 192t, 199, 203t, 204t, 205t, 209t, 212, 213t, 214t

Mbinda 150

Meat 28, 62, 102, 167

Mechanized farming 25–6, 29, 54, Plate 6

Medical facilities **9**, 33, 175, 184

Menongue 151, 152m

Middle East 61, 190t, **199**, 207b

Miferma 85, 94

Migration 5–6, **175**, 178, 187, 188b, 190, 200

Milk 28, 38

Millet 38

Mining 18t, 20, **76–98**, 102–3, 139, 142–3, 144, 147, 148–9, 153, 174, 178, 200, 216, Plates 9–11

Moanda 87

Moçamedes 68, 140, 151
Mogadishu 140
Mombasa 108t, 114m, 131, 140, 141m, 177t, 181, Plate 17
Monrovia 85m, 91, 95, 108t, 140, 164t
Mossi 6
Motor assembly 107–8
Mounana 91
Mount Coffee 132
Mozambique 4t, 6, 12, 18t, 31, 46t, 51, 54, 58t, 59, 81, 86, 102, 104t, 105, 107t, 108t, 115–16, 117t, 121t, 133, 139–40, 147, 150t, 151, 155t, 156, 158, 173t, 191t, 196, 199–200, 204t, 205t, 206, 213t
Mufulira 82, 93, 182t
Mushin 181
Mwea-Tebere 36

Nacala 140, 151
Nairobi 100, 101, 113, 114m, 162, 165, 167t, 177t, 181, 184, 185m, 186, Plate 22
Nakambala 60
National income (or GNP) 15–16, 18t, 19, 89, 90, 208, 209t, 210m, 211–13
National integration 13–14, 15, 21b
Natural gas 80, 93, 110, 128, 130
Nchanga 82
N'djamena 167t
Ndola 92, 108t, 182t, 183
Neo-colonialism 18, 189
Netherlands 163t, 194
Ngaoundéré 150t, 151m, 153
Nickel 90
Niger 4t, 8, 20, 22t, 28, 38, 48, 49, 62, 63, 91, 102, 104, 105, 108, 111, 118, 121t, 155, 173t, 191, 192t, 202, 204t, 205t, 213t, 214t
  river 34, 36, 61, 69, **128–30**, 145
Nigeria 3, 4t, 6, 7, 8t, 9, 12, **14**, 15m, 17t, 18t, 22t, 24, 25, 26, 27, 36, 37, 44t, **45**, 46t, 47, 48t, **49**, 50, 52, 57–8, 59t, 61, 62, 64, 66b, 68t, 69, 72, 74, 75b, 78, **79–80**, 81, 87, 89t, **90**, **93–4**, **94–5**, 97, 99, 101, 102t,

104, 105, 106, 107, 108, **109–10**, 117t, 118, 119b, 121t, **128–30**, 136b, 139, 145, 147t, 148, 150, 155t, 157–8, 160, 162t, 164, 165, 171, 173, 174, **177**, **180–1**, 188b, 191t, 193t, 194, 195, 196, 197, 203, 204t, 205t, 209t, 213, 215, 216, 219b, Plates 9, 10, 15, 16, 21
Nile river 34–5, 36, 46, 70, 123m, 131, 132, 146
Nimba mountains 84, 85m, 91, 149
Nkana 82, Plate 11
Nkrumah, K. 126, 128
Nkula Falls 132
Nouadhibou 142, 148
Nouakchott 176
Nyala 139t, 140m
Nyerere, J. 13, 32

OAU 200
OCAM 200–1
Oil, mineral 17t, **77–80**, 90, 93–4, 94–5, 97b, 120, 128, 130, 195, 196, 199, 203, Plates 9, 10
Oil refining 92, **108**, 109, 112
Oil, vegetable 48, 49–51, 101–2, 103–4, 109
Omdurman 181
OPEC 78, 199
Owendo 144
Owen Falls 114, 123, **131**, 136b
Ox ploughing 25, Plate 5

Pakwach 150t, 151
Palm kernels 39t, **49–51**, 101
Palm oil 39t, **49–51**
Paper 74
Pastoralism *see* Livestock
Paysannats 30
Petroleum *see* Oil
Phosphates 26, 77m, 78t, **88–9**, 91, 95, 105
Pigs 29
Pineapples 102
Pipelines 79, 80, 154, 169, Plate 10

Plantations 31m, 51, 52, **54–61**, Plate 8
Plywood 72t, 112
Pointe Noire 112, 139, 144
Poland 198
Political change **9–14**, 21b, 52, 125–6, 140, 165–6, 178–9, 186, 199–200, *see also* Independence
Political problems 6, 13–14, 44, 53, 55, 64, 79, 112, 133, 145, 147, 153–4
Political relationships 10–11m, 12–13, 168, 174, 189–207 *passim*
Population 3–7, 21b, 24, 172–88 *passim*
 growth 3–5, 171, 175, 178
 pressure 3, 23, 38, Plate 2
Port Gentil 79, 108t, 112, 167
Port Harcourt 79, 93, 106, 108t
Port Sudan 108t, 113, 181
Ports 91–2, **139–44**, 168, 169, 170b, 174, 178, Plates 17, 18
Portugal 6, 10–11m, 12, 44–5, 54, 59, 85, 133, 151, 158, 190, 191t, 193
Potash 26, 91
Poultry 29
Power supplies 92, **120–37**
Pyrethrum 51, 53, 102

Que Que 115, 183t

Railways 74, 85m, 91, 138, **146–54**, 159, 168, 169, 170b, Plate 19
Rainfall *see* Drought
Ranching 61–2
Redcliff 86, 115
Regional co-operation 201–4, 206, 207b, 208, *see also* Economic integration
Regional disparities 18–19, 45, 65, 118, 120, 135, 184, 208, **215–16**, 217, 218, 219b
Regional planning 119, 216, 218, 219b
Resettlement **30–3**, 52–3, 66b, Plates 15, 16
Rhodesia 3, 4, 6, 9, 12, 18t, 22, 26, 30, 36, 46, 51, 52, **53**, **59–60**, 62, 71, 81, 83, 84, 86, 87, 89, 90, 101, 103, 104, 105, 106, 108t, **115**, 117, 118, 121t, **122–6**, 136b, 147, 150t, 153–4, 155, 158, 166, 172, 173t, 174, 179, **183**, 186, 200, 203, 204t, 205, 209t, 212, 213t, 215, Plate 13
Rice 36, 37, 39
Richard–Toll 36, 61
River transport 73, 138, **145–6**, 170b, 174
Road transport 85m, 91, 138, 146, 147, 148, 152, **154–61**, 169, 170b, Plate 20
Roan Antelope 82
Roseires 35, 123m, 132
Ruaha river 123m, 132
Rubber 39t, **57–8**
Rutenga 150t, 152m
Rwanda 1, 3, 4t, 5, 8, 9, 12, 20, 44, 57, 64, 87, 107t, 118, 119, 121t, 155t, 162, 173t, 178, 191t, 193, 204t, 205t, 211, 213t, Plate 2

Salisbury 115, 125, 166, 167t, 177t, 179, 183, 186, 187
Sanaga river 123m, 130–1
Sangaredi 86, 150t, 153
San Pedro 142
Sarh 153
Saudi Arabia 28, 199
Sawmilling 73–4
Sea transport **138–45**, *see also* Ports
Senegal 4t, 12, 18t, 26, 36, 37, 48t, **49**, 61, **68–9**, 89, 101, 102t, 104t, 105, 107, 108t, **111**, 121t, 139t, 147, 155t, 165, 170b, 173t, 191, 192t, 203t, 204t, 205t, 209t, 212, 213t, 214t
Settlement schemes 30–3, 66b, *see also* Resettlement
Seven Forks 123m, 131
Shaba 14, 83, 94, 101, 132, 134, 153
Sheep 28
Shifting cultivation 24, 30, 71
Shipping 144–5
Shire river 60, 132
Shiroro 129m, 130
Shoes 99, 104, 111, 112, 113

Sierra Leone 4t, 39, 50, 64, 70, 84, 87, **88**, 89t, 91, **95**, 98b, 101, 103, 104t, 107t, 108t, 111, 118, 121t, 139t, 147t, 148, 155t, 173t, 181, 203t, 204t, 205t, 213t, 219b
Sisal 39t, **58–9**, 102
Soap 103–4
Social change 7–9
Somalia 1, 4t, 7, 12, 24, 28, 59t, 61, 62, 70, 108, 118, 121t, 139, 140, 155t, 173t, 191t, 193, 197t, 198, 199, 201, 204, 205t, 206, 212, 213t
Sorghum 38
South Africa 133, 165–6, 190t, **199–200**, 207b
Soviet Union *see* USSR
Spain 10–11m, 12, 73
Squatter settlements 186, 188b
State farms 54
Steel 86, 103, **106–7**, 110, 112, 114
Subsistence 15, 16–17, 20, 37
Sudan 4t, 5, 8t, 9, 12, **14**, 17t, 18t, 22t, 25–6, 29, **34–6**, **46**, 48t, 49, 51, 59t, **61**, 64, 70, 99, 102, 104, 107, 108t, **113**, 118, 121t, 132, 138, 139t, 146, 147, 149–50, 155t, 156, 159, 162t, 173t, 181, 191t, 196t, 197, 198, 199, 204t, 205t, 206, 213t, 216
Suez Canal 138–9
Sugar 35, 36, 55, **59–61**, 66b, Plate 8

Taabo 130
Taiba 89
Takoradi 110, 140, 141, 180t
Tana river 123m, 131
Tanga 58, 182t
Tanzania 4t, 5, 7, 8, 9, 13, 18t, 21b, 22t, 25, 26, **32–3**, **42**, 43m, 46–7, 51, 56, **58**, 59t, 61, 62, 65, 66b, 68t, 72t, 81, 87, 88, 102, 104, 105, 106, 107, 108t, **114**, 117t, 119, 121t, 132, 139t, 147t, 150t, 152, **153–4**, 155t, 160, 170b, 173t, 178, 181, 182t, 191t, 197t, 198, 201, 203t, 204t, 205t, 206, 209t, 213t, 215, 216, 219b, Plate 1
Tazadit 86, 148

Tchad *see* Chad
Tea 33, 39t, 51, **55–7**
Tema 69, 103, 108t, 110, 118, 141, 142, 144, 176, 180, Plate 18
Textiles 101, 102, **104**, 105m, 109, 111, 112, 113, 114, 116, 117t, 119b, 198
Thika 113, 114m, 118, 181
Timber **71–5**, 144, 153
Tin 77m, 78t, **87**, 102
Tobacco 39t, **51–2**, 53, 71
Togo 4t, 44t, 50, 89, 91, 104t, 107t, 108, 111–12, 121t, 135, 139, 142, 143–4, 147t, 155t, 160, 167, 173t, 181, 192t, 202, 204t, 205t, 209t, 213t
Tractors 25–6
Trade 16, 17–18, 37–8, 171, 189, 190–200, 203–4, 214, *see also* Exports, Imports
Transport 48, 73, 74, 82, 91–2, **138–70**, 174, 203, Plates 10, 17–20

Ubangui river 73, 145
UDEAC (Equatorial Customs Union) 90, 112, **202**
Uganda 4t, 7, 9, 14, 18t, 33, **41**, 43m, 46–7, 48t, 49, 54, 56, 59t, 60–1, 62, 68t, 72t, 73, 81t, 83, 89, 91, 104, 105, 107, **114**, 117, 118, 121t, **131**, 136, 146, 147t, 150t, 151, 155, 159–60, 170b, 173t, 174, 178, 194t, 197t, 198, 201, 203t, 204t, 205t, 213t, 215, Plates 4, 5, 8, 12, 19
Ughelli 79, 93, 128, 129m
Ujamaa 13, 32, 66b, 136
Umtali 108t, 115, 183t
Unemployment 17, 175, 187
UK (Britain) 10–11m, 12, 60, 163t, 190, 191t, **192**, 207b
United States 12, 78, 86, 127, 157, 190t, 191, **194–5**
Upper Volta 4t, 6, 9, 28, 47, 49, 61, 62, 63, 64, 96, 107t, 108, 111, 118, 119, 121t, 147t, 155, 160, 173t, 191, 192t, 202, 203t, 204, 205t, 206, 209t, 211, 212, 213, 214

Uranium   77m, 91
Urbanization   6, 7, 37, 94, **171–88**,
    Plates 21, 22
USSR (Soviet Union)   69, 86, 111, 163t,
    190t, 191, **196–8**, 206, 207b

Victoria, Lake   70, 131, 146
Vila Cabral   150t, 151, 152m
Volta river   32, 70, 123, **126–8**, 136b,
    146, Plate 14

Wad Medani   113, 181
Wankie   81, 183t
Warri   79, 80m, 109
Water supplies   24, 32, 186
Waterways   73, 138, 145–6, 170b, 174
Wau   135, 139t, 140m
Wheat   35, 53
Wood   71–5

Yaoundé   113
Yoruba   45, 171, 174

Zaire   4t, 6, 8, 9, 12, 13, **14**, 17t, 18t,
    30, 37, 44, 46t, 48, 50, 55, 57, 59t,
    64, 68t, 72t, 73, 79, 81–2, **83**, 87, 88,
    89, 92, 94, 101, 102, 104t, 105, 106,
    107, 108, **112**, 117t, 118, 119b, 121t,
    132, **133–4**, 139t, 145, 146, 147t, 148,
    150t, 152, 153, 155t, 162t, 163, 170b,
    173, 191t, 192–3, 194t, 195, 196, 202,
    204t, 205t, 213t, 214t, 215
  river   92, 123m, **133–4**, 145
Zambezi river   36, **123–6**, **133**, 146,
    Plate 13
Zambia   3, 4, 6, 8, 9, 12, 13, 17t, 18t,
    20, 22, 36, 52, 53, 59t, 60, 66b, 81,
    82–3, 89, 92, **93**, **94**, 96, 97b, 98b,
    102, 104, 105, 107t, 108, **115**, 117t,
    118, 119b, 121t, **122–6**, 146, 147,
    150t, **153–4**, 155t, 160, 162t, 166,
    172, 173, **182–3**, 186, 187, 188b,
    193t, 194, 196, 197t, 198, 200, 201,
    203, 204t, 205t, 209t, 211, 213, 214t,
    216, 217t, 218, Plates 11, 13, 20
Zanzibar   13, 198
Zimbabwe   *see* Rhodesia
Zinc   78t, 83
Zomba   182
Zouérate   150t